Kasparov versus Deep Blue

Springer
New York
Berlin
Heidelberg
Barcelona
Budapest
Hong Kong
London
Milan
Paris
Santa Clara
Singapore
Tokyo

Kasparov versus Deep Blue
Computer Chess Comes of Age

Monty Newborn

Springer

Library of Congress Cataloging-in-Publication Data
Newborn, Monroe.
    Kasparov versus Deep Blue : computer chess comes of age / Monty
Newborn.
      p.   cm.
    Includes bibliographical references and index.
    ISBN 0-387-94820-1 (hard : alk. paper)
    1. Computer chess.   2. Kasparov, G. K. (Garri Kimovich)
I. Title.
OV1449.3.N48   1996
794.1'72416—dc20   96-24220

Printed on acid-free paper.

Production managed by Steven Pisano; manufacturing supervised by Jeffrey Taub.
Photocomposed by Impressions Book and Journal Services, Inc., Madison, WI.
Printed and bound by R. R. Donnelley and Sons, Harrisonburg, VA.
Printed in the United States of America.

9 8 7 6 5 4 3 2 1

ISBN 0-387-94820-1   Springer-Verlag New York Berlin Heidelberg   SPIN 10541579

Contents

Preface

This is a book about efforts to design a chess program that can defeat the world's best human player. Today, that human is Garry Kasparov. He has been world champion for the last decade, winning the title from Anatoly Karpov, who reigned during the previous decade. Although Kasparov is thirty-two years old now, and in spite of the fact that there are several young grandmasters chasing after him, his successful title defense against Vishwanathan Anand last year suggests that he may remain on top for a number of years to come; Mikhail Botvinnik, Kasparov's mentor, was over fifty and still world champion in the early 1960s.

However, challenging Kasparov from a totally different direction are the best of mankind's computer creations. For almost fifty years, developing a world-class chess program has been a goal of the computer science community. Over this period of time, computers have continually improved in strength, until today at least one program, IBM's DEEP BLUE, is on a par with the world's best players, perhaps not quite up to Kasparov, but not much behind either.

This book attempts to chronicle progress in computer chess from the 1950s through the six-game ACM* Chess Challenge between Kasparov and DEEP BLUE in Philadelphia, in February of this year. Many games are presented; as is said, the proof is in the pudding.

In Chapter 2, we begin by presenting the seminal work of Claude Shannon and Alan Turing. Some technical material on the minimax algorithm and the alpha-beta algorithm is presented for those interested in understanding the programming or even perhaps interested in learning how to develop one's own program. For those without a technical background, this material can be skipped, as can similar technical material in several other early chapters.

---

*The Association for Computing, which in its early days was known as the Association for Computing Machinery, hence ACM.

The chess programs developed at MIT in the 1960s and at the Institute of Theoretical and Experimental Physics (ITEP) in Moscow are the subject of Chapter 3. The ITEP Program was first to demonstrate the effectiveness of Shannon's Type A strategy and the power of deeper search. KAISSA, a descendent of the ITEP Program, was the first world champion chess program.

In Chapter 4, Richard Greenblatt's MAC HACK is described. MAC HACK was the first program to compete successfully in human tournaments, doing so for the first time in 1967. His program was also the first to use transposition tables to store chess positions as they were encountered in the search for later use, reducing the size of the search space that needed to be examined. Technical material on the way transposition tables are used in conjunction with alpha-beta search is presented.

Chapter 5 is devoted to the greatest winning team in Northwestern University's history, the chess programming team of David Slate, Larry Atkin, and Keith Gorlen. Their program was the first to play expert-level chess and did so beginning in 1976, when it took first place in the Minnesota State Championship with a 5-1 score.

Play by computers moved up to the next plateau, to that of master, in 1983, when BELLE was awarded that title by the United States Chess Federation (USCF). BELLE, developed by Ken Thompson with help from Joe Condon, used special-purpose circuitry to generate chess positions at a rate of 120,000 per second. Chapter 6 surveys Thompson's contributions to the field, including his work on opening books, special-purpose hardware, and endgame databases. The rules of chess were changed because of Thompson's work on endgame databases.

When defending its title as world champion in 1983, BELLE was defeated by Robert Hyatt, Bert Gower, and Harry Nelson's CRAY BLITZ. The power of the multiprocessor Cray computer was too much for BELLE. From then until 1985, CRAY BLITZ was the best chess program, but in 1985, and while still world champion, it was surpassed by Hans Berliner's HITECH. CRAY BLITZ went on to retain its title at the 1986 world championship—the first program to repeat as title holder—while HITECH advanced to new levels of excellence against human competition. Chapter 7 surveys the accomplishments of these two programs.

IBM's DEEP BLUE team has synthesized and modified the many ideas that have evolved over the years, adding some of their own, and creating a super-powerful machine; its rise to the top of the chess world is chronicled in Chapter 8. The chapter records its exciting matches against some of the world's best humans and its ascendancy to the top of the computer world. Forty-one games played by DEEP BLUE are presented. Its two-game match in 1989 with Kasparov was the first formal match with a world champion. At the end of the same year it defeated international master David Levy, who had offered himself up as a milestone in the progress of chess programs. Two months later, it played a one-game match with Karpov, losing but putting up a good battle. In 1993, the IBM program showed that it had made significant progress when it defeated Judit Polgar in a two-game match. Since 1987, it has been the best of the computer programs, winning the world championship in 1989 and dominating the ACM tournaments. It is about ten years old, and as great as has been its progress to date, its future progress may take it to unrivalled levels of play. Chapter 8 also includes seven encounters that Kasparov had against other programs: PENTIUM CHESS GENIUS, FRITZ 3, and FRITZ 4. These games were played at accelerated speeds.

Chapter 9 presents the recent ACM Chess Challenge between Kasparov and DEEP BLUE. The six-game match attracted world-wide media attention as Kasparov, losing the first game and then playing very cautiously for the next four games, won the match with a 4-2 score. Kasparov won a purse of $400,000 for a hard week of work—much harder than he ever imagined when he accepted the challenge.

The concluding chapter, Chapter 10, examines the implications of progress in computer chess for the future of chess and computing.

My own role has been as a participant, organizer, and author over the years. In 1970, Ken King, then the director of the Columbia University computer center, and I, then an assistant professor in Columbia's Department of Electrical Engineering and Computer Science, organized the first chess tournament exclusively for computers as part of the ACM annual conference at the New York Hilton. Named the United States Computer Chess Championship, the event featured six programs and loud laughter from the experts in the audience. The next year, I assisted Ben Mittman, the director of Northwestern University's Vogelback Computer Center, in organizing the second U.S. Computer Chess Championship, and the two of us went on to organize events around the world over the next fifteen years. In 1977, the International Computer Chess Association (ICCA) was formed. Mittman initially served as president and I as vice-president; later, from 1983–1986, I served as president. In the early 1980s, the ACM set up their

Computer Chess Committee and I have served as chairman of that committee since its inception. Other members are Tony Marsland, who is also the president of the ICCA; Hans Berliner; Ken Thompson; Robert Hyatt; and Chung-Jen Tan, who is in charge of the DEEP BLUE team. It is our committee that was responsible for the ACM computer chess events over the years and the ACM Computer Chess Challenge.

My program OSTRICH, developed with Columbia University undergraduate student George Arnold, participated in many events from 1972 through 1987. It participated in five world championships, narrowly missing a tie for first place at the first, in Stockholm in 1974. Written in the assembly language of the Data General Nova series computers, the program was tied to a computer that gradually lost ground to the newer and more powerful systems.

In putting together the ACM Chess Challenge, I have worked closely with many people. The main organizing committee consisted of Joe De-Blasi; executive director of the ACM and former IBMer; "CJ" Tan; and me. Public relations was handled by ACM's Terrie Phoenix and IBM's Marcy Holle. Mike Valvo served as tournament arbiter, assisted by Ken Thompson, while Yasser Seirawan and Maurice Ashley provided commentary to the large audiences, assisted by Hans Berliner, Danny Kopec, Dan Heisman, and David Levy. The layout in the Pennsylvania Convention Hall and the audio-visual equipment at the event were handled by IBMers Jennifer Hall and Matt Thoennes. The match was perhaps the greatest event in the history of chess and it may serve as the forerunner of even more exciting events.

Five appendices are included. Appendix A lists the top two finishers of the eight world championships and the twenty-four ACM championships. Appendix B presents the rules used at the ACM Chess Challenge. Appendix C summarizes the matches played by DEEP BLUE since its inception as CHIPTEST. Appendix D summarizes Kasparov's encounters with computers. Finally, Appendix E describes the algebraic chess notation used in this book. The description used herein is concise, and is currently the one used by the ICCA.

I wish the readers an enjoyable time following the great progress that has taken place in this exciting area of science. You can be assured that the story is far from over!

Monty Newborn

Foreword

I t is with great delight that I write this Foreword for Monty Newborn's book *Kasparov versus* DEEP BLUE. The book features two stories. The first chapters explore an extraordinarily well researched work on the development of chess computer programs, written with the sure hand of an insider. Also, it tells the story of the 1996 match-up between PCA Champion Garry Kasparov and IBM's DEEP BLUE program. The latter was a watershed event in the history of chess and computers. For the first time the world's best chess player (human) sat down and faced a computer in world chess championship match conditions. The match itself could not have been more compelling or better scripted. For more than a week the match took front page headlines on newspapers throughout the world. Why?

For millennia, man has been fascinated with tools, then machines, and now computers. In 1996, at the Philadelphia Convention Center, the ACM celebrated fifty years of ENIAC—the world's first computer. Man was creating a machine that could mimic its creator. The machine was being designed to "think." And what sterner test of "thinking" is there than a game of chess? Chess has agonized its adherents since it evolved centuries ago. A sterner intellectual challenge is hard to find. After all, what on earth are we doing when we play a game of chess if not thinking? Surely, if machines could best man at chess, what more proof need we have that machines indeed can and do think?

Which leads us into ever more questions. If computers can think, can they teach? Can they teach only other machines or their creators too?

The story of how chess-playing computers have evolved into strong chess opponents is exhaustively researched and beautifully presented in this work. As an International Chess Grandmaster, I found myself engrossed in this book right away. I became a bird. In Chapter 1, Monty Newborn describes a bird watching airplanes fly: Lots of laughter following the frantic

wing flapping and inevitable crashing. Then stunned silence while a sleek metallic 300-ton vessel slices its way through the air.

When watching a computer play a game of chess, I too was in denial. The computer is certainly not playing as I do. Nor does it evaluate a position as I do. While a chess grandmaster may intuit a solution, computers come to a similar solution but from a wholly different perspective. Can intuition be programmed?

Computers play a mean, calculating game of chess. Their impact on chess—especially in the endgame—has even caused the rules of this ancient game to be rewritten. Like that bird, I laughed at first at the computer's struggles. But now I laugh no longer, and watch in glum silence, as the fastest computers in the world race to discover the secrets of chess.

In 1995, I received an invitation from Monty to join the ACM in Philadelphia and act as a commentator during the Kasparov versus DEEP BLUE match. I cheerfully accepted and enjoyed the experience immensely. When I learned that the prize fund was $400,000 to the winner, I was quite surprised. What a wonderful charitable donation to Kasparov's bank account! In my view, Garry would easily beat DEEP BLUE. The only question for me was whether or not it would be a whitewash with Garry winning 6–0! Later we will discover that Garry worked hard for his prize.

Game One left me in utter disbelief. In Garry's own words he was rightfully massacred. At the prematch press conference both sides were boastful and confident. C.J. Tan, the leader of IBM's DEEP BLUE team, had modestly identified his protégé's playing strength as 3000. In chess speak, this would have placed his computer at several levels superior to Garry Kasparov—one of history's greatest players ever!

Having laughed, I had been happy to accept an invitation to be interviewed on the PBS News Hour with Jim Lehrer later in the week. C.J. Tan would also be a guest. I had secretly nursed the ambition to put C.J. back into his place. 3,000 indeed! What now? If Garry would lose Game Two, what could I possibly say? "Garry's got the computer right were he wants it?" I sweated throughout the moves of Game Two. Garry ground the computer down in a masterful ending, leveling the score of the match. Now I could face the cameras, but C.J. had proven his point before I could open my mouth.

How in the world did the computer ever get so strong? If the computer isn't thinking when it plays a game of chess, then what is it doing? Is it merely going through a calculation exercise of some complex algorithm?

And even if that is true, what isn't reducible to a complex equation with a working solution? Will computer scientists be able to duplicate man's emotions including fear and exhilaration? Why not?

Read this most enjoyable and seminal work on one of the most fascinating and challenging milestones in man's history. Monty Newborn has done both the computer and chess world great credit with this work.

Yasser Seirawan
International Chess Grandmaster
Three Times U.S. Champion
Seven Times U.S. Olympic Chess Team Member
1996 AEGON Computer Tournament winner

1 Learning to Fly

Once upon a time, I imagine, all birds wore smiles on their fine feathered faces, watching mankind's efforts to fly. Venturesome human aviators taped wings to their backs, jumped off cliffs, flapped their arms like mad and crashed to the ground. Certainly they will never learn to fly like us, thought the birds. For many years, the birds laughed and laughed, but slowly they became fascinated with the progress being made, and they began to sit quietly on their branches watching their world change. As they watched, they remained in a state of denial, contending that although mankind was making some progress, what they were watching couldn't be called flying. Today, we have built aircraft that have gone to the moon and beyond, and the birds are resigned to sharing their space with these sleek metallic marvels, but there is still no bird that would agree that these inflexible contraptions really can fly.

The birds in the world of chess are the grandmasters, some several hundred of them, scattered around the globe. Beginning in the 1970s, they observed the attempts of scientists to program computers to play their game and they smiled in great amusement. They laughed and laughed until 1976, when Northwestern University's CHESS 4.6 finished first in the B Section of the Paul Masson Chess Classic and then several weeks later won the Minnesota Open. Beginning then, the grandmasters started watching. Though watching, they remained in a state of denial. While the programs weren't playing too badly, they certainly weren't playing like grandmasters, and the grandmasters thought they never would. Then one by one, through the late 1980s and early 1990s, the grandmasters fell to computers. Even

world champion Garry Kasparov had his problems. Now, in 1996, it is fair to say that computers are playing on a par with the best grandmasters, and these strong human competitors are slowly learning to share their space. But are these new marvels of mankind, characterized by megabytes and megahertz, really playing chess? You can be the judge!

While building flying machines was a goal unto itself, initially programming computers to play chess was regarded by scientists as a means to a goal. The goal was to understand how the human mind worked—how it thought, how it solved difficult problems, what intelligence was all about, how learning occurred. The corollary, of course, was that once these processes were understood, they could be replicated on a computer. Thus, chess served this group of scientists, the artificial intelligence (AI) community as it became known, in much the same way as the fruit fly served the geneticists. The game was sufficiently complex, but not too complex, and it had many of the ingredients of the more complex problems that really needed to be understood.

To program a computer to play chess is no great trick. The trick, of course, is to have it play strong chess. The definition of strong has changed as the programs improved, and in 1996, with defeated grandmasters everywhere, the definition of strong has become synonymous with playing chess better than any human on planet Earth. It was once thought that if a strong program could be written, something about the human thought processes would be learned. Some went further and contended that before a computer could play strong chess, it was necessary to understand how the mind managed it. Computers, then, would be programmed to do the same.

But learning how birds fly was a relatively easy task. They could be watched in flight. Pictures of them could be drawn. They could even be caught and dissected. However, at first there were major problems. When attempts were initially made to fly, the technology in existence to remain afloat was inadequate; there was no appropriate source of power. There was also an unawareness of the laws governing the dynamics of flight. Once these problems were solved at the turn of the twentieth century, our beaked buddies found themselves sharing the skies with machines that made horrible noises, needed vast fields to take off and land, and maneuvered at best like oxen.

Learning how man plays chess is an even more elusive matter. So far, it has been impossible to see exactly how we do it. Evidently electrical and chemical signals race around inside the brain, and somehow that does the trick. Nevertheless, early attempts to design chess programs were aimed at replicating our poorly understood thought process. Alan Newell and Herb Simon studied the eye movements of chess players as they looked for a move, hoping that would shed some light. Our ability to recognize patterns on the chessboard was considered fundamental to the process by many. Some attributed our success to "intuition," an overused word by those who particularly imagined that a computer would never play strong chess because this mystical human attribute was too complex to replicate. Most contended that our mind carried out some sort of search, examining certain lines of play, or continuations, to great depths while giving others little attention. Good players were better at this process of selective search than were weak players.

Programming a computer to play strong chess was too challenging an activity to sit back and wait for the AI world to figure out how the mind works, however. Programs slowly evolved using techniques that the discipline of operations research might more appropriately claim as their own, although the programmers were unconcerned about who took credit. They used programming languages—assembly language and C—that made AI purists shudder. And from the very beginning, they saw countless ways to improve their programs, with no shortage of ideas to implement and test. Even today, the DEEP BLUE team is filled with more ideas for improving their program than time permits. Chess programmers have seen gradual, steady improvement in their creations and they have worked with an unmatched passion.

In the beginning there was a love affair between the chess programmers and the AI community, but the latter gradually divorced the former, perhaps disappointed that the techniques being used so successfully in chess programs weren't theirs. Knowledge-based programs, founded on high-level programming languages, became a rage in the AI world, knowledge engineering a buzzword, and later, failures to perform up to expectations commonplace. Unlike chess programs, where knowledge got tucked away in the cleverest of ways, these programs were often bulky and very inefficient. Some minor successes were achieved by medical diagnosis programs and programs that searched for earth resources such as oil, for example, but these programs had a much simpler task than playing strong chess. Many AI-oriented companies that had made their way onto the major stock exchanges of North America disappeared in the early 1990s when they failed

to deliver. In the middle 1980s, however, there was some recognition that techniques developed for chess programs could be applied to other AI problems, in particular, automated reasoning, or more abstractly, automated theorem proving. This area is fundamental to intelligent systems.

This book leads the reader through the developments in computer chess over the last fifty years, developments that have produced DEEP BLUE, a program that competes with the world's best humans. Over most of these years, certainly from 1967 on, there has been coincidentally a succession of programs that have moved, one after the other, to the head of the pack. Each dominated for a number of years and then gave way to the next. Our story of this exciting, continual progress of computer chess will focus on these standouts. It should be kept in mind that they were each built on the shoulders of their predecessors, through a process of natural evolution. Good ideas and techniques quickly spread, while those that didn't pan out were dropped.

The ACM and the ICCA have been major catalytic forces in the field of computer chess. Beginning in 1970, the ACM held a yearly championship at which the best programs in North America and some of the best from Europe competed. The ICCA was formed in 1977 at the second World Computer Chess Championship and has been responsible for holding a world championship every three years. In addition to being responsible for holding major competitions, these two organizations have published many of the most important papers on the subject. The ACM events usually included technical presentations and panel discussions. The ICCA Journal is the most important publication on the subject of chess, not alone computer chess, for the last sixteen years.

Claude Shannon, Alan Turing	Minimax search with scoring function	1950
KOTOK/MCCARTHY Program & ITEP Program	Alpha-beta search, brute force search	1966
MAC HACK	Transposition tables	1967
CHESS 3.0–CHESS 4.9	Iteratively-deepening depth-first search	1975
BELLE	Special-purpose circuitry	1978
CRAY BLITZ	Parallel search	1983
HITECH	Parallel evaluation	1985
DEEP BLUE	Parallel search and special-purpose circuitry	1987

Figure 1.1. Some significant ideas in computer chess

Our story begins with Claude Shannon and Alan Turing, who laid the foundations for all that followed. It continues with the KOTOK/MCCARTHY program at MIT and the ITEP program and KAISSA in Moscow in the 1960s and early 1970s. It then goes on to MAC HACK, CHESS 3.0 through CHESS 4.9, BELLE, CRAY BLITZ, HITECH, and finally DEEP BLUE. Oversimplifying greatly, Figure 1.1 attempts to associate some of the main ideas in computer chess with the first person or program to demonstrate their applicability.

2 The Foundations

The game of chess consists of three phases: an opening phase, a middle-game phase, and an endgame phase, as depicted in Figure 2.1. The opening phase lasts anywhere from five to fifteen moves. Computers access large databases that assist in selecting moves during this stage, although when playing the leading players, these databases serve more as damage-control devices than as anything else. In Chapter 9, it will be seen that DEEP BLUE did not outplay Kasparov during this phase. Although computers play endgames quite well and probably better than they are given credit for, this stage also favors the leading players since many endgames involve subtle moves that cannot be understood by even the strongest programs. However, if the endgame is reached with five or fewer pieces on the board, not counting pawns, it favors the computers since a database of all five-piece endgames exists. Of course, to reach this phase is no simple matter.

It is in the middle-game, when the opening book no longer provides guidance, and before the endgame databases are useful, that the main programming effort has been invested. In typical middle-game positions there are about thirty to forty moves that each lead to thirty to forty new positions, which in turn each have thirty to forty moves that each lead to thirty to forty more new positions. For round numbers, about a thousand positions arise after exploring, or searching, one move by each side. A search of two moves by each side leads to about a million positions. This large tree of moves and positions grows at an exponential rate, and after only a few moves contains far too many positions for any computer to hope to

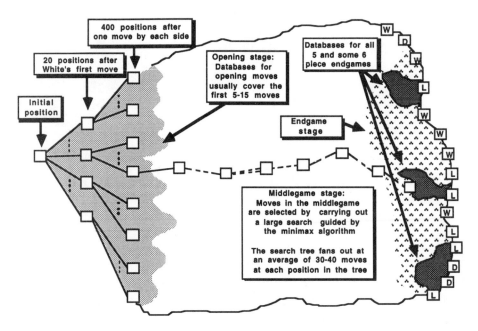

Figure 2.1. The chess tree.

search. Even in the endgame, where the size of the tree grows at a considerably slower rate, the computer can hope to search only a small part of the tree. Of course, if it could see the entire tree, it would know exactly how to play. Given that that is impossible, Claude Shannon's approach became the leading alternative.

Claude Shannon

In 1950, Claude Shannon, a scientist at Bell Telephone Laboratories at Murray Hill, New Jersey, published a paper entitled "Programming a Computer for Playing Chess" in the *Philosophical Magazine,* giving birth to the field of computer chess. Shannon had become prominent for his contributions to the theory of computer circuit design and for his contributions to the field of information theory. He is one of the most distinguished computer scientists in North America.

Shannon proposed two approaches to programming chess. The first is best described as a "fixed-depth" search, called a Type A search by Shannon, while the second is best described as a "variable-depth" search, called a Type B search by Shannon. No program has ever been built precisely as he described, but almost every program follows his general ideas.

In Shannon's Type A strategy, a move is picked from a given position by exploring all lines of play to some fixed depth and then assigning a score to the position at the end of each continuation. The score assigned to the position by a "scoring function" is a measure of how good the position is for the side on the move. To decide on the score to assign, Shannon suggested that a number of factors be taken into account. He began by suggesting the following three:

1. *Material:* Assign pieces values as follows: queen = 9, rook = 5, bishop = 3, knight = 3, pawn = 1 and king = 200. The value of the king must exceed that of all the other pieces to make sure it is never traded off!
2. *Pawn formation:* A penalty of 0.5 for each doubled (*DP*), isolated (*IP*) or backward (*BP*) pawn.
3. *Mobility:* It is desirable to have many moves available for yourself and few for your opponent. Thus Shannon suggested 0.1 points be credited for each move available.

Based on these three factors and assuming White to move, the score of a position *P*, denoted SCORE(*P*), is given by the formula

$$\text{SCORE(P)} = 200(K - K') + 9(Q - Q') + 5(R - R')$$
$$+ 3(B - B' + N - N') + (P - P') - 0.5(DP - DP' + IP - IP' + BP - BP')$$
$$+ 0.1(MVS - MVS')$$

where *K, Q, R, B, N,* and *P* are the numbers of kings, queens, rooks, bishops, knights, and pawns for White; *DP, IP,* and *BP* are the numbers of doubled, isolated, and backward pawns for White; and *MVS* is the number of legal moves for White. Primed variables represent similar variables for Black. If SCORE(*P*) is positive, it means that the evaluation function thinks White has the better position.

Other factors were suggested later in his paper. He suggested that central pawns should receive credit, passed pawns should receive credit, and weak pawns near the king should be penalized. In addition, he suggested credit for good placement of the knights and rooks and for certain attacks and pins, but he didn't specify how much.

It is surprising how well his "three-component" scoring function works. In the great majority of positions, material turns out to be the dominant

factor. Simply adding up the material for both sides is often sufficient to determine which of two positions is better.

Comparing the scores for the positions in Figure 2.2a and Figure 2.2b, it can be seen that Shannon's scoring function will recommend opening with 1 e4 rather than 1 d4 based on a one-move lookahead. The mobility component of the scoring function is the determining factor for deciding between these two moves. After 1 e4, White has thirty moves (one king move, four queen moves, five bishop moves, five knight moves, and fifteen pawn moves) and Black has twenty, giving White ten more moves and thus a 1.0 point advantage. After 1 d4, White has only twenty-eight moves, resulting in a 0.8 point advantage.

Although this simple scoring function works surprisingly well, nevertheless there are countless positions where it fails. Figures 2.3a, 2.3b, and 2.3c show some of the problems with it. These three positions are all assigned an unrealistic score of zero. In Figure 2.3a, the position is a win for Black no matter whose turn it is. In Figure 2.3b, the opposite is true. In Figure 2.3c, whoever is to move wins.

Shannon's scoring function has a "granularity" of 0.1 pawns; that is, the minimum difference in score between any two positions is 0.1 pawns. The granularity of scoring functions in the best programs of today is approximately 0.01 pawns. Those functions take into account many factors suggested by Shannon as well as many others not considered. They are very

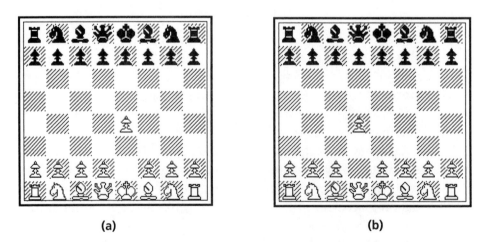

(a)   (b)

Figure 2.2. Comparison of 1 e4 and 1 d4. (a) Position after 1 e4—assigned a
score of 1.0. (b) Position after 1 d4—assigned a score of 0.8.

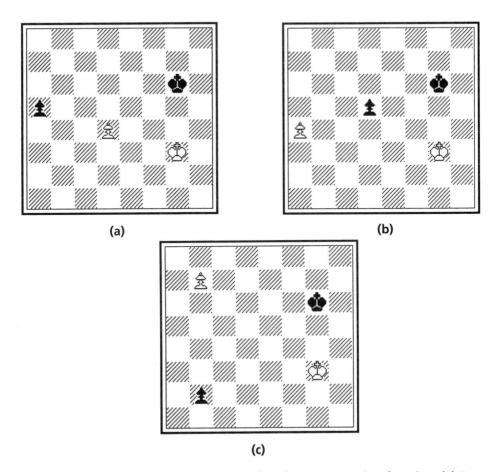

Figure 2.3. Three pathological positions for Shannon's scoring function. (a) Position with a score of 0.0 but Black winning. (b) Position with a score of 0.0 but White winning. (c) Position with a score of 0.0 and the side to move winning.

smart on deciding when to trade pieces, on pushing pawns toward queening squares, on castling and defending the king, on placing rooks on the seventh rank, and eventually, as the game reaches the endgame stage, on using the king offensively. One component of many scoring functions is a "contempt factor." Before starting a game a contempt factor can be entered by the operator of the program. If the opponent is thought to be much weaker than the computer, a value of, say, two pawns (big contempt!) is added to every position. A position that would receive a score of zero without this factor would be assigned a score of +2 with it. This would effectively tell the computer to avoid a draw even when behind as much as two pawns.

Shannon went on to discuss the problems with the proposed type A strategy. As said previously, in a typical middle-game position there are thirty to forty moves to choose from. After just one move by each side there are roughly a thousand positions to be evaluated, after two moves there are about a million positions, and after three moves by each side there are about a billion positions. This means that a computer evaluating one terminal position every microsecond (0.000001 second) would require about sixteen minutes to make a move. Shannon realized that an exhaustive search to a depth of six half-moves or plies (a ply is a half-move) would not play chess at a high standard because of the number of important variations that were more than six plies long. Since it seemed to Shannon that a human chess master examines some variations to a depth of only a few plies and others to a much greater depth, Shannon argued that it is therefore necessary that a chess program be given the same capability.

Thus, Shannon introduced the notion of quiescence (or "stability," as he called it) into his second, type B, strategy, which searched all lines to some minimum depth and others that were unstable deeper yet. He suggested that this strategy could be improved further if "forward pruning" was used: that at each position in the search tree, a preliminary screening of moves be made and "obviously bad" moves eliminated. At positions near the root of the tree, the pruning would eliminate fewer moves than it would at deeper levels. The idea of forward pruning appealed to the early programmers, and great efforts were made to find rules for calling moves bad. As the programs improved in the 1970s, there turned out to be too many exceptions to any rule proposed.

The minimax algorithm

Shannon then described how to use the scoring function. First, decide upon a maximum depth of search based on the allotted time and the capabilities of the computer. Then, construct a tree of all move continuations to this depth and assign a score to all positions at this depth. These positions are called terminal positions. Next assign scores to the other positions, the nonterminal positions, those at shallower levels in the tree, as follows: If a nonterminal position is at an even (odd) level in the tree, assign to it—or as is usually said, "back-up" to it—the maximum (minimum) score of its successor positions. Eventually a score will be assigned, or backed up, to every position in the tree, including the root. The move to make is the one leading to the position at the first level whose score is backed up to the root. The sequence of moves on the path from the root to the terminal position whose score is eventually backed up to the root is called the principal continuation. This continuation is the way the game should be played by both players when the only information they have available is that gathered by the search.

The minimax algorithm is illustrated in Figure 2.4, where it is White's turn to move in the root position A. The depth of search was chosen as two to make the example as easy as possible to understand, and for the same reason, only two moves in each position were generated. The tree was then constructed and the scores of the four terminal positions D, E, F, and G were calculated. Next, positions B and C were assigned backed-up scores equal to the minimum score of their successors. For position B, the minimum was +1, and for position C, the minimum was −3. Then position A was assigned a backed-up score of +1, equal to the maximum score of its successors, with move 1 B×c3 found to be the best move to play. The principal continuation was found to be 1 B×c3 R×d4, leading to a one pawn advantage for White.

Depth-first search and the minimax algorithm

Shannon suggested that the search of the chess tree using the minimax algorithm be carried out in a depth-first fashion. Essentially, the procedures for growing the tree, scoring the terminal positions, and backing up the scores to the root are combined and carried out in tandem. The minimax algorithm based on depth-first search uses the data structures presented in Figure 2.5 and described here. They represent a simplification of the data structures used by the typical chess-playing program. These programs use many other data structures, the main one being a large table for storing information about positions that have been searched and scored.

BOARD(8,8): Every chess program must keep an internal representation of the pieces on the board. This is done in a two-dimensional array, BOARD(8,8). The squares are assigned names as shown on the left in Figure 2.6a, while the right side of Figure 2.6a indicates how they are typically encoded by a chess program. White's pieces are assigned integers:

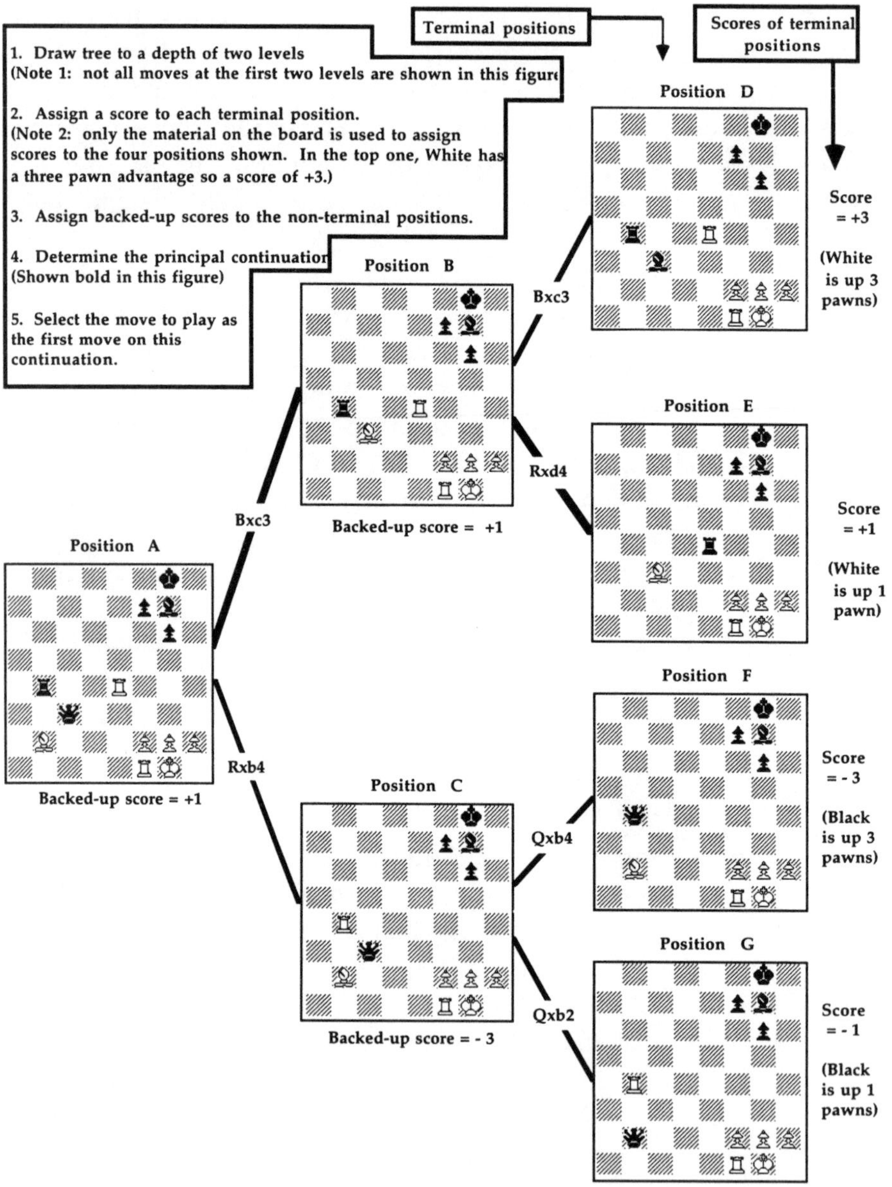
Terminal positions
Scores of terminal positions
1. Draw tree to a depth of two levels
(Note 1: not all moves at the first two levels are shown in this figure
2. Assign a score to each terminal position.
(Note 2: only the material on the board is used to assign scores to the four positions shown. In the top one, White has a three pawn advantage so a score of +3.)
3. Assign backed-up scores to the non-terminal positions.
4. Determine the principal continuation
(Shown bold in this figure)
5. Select the move to play as the first move on this continuation.
Position A
Backed-up score = +1
Bxc3
Rxb4
Position B
Backed-up score = +1
Position C
Backed-up score = - 3
Bxc3
Rxd4
Qxb4
Qxb2
Position D
Score = +3
(White is up 3 pawns)
Position E
Score = +1
(White is up 1 pawn)
Position F
Score = - 3
(Black is up 3 pawns)
Position G
Score = - 1
(Black is up 1 pawns)

Figure 2.4. Tree of depth 2 illustrating the minimax algorithm.

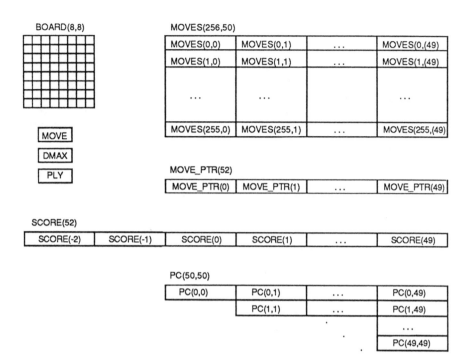

Figure 2.5. Data structures used by the minimax algorithm.

pawn = 1, knight = 2, bishop = 3, rook = 4, queen = 5, and king = 6. Black's pieces are assigned the corresponding negative numbers. A blank square is assigned a 0. Figure 2.6b shows a chess position and how it would be represented in BOARD(8,8).

MOVES(256,50): In Figure 2.7, the left most column shows a partial list of the moves in the opening position in basic chess notation, the next column shows the move notation used in this book, and the third column shows how they would be represented inside a computer. Chess programs use a two-dimensional array, MOVES(256,50), in which the moves at each level in the tree are stored as they are generated. MOVES(256,50) has sufficient space for a search to a depth of fifty plies with up to 256 moves in a position. No position has more than 256 moves. In a depth-first search, only those moves at positions on the continuation under search need be kept in MOVES(256,50). The rest can be removed from the list after they have been considered, or added to the list when their turn comes up.

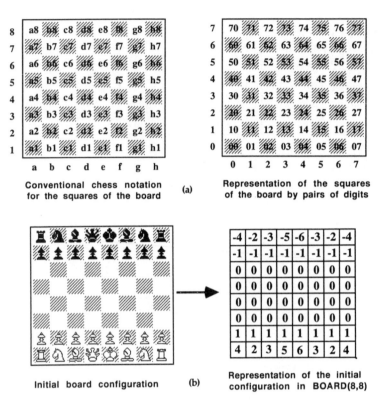

Figure 2.6. Notation used to describe pieces and squares. (a) Left: Conventional chess notation for the squares of the board. Right: Representation of the squares of the board by pairs of digits. (b) Left: Initial board configuration. Right: Representation of the initial configuration in BOARD(8,8).

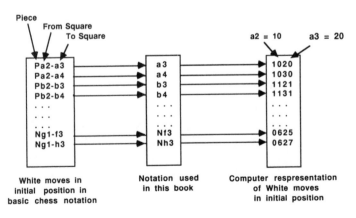

Figure 2.7. Encoding of moves.

MOVE_PTR(50): An array of move pointers, MOVE_PTR(50), is used to keep track of what continuation is under search. MOVE_PTR(*i*) points to the move at ply *i* that is currently under search. For example, in Figure 2.4, when terminal position *F* at the end of the move sequence 1 R×b4 Q×b4 is reached, the value of the move pointers will be MOVE_PTR(0) = 2, MOVE_PTR(1) = 1.

SCORE(52): This array keeps track of the scores assigned to positions on the continuation under search. One score must be kept for each position on the continuation. SCORE(*i*) maintains the best score found thus far for the position at level *i* on the continuation under search. Before the search begins, SCORE(–2) and SCORE(–1) are set to $-\infty$ and $+\infty$ respectively.

PC(50,50): This triangular array is used to help determine the principal continuation. When the search ends, the principal continuation of length, say *L*, is in the top row of this array, that is, in PC(0,0), PC(0,1), ..., PC(0,*L*–1).

MOVE, DMAX and PLY: Three additional variables are necessary. MOVE contains the current move under search, PLY denotes the current search depth, and DMAX denotes the maximum search depth as the search progresses.

Functions called by the minimax algorithm

A pseudo-C version of the depth-first minimax algorithm is shown in Figure 2.8. The main program calls seven functions. Two are called before the search begins, ENTER_POSITION and SET_DMAX, and they will not be discussed further. Five are called during the search: GENERATE_MOVES, SCORE_POSITION, SUCCESSOR, PREDECESSOR, and CALC_PC.

GENERATE_MOVES(BOARD,PLY) generates the legal moves in a given board position BOARD at ply PLY. The moves are placed on MOVES in column PLY. The list is terminated with a zero. Coupled with generating moves in most programs are heuristics for ordering the moves from the most to least promising. Generating moves is a computationally expensive procedure and considerable effort is made to optimize this part of the code. It is move generation that has been the primary purpose of special-purpose chess hardware.

SCORE_POSITION(BOARD), the scoring function, assigns a score to a position using the various factors that have been discussed earlier.

```
/* PSEUDO-C CODE FOR THE DEPTH-FIRST MINIMAX ALGORITHM                      */

/* - - - - - - - - - - -DATA STRUCTURES - - - - - - - - - - - - - - - - - - - - - - - - - - - - - - - - - */

INTEGER BOARD(8,8), MOVES(50,256), MP(50), SCORE(52),
INTEGER PC(50,50), MOVE, DMAX, PLY;

/* - - - - - - - - - - -FUNCTIONS CALLED - - - - - - - - - - - - - - - - - - - - - - - - - - - - - - - */
/*        ENTER_POSITION(), SET_DMAX(), GENERATE_MOVES(),                    */
/*        SCORE_POSITION(), SUCCESSOR(), PREDECESSOR(), SET_PC()             */
/* - - - - - - - - - - - - - - - - - - - - - - - - - - - - - - - - - - - - - - - - - - - - - - - - - - -*/

/* - - - - - - - - - - - - - - INITIALIZE - - - - - - - - - - - - - - - - - - - - - - - - - - - - - - - - -*/
/*        1. ENTER POSITION IN BOARD(8,8)                                    */
/*        2. SET MAXIMUM SEARCH DEPTH, DMAX                                  */
/*        3. SET INITIAL VALUES OF SCORE(-2) AND SCORE(-1)                   */
/*              TO EFFECTIVELY -∞ AND +∞ RESPECTIVELY                        */
/* - - - - - - - - - - - - - - - - - - - - - - - - - - - - - - - - - - - - - - - - - - - - - - - - - - - -*/

ENTER_POSITION();
SET_DMAX();
PLY = 0;
SCORE(-2) = -100000;
SCORE(-1) = +100000;

/* - - - - - - - - - - -A NEW POSITION IS REACHED - - - - - - - - - - - - - - - - - - - - - - - - - */
/*        IF AT MAXIMUM DEPTH, GO TO TERMINAL_POSITION.                      */
/* - - - - - - - - - - - - - - - - - - - - - - - - - - - - - - - - - - - - - - - - - - - - - - - - - - -*/

NEW_POSITION:
IF (PLY EQUALS DMAX) GOTO TERMINAL_POSITION;

/* - - - - - - - - - - - - - OTHERWISE, IF NOT AT MAXIMUM DEPTH - - - - - - - - - - - - - - - - - - -*/
/*        1. BRING DOWN THE SCORE FROM TWO LEVELS HIGHER,                    */
/*        2. GENERATE MOVES, PLACE THEM IN THE MOVES ARRAY,                  */
/*              IN LOCATIONS MOVES(0,PLY), MOVES(1,PLY), . . . ,             */
/*              AND PLACES A "0" AT THE END OF THE LIST,                     */
/*        3. SET THE MOVE POINTER AT DEPTH "PLY" TO THE FIRST MOVE,          */
/* - - - - - - - - - - - - - - - - - - - - - - - - - - - - - - - - - - - - - - - - - - - - - - - - - - - */

SCORE(PLY) = SCORE(PLY - 2);
GENERATE_MOVES(BOARD,PLY);
MOVE_PTR(PLY) = 0;

/* - - - - - - - - - - - - -MOVE FORWARD TO SUCCESSOR POSITION - - - - - - - - - - - - - - - - - - - -*/
/*        1. GET THE NEXT MOVE                                               */
/*        2. TEST MOVE                                                       */
/*              A. IF NO MOVE AND PLY IS 0, EXIT                             */
/*              B. IF NO MOVE AND PLY IS NOT 0, GO TO TERMINAL_POSITION      */
/*              C. OTHERWISE, IF NO MORE MOVES, BACKUP                       */
```

Figure 2.8. Pseudo-C version of the depth-first minimax algorithm.

```
/*        3. CONSTRUCT SUCCESSOR POSITION                                  */
/*        4. INCREMENT CURRENT SEARCH DEPTH                                */
/*        5. GO TO NEW POSITION                                            */
/* ---------------------------------------------------------------------- */

ADVANCE:
MOVE = MOVES(MOVE_PTR(PLY),PLY);
IF (MOVE EQUALS 0) {
        IF (PLY EQUALS 0) EXIT;
        IF (MOVE_PTR(PLY) EQUALS 0) GOTO SCORE_POSITION;
        GOTO BACKUP;}

BOARD = SUCCESSOR(BOARD,MOVE);
PLY++;
GOTO NEW_POSITION;

/* ------------------------ AT A TERMINAL POSITION --------------------- */
/*        DETERMINE ITS SCORE                                             */
/* ---------------------------------------------------------------------- */

TERMINAL_POSITION:
SCORE(PLY) = SCORE_POSITION(BOARD);

/* -------------- BACK UP TO PREDECESSOR POSITION ---------------------- */
/*        1. DECREMENT THE CURRENT SEARCH DEPTH                           */
/*        2. GET MOVE TO BACK UP ON                                       */
/*        3. RECONSTRUCT PREDECESSOR POSITION                             */
/* ---------------------------------------------------------------------- */

BACKUP:
PLY--;
MOVE = MOVES(MOVE_PTR(PLY),PLY);
BOARD = PREDECESSOR(BOARD,MOVE);

/* ------------------------------ MINIMAX NOW ------------------------- */
/*        IF MOVE IS GOOD, BACK UP SCORE, SAVE IN PC ARRAY                */
/* ---------------------------------------------------------------------- */

IF (((PLY IS EVEN) AND (SCORE(PLY) LESS THAN SCORE(PLY + 1)) OR
        ((PLY IS ODD) AND (SCORE(PLY) GREATER THAN SCORE(PLY + 1)) {
        SCORE(PLY) = SCORE(PLY + 1);
        SET_PC(MOVE),PLY);}

MOVE_PTR(PLY)++;
GOTO ADVANCE;
```

Figure 2.8. (continued)

SUCCESSOR(BOARD,MOVE) and PREDECESSOR(BOARD,MOVE) are called to construct the successor and predecessor, respectively, of a board position BOARD, when move MOVE is made or taken back. These functions require only a few lines of code. Note that a computer need keep only one representation of the board in memory when searching the tree. As the computer goes from one position to another it moves the pieces on this one board.

CALC_PC(MOVE,PLY) saves good moves in the principal continuation array PC in row PLY. Whenever a good move is found in some position at some ply, say PLY, it is placed in PC(PLY,PLY) and the continuation in row PLY+1 is moved up, column for column, to row PLY. A good move is defined as a move for which a score is backed up to the position where the move originates.

The depth-first minimax search of a tree: an example

Figure 2.9 illustrates a depth-first minimax search of an abstract game tree of depth four with twelve terminal positions. The same tree is used to illustrate the alpha-beta algorithm later in this chapter. In Chapter 5, it is used again to illustrate the use of transposition tables. Positions at even levels in the tree are drawn as squares and those at odd levels as circles. Moves label each branch; note that some moves appear several times in the tree. The scores of the terminal positions are shown to their right. Arrows show the path of the search. It is a top-down depth-first search: terminal positions are encountered from the top of the page down to the bottom.

The search path begins at the root of the tree, position A. The minimax algorithm begins by setting the score of the root to $-\infty$. Later on, the algorithm will back up a score to the root whenever one of its children is found to have a more positive value. Thus a score will be backed up to the root when the search of the first move, move a, has been completed. Moves a and b are then generated and listed in MOVES(0,0) and MOVES(1,0). The successor of position A when move a is made, that is, position B, is then constructed. A score of $+\infty$ is then assigned to position B. Here, the algorithm will back up a score to position B whenever one of its children is found later to have a more negative score. The moves at position B, moves c and d, are then generated and listed in MOVES(0,1) and MOVES(1,1).

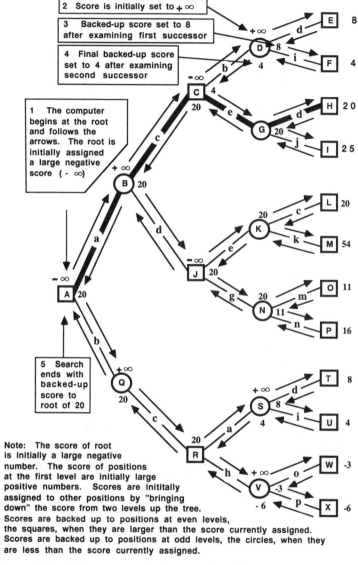

2 Score is initially set to $+\infty$

3 Backed-up score set to 8 after examining first successor

4 Final backed-up score set to 4 after examining second successor

1 The computer begins at the root and follows the arrows. The root is initially assigned a large negative score ($-\infty$)

5 Search ends with backed-up score to root of 20

Note: The score of root is initially a large negative number. The score of positions at the first level are initially large positive numbers. Scores are initially assigned to other positions by "bringing down" the score from two levels up the tree. Scores are backed up to positions at even levels, the squares, when they are larger than the score currently assigned. Scores are backed up to positions at odd levels, the circles, when they are less than the score currently assigned.

Figure 2.9. Minimax search of a four-level abstract game tree.

The successor of position B when move c is made, that is, position C, is then constructed and assigned a score of $-\infty$. This process of going deeper in the tree continues until position E is constructed. The scoring function is then called to evaluate E, and it returns a value of 8. The predecessor of E, that is, position D, is then reconstructed and a score of 8 is backed up to it since 8 is less than the $+\infty$ that was initially assigned to it. This continues until the search of move *b* in position A has been completed.

The root will then have been assigned a score of 20 and the principal continuation, the line of play that the search concludes is best for each side, is *a-c-e-d* as the bold line indicates.

Figure 2.10 shows how moves are placed in the PC array as search is carried out. Whenever a score is backed up on move MOVE from one position to its predecessor at ply PLY, MOVE is placed in the PC array. It is placed in PC(PLY,PLY), and moves in PC in the next lower row are moved up one location. That happens fourteen times, and thus fourteen calls to

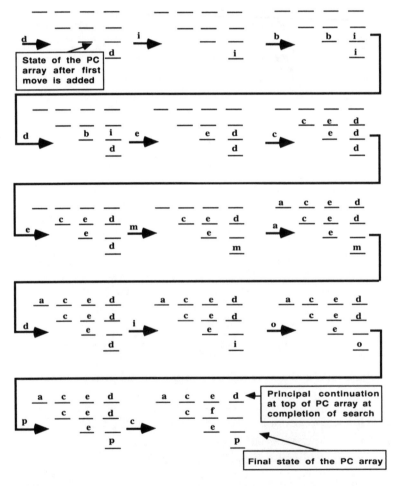

Figure 2.10. Forming the principal continuation in the PC array.

SET_PC are made. The ninth call places the continuation *a-c-e-d* in the top row, where it remains.

Depth-first search requires memory space that grows linearly with the depth of search, while breadth-first search, the other basic search strategy, requires memory space that grows exponentially with the depth of search. In the old days, the large amount of memory required by breadth-first search virtually ruled it out for chess. Even now, when memory space is a much less important criterion for choosing a search strategy, almost all chess programs continue to use depth-first search because of its simpler implementation.

The horizon effect, ostriches, and Alan Turing

In 1951, Alan Turing reported his work on computer chess at the University of Manchester. Like Shannon, Turing was one of the outstanding pioneers of computer science: every student in the field has learned how to program a Turing machine to scan a tape for some strange set of sequences. Turing is also credited with cracking the German coded messages of the Second World War.

Turing was the first person to design and execute—by hand!—a chess playing program. He designed a simple scoring function in which material was the dominant factor. All lines of play from the current position to a

Claude Shannon, father of computer chess.

depth of two plies were examined and then all "considerable" moves were followed, stopping when a "dead" position was reached. A dead position was one in which there were no considerable moves, defined as those that (a) capture an undefended piece, (b) recapture a piece, (c) capture a defended piece with one of lesser value, or (d) give mate.

To play a game by hand using such a scheme had the potential of taking a great deal of time and patience. With thirty to forty moves in the typical position, Turing might have had to consider more than a thousand terminal positions and perform evaluations for many of them. Turing probably avoided scoring all of them by using a variation of the alpha-beta algorithm which is discussed shortly, although he might not have done so conscientiously. If the material evaluations were equal for two or more positions at depth one, positional factors were used to break the tie. This positional value did not take into account all the pieces on the board but only those of the side to move as well as the opponent's king. The components of Turing's positional evaluation were as follows:

1. Mobility: For the queen, rooks, bishops, and knights, add the square roots of the number of moves that the piece can make, counting a capture as two moves. (For the sake of simplicity Turing approximated square roots to one decimal place.)

2. Piece safety: For the rooks, bishops, and knights add 1 point if there is one defender, and 1.5 if there is more than one.

3. King mobility: For the king use the same method of scoring as for the pieces, but do not count castling.

4. King safety: Deduct points for the king's vulnerability, defined as the number of moves that a queen could make were it on the square of the king.

5. Castling: Add 1 point if castling is still legally possible after this move (i.e., if neither the king nor the rook has yet moved). Add another point if castling is immediately possible or if a castling move has just been made.

6. Pawn credit: Score 0.2 points for each rank advanced and 0.3 points for each pawn defended by one or more non-pawns.

7. Check and mate threats: Score 1 point for the threat of mate and 0.5 points for a check.

The material values assigned to each of the pieces were pawn = 1, knight = 3, bishop = 3.5, rook = 5, queen = 10.

The following game was played in Manchester in 1951 between Turing's hand simulation and Alick Glennie, then twenty-six years old and a weak chess player.

1951, Manchester
White: Turing's program (simulation)   *Black: Alick Glennie*
Vienna Game

---

1 e4 e5 2 Nc3 Nf6 3 d4 Bb4 4 Nf3 d6 5 Bd2 Nc6 6 d5 Nd4 7 h4

We see very early in the history of computer chess that computers have a mind of their own. Turing's evaluation function, as well as the evaluation functions of many of the more recent programs, encourage advancing pawns (exemplified by a credit of 0.3 points for each rank advanced) and increasing mobility (score the square root of the number of moves that a piece can make). The move 7 h4 receives a credit of 0.6 points for advancing the pawn two ranks, and it increases the mobility of the rook on h1 from two moves (for which it receives a credit of 1.4 points) to four moves (for which it receives a credit of 2 points).

7 . . . Bg4 8 a4

Given White's previous move, this one should be no surprise!

8 . . . N×f3+ 9 g×f3 Bh5 10 Bb5+ c6

Obviously 10 . . . Nd7 would be better. The simulation should have seen that 10 . . . c6 11 d×c6 b×c6 12 B×c6+ loses a pawn, even if it didn't see that it also led to the loss of an exchange as well.

11 d×c6 O-O 12 c×b7 Rb8 13 Ba6 Qa5 14 Qe2 Nd7 15 Rg1

Increasing White's mobility while leaving queen-side castling still possible.

15 . . . Nc5

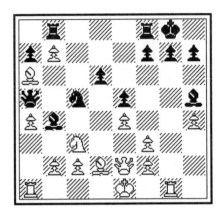

Figure 2.11. Position after 15 . . . Nc5.

16 Rg5

The "horizon effect" is born! Turing and others have commented that this move was made using the "heads in the sand" approach, like an ostrich. The program is faced with the loss of a pawn on b7 and delays this happening for as long as possible.

By playing 16 Rg5 the program tries to close its eyes to reality—it simply pushes reality, in this case the loss of the pawn on b7, over its search horizon. Now, after Black moves his attacked bishop and White retreats his own bishop, the threat of the capture of the pawn on b7 still remains, but its capture will occur beyond the program's search horizon.

It is a coincidence that 16 Rg5 is actually White's best move, but Turing and many later commentators on this game have overlooked the reason.

16 . . . Bg6 17 Bb5

Better for White was 17 Bc4 since if Black were then to capture the pawn on b7 White could play 18 h5, trapping the bishop (18 . . . h6 19 R×g6). If Black counters 17 Bc4 with 17 . . . Kh8, avoiding the pin on the g8–a2 diagonal, White wins by 18 h5. For example, 18 . . . f6 19 R×g6 h7×g6 20 h×g6, and Black's pieces are so out of play that it is unable to prevent White from mating him by Qf1 followed by Qh1, or f4 followed by Qh5. To play 17 . . . Kh8 18 h5 h6 is also no good because of 19 h×g6 h×g5 20

Qf1 etc. It seems that Black must reply to 17 Bc4 with 17 . . . Ne6 18 B×e6 f×e6, when White has an excellent position. Moreover, 17 h5 at once is not good enough because of 17 . . . Ne6. So by playing 17 Bc4, Turing's program would have had a clear advantage.

17 . . . N×b7 18 O-O-O

Again, 18 Bc4, threatening 19 h5, probably gives White a won game. Even 18 h5 h6 19 h×g6 h×g5 20 Bc4 is clearly better than castling. The program, however, is more attracted by the bonus attached to the move played.

18 . . . Nc5 19 Bc6 Rfc8

19 . . . Ne6 was essential, for obvious reasons.

20 Bd5 B×c3 21 B×c3 Q×a4 22 Kd2 Ne6 23 Rg4 Nd4 24 Qd3 Nb5 25 Bb3 Qa6 26 Bc4

26 Rdg1 gives White a winning attack, but the fruits of the move are too far off for White to see.

26 . . . Bh5 27 Rg3 Qa4 28 B×b5 Q×b5

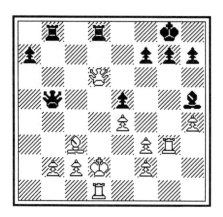

Figure 2.12. Position after 23 . . . Qxb5.

29 Q×d6 29 . . . Rd8 White resigns.

White had overlooked the strength of this "deep" move. The program only looked to a depth of two plies, and so when it considered 29 Q×d6 it was unable to see as far as the position in which its queen was captured (which was at depth 4).

Turing summed up the weakness of his "program" by describing it as a caricature of his own play. "It was in fact based on an introspective analysis of my thought processes when playing, with considerable simplifications. It makes oversights which are very similar to those which I make myself, and which may in both cases be ascribed to the considerable moves being inappropriately chosen."

The first programs for electronic computers

The first working programs appeared in the late 1950s. The first was the LOS ALAMOS chess program, developed at the Los Alamos Scientific Laboratory in New Mexico. It was developed by a group of prominent scientists—James Kister, Paul Stein, Stanislaw Ulam, William Walden, and Mark Wells—and ran on a Univac MANIAC I computer. The MANIAC I executed about eleven thousand instructions per second, at least a million times slower than the fastest computers now available. Of course, operating systems had not yet been developed, and programming was a slow, tedious process. To simplify matters, they developed their program for a 6×6 chess board, with no bishops and six pawns per side. Their program examined all continuations to a depth of four in about twelve minutes. Its level of play was unimpressive.

The first full-fledged chess program was written by Alex Bernstein, Michael de V. Roberts, Thomas Arbuckle, and Martin A. Belsky. It was designed for the IBM 704, one of IBM's last vacuum tube computers. The 704 executed about forty-two thousand instructions per second, four times as fast as the MANIAC I. The program was designed to search four plies deep and to search seven moves at each position in the tree. Thus there were 7×7×7×7 terminal positions and 1 + 7 + 7×7 + 7×7×7 nonterminal positions in the trees searched. A move typically took eight minutes. In making a move, then, 42,000×8×60 instructions were executed. If the number of instructions executed at nonterminal positions was eight times as many as at terminal positions, there were 28,800 instructions executed at each nonterminal position and 3,600 instructions executed at each terminal position. Its level of play was also unimpressive.

Carnegie Mellon University has been one of the leaders in the field of artificial intelligence, led on by Nobel Prize winner Herb Simon (for his work in economics!) and Alan Newell. The two teamed up with John Shaw and developed the NEWELL, SHAW, and SIMON (NSS) chess program in the middle 1950s. It attempted to use various goals to guide the search. A material advantage was the first goal. It was the first chess program to use a high-level language (IPL-4). Its performance was also unimpressive.

The alpha-beta algorithm

The alpha-beta algorithm seems to have been implemented for the first time in the NSS chess program. It takes advantage of the fact that when carrying out a depth-first minimax search of a game tree, not all continuations must be examined to determine the principal continuation. For example, referring again to Figure 2.4, after the computer finds that 1 B×c3 leads to a score of +1, it then examines the continuation 1 R×d4 Q×b4 and finds that it leads to a score of −3. When it discovers this, it concludes that Black's 1 . . . Q×b4 refutes 1 R×d4, that is, 1 . . . Q×b4 makes 1 R×d4 look bad when compared to 1 B×c3. Because Black's 1 . . . Q×b4 refutes 1 R×d4, there is no need to consider any other Black reply to White's 1 R×d4. Search can be stopped or cut off at position C after move 1 . . . Q×b4 has been examined. This means that only three of the four terminal positions need be scored.

The cutoff described in the previous paragraph is a shallow cutoff. Deep cutoffs can also occur as illustrated in Figure 2.13. In this abstract position, the computer first searches White's move A and finds it leads to a score of 10. Then move sequence B-C-D-E is followed out to position Q, and position Q is assigned a score of 2 by the scoring function. At this point, the computer realizes it would be foolish to allow the game to proceed to position P with a score of at most 2 when it can play move A leading to a score of 10. The score is at most 2 because there may be another move in position P that has not yet been searched and that is even better for Black than move E. Move E is a refutation of move D, and no other

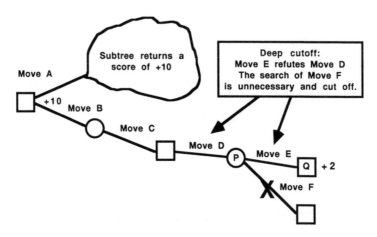

Figure 2.13. Partially drawn game tree showing deep alpha-beta cutoff.

move in position P need be searched. Move E leading to position Q is said to be a deep refutation and search is cut off at position P.

Only minor programming modifications must be made to the minimax algorithm to include code for causing these cutoffs. This modified minimax algorithm takes the name "alpha-beta algorithm" and is shown in Figure 2.14. Note that the pseudo-C code in Figure 2.14 is identical to that in Figure 2.8 except for the five additional lines following the label ALPHA_BETA. When the game tree presented in Figure 2.9 is searched by the alpha-beta algorithm as shown in Figure 2.15, three moves are found to be refutations.

The effectiveness of the alpha-beta algorithm depends on the order in which moves are searched at each position in the tree. If at each position the best move is always searched first, the maximum number of refutations occur and the minimum number of positions are scored. Analysis will show that in a tree with F moves in each position and searched to a depth $DMAX$, the minimum number of terminal positions is:

$$2F^{DMAX/2} - 1 \qquad \text{for } DMAX \text{ even}$$
$$F^{(DMAX+1)/2} + F^{(DMAX-1)/2} - 1 \qquad \text{for } DMAX \text{ odd}$$

These two expressions essentially say that a program that incorporates the alpha-beta algorithm is able to search twice as deeply as one without it. This is an incredible bonus for simply adding a few lines of code to the

```
/* PSEUDO-C CODE FOR THE ALPHA_BETA ALGORITHM - - - - - - - - - - - - - - - - - - - - - - - - - - - - - - - - - -*/

/* - - - - - - - - - - - - - - - - DATA STRUCTURES - - - - - - - - - - - - - - - - - - - - - - - - - - - - - - - - - - - - -*/

INTEGER BOARD(8,8), MOVES(50,256), MP(50), SCORE(52),
INTEGER PC(50,50), MOVE, DMAX, PLY;

/*- - - - - - - - - - - - - - - - FUNCTIONS CALLED- - - - - - - - - - - - - - - - - - - - - - - - - - - - - - - - - - - -*/
ENTER_POSITION(), SET_DMAX(), GENERATE_MOVES(),                                      */
/*       SCORE_POSITION(), SUCCESSOR(), PREDECESSOR(), SET_PC()                      */
/*- - - - - - - - - - - - - - - - - - - - - - - - - - - - - - - - - - - - - - - - - - - - - - - - - - - - - - - - - - - - - - - */

/*- - - - - - - - - - - - - - - - - INITIALIZE - - - - - - - - - - - - - - - - - - - - - - - - - - - - - - - - - - - - - - - -*/
/*       1. ENTER POSITION IN BOARD(8,8)                                             */
/*       2. SET MAXIMUM SEARCH DEPTH, DMAX                                           */
/*       3. SET INITIAL VALUES OF SCORE(-2) AND SCORE(-1)                            */
/*              TO EFFECTIVELY -∞ AND +∞ RESPECTIVELY                               */
/*- - - - - - - - - - - - - - - - - - - - - - - - - - - - - - - - - - - - - - - - - - - - - - - - - - - - - - - - - - - - - - - */

ENTER_POSITION();
SET_DMAX();
PLY = 0;
SCORE(-2) = -100000;
SCORE(-1) = +100000;

/*- - - - - - - - - - - - - - - - A NEW POSITION IS REACHED - - - - - - - - - - - - - - - - - - - - - - - - - - - - -*/
/*       IF AT MAXIMUM DEPTH, GO TO TERMINAL_POSITION.                               */
/*- - - - - - - - - - - - - - - - - - - - - - - - - - - - - - - - - - - - - - - - - - - - - - - - - - - - - - - - - - - - - - - */

NEW_POSITION:
IF (PLY EQUALS DMAX) GOTO TERMINAL_POSITION;

/*- - - - - - - - - - - - - - - - OTHERWISE, IF NOT AT MAXIMUM DEPTH - - - - - - - - - - - - - - - - - - - - - -*/
/*       1. BRING DOWN THE SCORE FROM TWO LEVELS HIGHER,                             */
/*       2. GENERATE MOVES, PLACE THEM IN THE MOVES ARRAY,                           */
/*          IN LOCATIONS MOVES(0,PLY), MOVES(1,PLY), . . . ,                         */
/*          AND PLACES A "0" AT THE END OF THE LIST,                                 */
/*       3. SET THE MOVE POINTER AT DEPTH "PLY" TO THE FIRST MOVE,                   */
/*- - - - - - - - - - - - - - - - - - - - - - - - - - - - - - - - - - - - - - - - - - - - - - - - - - - - - - - - - - - - - - - */

SCORE(PLY) = SCORE(PLY - 2);
GENERATE_MOVES(BOARD,PLY);
MOVE_PTR(PLY) = 0;

/*- - - - - - - - - - - - - - - - MOVE FORWARD TO SUCCESSOR POSITION - - - - - - - - - - - - - - - - - - - - - -*/
/*       1. GET THE NEXT MOVE                                                        */
/*       2. TEST MOVE                                                                */
/*              A. IF NO MOVE AND PLY IS 0, EXIT                                      */
/*              B. IF NO MOVE AND PLY IS NOT 0, GO TO TERMINAL_POSITION              */
/*              C. OTHERWISE, IF NO MORE MOVES, BACKUP                               */
/*       3. CONSTRUCT SUCCESSOR POSITION                                             */
/*       4. INCREMENT CURRENT SEARCH DEPTH                                           */
/*       5. GO TO NEW POSITION                                                       */
/* - - - - - - - - - - - - - - - - - - - - - - - - - - - - - - - - - - - - - - - - - - - - - - - - - - - - - - - - - - - - - - */

ADVANCE:
MOVE = MOVES(MOVE_PTR(PLY),PLY);
IF (MOVE EQUALS 0) {
        IF (PLY EQUALS 0) EXIT;
        IF (MOVE_PTR(PLY) EQUALS 0) GOTO SCORE_POSITION;
        GOTO BACKUP;}
```

Figure 2.14. Pseudo-C version of the alpha-beta algorithm.

```
BOARD = SUCCESSOR(BOARD,MOVE);
PLY++;
GOTO NEW_POSITION;

/*--------------------- AT A TERMINAL POSITION  ---------------------------------*/
/*        DETERMINE ITS SCORE                                                    */
/*------------------------------------------------------------------------------/

TERMINAL_POSITION:
SCORE(PLY) = SCORE_POSITION(BOARD);

/*----------- BACK UP TO PREDECESSOR POSITION ----------------------------------*/
/*        1. DECREMENT THE CURRENT SEARCH DEPTH                                 */
/*        2. GET MOVE TO BACK UP ON                                            */
/*        3. RECONSTRUCT PREDECESSOR POSITION                                   */
/*------------------------------------------------------------------------------*/

BACKUP:
PLY--;
MOVE = MOVES(MOVE_PTR(PLY),PLY);
BOARD = PREDECESSOR(BOARD,MOVE);

/*----------------------- MINIMAX NOW  -----------------------------------------*/
/*        IF MOVE IS GOOD, BACK UP SCORE, SAVE IN PC ARRAY                      */
/*------------------------------------------------------------------------------/

IF (((PLY IS EVEN) AND (SCORE(PLY) LESS THAN SCORE(PLY + 1)) OR
        ((PLY IS ODD) AND (SCORE(PLY) GREATER THAN SCORE(PLY + 1)) {
        SCORE(PLY) = SCORE(PLY + 1);
        SET_PC(MOVE,PLY);}

/*------------------ TEST FOR ALPHA-BETA CUTOFF --------------------------------*/
/*        IF CUTOFF IS FOUND, BACK UP AND CUTOFF SEARCH                         */
/*------------------------------------------------------------------------------*/

IF (((PLY IS EVEN) AND (SCORE(PLY) GREATER THAN SCORE(PLY - 1)) OR
        ((PLY IS ODD) AND (SCORE(PLY) LESS THAN SCORE(PLY - 1)) {
        PLY--;
        MOVE = MOVES(MOVE_PTR(PLY),PLY);
        BOARD = PREDECESSOR(BOARD,MOVE);
MOVE_PTR(PLY)++;
GOTO ADVANCE;
```

Figure 2.14. (continued)

minimax algorithm. Figure 2.16 shows the minimum number of positions that must be scored when searching to depths $DMAX = 2, 4, \ldots, 14, 16$, and with thirty moves in each position (or thereabouts where approximations have been introduced to keep numbers round). The table shows that a minimum alpha-beta search to a depth of sixteen levels must score at least two trillion positions, only a factor of fifty or so more than DEEP BLUE currently examines, and within the reach of computers in the next few years!

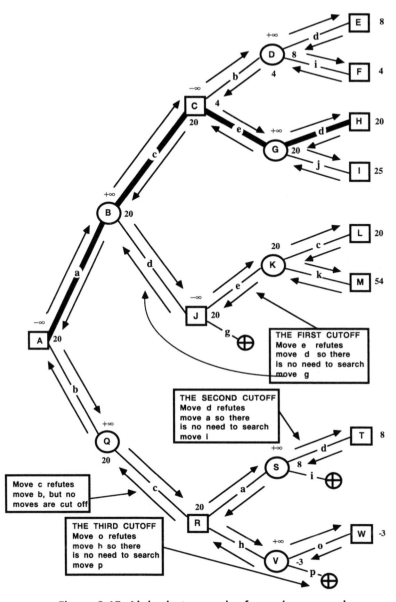

Figure 2.15. Alpha-beta search of ongoing example.

Search Depth (DMAX)	Minimum number of terminal positions in an alpha-beta search	
2	$\sim 2 \times 30^1 \approx 6 \times 10^1$	$= 60$
4	$\sim 2 \times 30^2 \approx 2 \times 10^3$	$= 2,000$
6	$\sim 2 \times 30^3 \approx 6 \times 10^4$	$= 60,000$
8	$\sim 2 \times 30^4 \approx 2 \times 10^6$	$= 2,000,000$
10	$\sim 2 \times 30^5 \approx 6 \times 10^7$	$= 60,000,000$
12	$\sim 2 \times 30^6 \approx 2 \times 10^9$	$= 2,000,000,000$
14	$\sim 2 \times 30^7 \approx 6 \times 10^{10}$	$= 60,000,000,000$
16	$\sim 2 \times 30^8 \approx 2 \times 10^{12}$	$= 2,000,000,000,000$

Figure 2.16. Minimum number of terminal positions scored in an alpha-beta search as a function of search depth, DMAX.

Of course, in the great majority of positions, the minimum number is not achieved. If it were, that would mean that the computer, as a minimum, first searched the principal continuation, and if it were smart enough to do that, then there would be no need to carry out the remainder of the search! However, by using move ordering techniques, most programs are able to come very close to these minimum figures.

References

C. E. Shannon, "Programming a computer for playing chess," *Philosophical Magazine* 41 (1950): 256–75.

A. M. Turing, "Digital computers applied to games," in *Faster Than Thought,* ed. B. V. Bowden (London: Pitman, 1953), 286–310.

J. Kister, P. Stein, S. Ulam, W. Walden, and M. Wells, "Experiments in chess," *Journal of the Association for Computing Machinery* (1957): 174–77.

A. Bernstein, M. de V. Roberts, T. Arbuckle, and M. A. Belsky, "A chess playing program for the IBM 704," *Proc. Western Joint Computer Conference* (1958): 157–59.

A. Newell, J. C. Shaw, and H. A. Simon, "Chess playing programs and the problem of complexity," *IBM Journal of Research and Development* 4, no. 2 (1958): 320–35. Also in *Computer and Thought,* eds. Feigenbaum and Feldman (McGraw-Hill: 1967).

3 Signs of Hope and KAISSA

The 1960s were the days of the Cold War between the United States and the former USSR, but as cold as relations were between these two adversaries, there was one area where some friendly cooperation took place. The authors of two chess programs, one in the United States and the other on the other side of the Iron Curtain and both the cream of the thin crop of those days, agreed to hold a friendly four-game match in 1966 with moves communicated across the Atlantic by telegraph.

Alan Kotok developed his program at MIT as his bachelor's thesis. His supervisor was John McCarthy, a prominent computer scientist who left MIT for Stanford around the beginning of the match. In addition to his contributions to computer chess, McCarthy is widely known for developing the programming language Lisp. The KOTOK/MCCARTHY program was written in FORTRAN and assembly language, and was modeled on Shannon's Type B strategy. It used the alpha-beta algorithm along with graduated forward pruning. During the match, the program ran on Stanford's IBM 7090 computer.

The ITEP (Institute of Theoretical and Experimental Physics) Program was developed by the Moscow-based group of George Adelson-Velsky, Vladimir Arlazarov, Alexander Uskov, Alexander Bitman, and Alexander Zhivotovsky. Arlazarov was the head of the group, Adelson-Velsky was its sage, and Bitman the chess whiz. The program ran on a Soviet M-20 computer and used Shannon's Type A strategy.

On November 22, 1966, the two groups began their match. After about nine months the ITEP program emerged the winner with a 3-1 score.

Games were adjudicated as drawn when the fortieth move was reached. It is likely that the Soviet program would have won all four games if they had been played to completion. In its two victories—mating in nineteen moves in one game and in thirty-seven moves in the other—the ITEP program was searching to a depth of five plies. In its two draws, it was searching to a depth of three plies. The KOTOK/MCCARTHY program was searching to a depth of four plies in all four games.

The results of this match showed very vividly for the first time that deeper search pays off. It was also one example of a Type A search being superior to a Type B search. Mikhail Botvinnik, when discussing the games, said that the heuristics for pruning moves in the KOTOK/MCCARTHY program were inadequate and threw away the baby with the bath water too often. This match also marked the beginning of the dominance of Arlazarov's group in the world of computer chess. It reigned for a decade—until the second world championship in Toronto in 1977.

Vladimir Arlzarov of the KAISSA team, 1983.

November 22, 1966
Game 1, ITEP program versus KOTOK/MCCARTHY program
Four-game match
White: ITEP program   Black: KOTOK/MCCARTHY program
Four Knights Game

In this game and in the next, the ITEP program is searching to a depth of three plies on each move using no forward pruning while the KOTOK/MCCARTHY program is searching to a depth of four plies but using forward pruning.

1 e4 e5 2 Nc3 Nc6 3 Nf3 Bc5 4 Bc4 Nf6 5 O-O O-O 6 d3 d6 7 Be3 Bg4 8 h3 Bh5
9 Bd5 Bd4 10 g4 B×c3 11 b×c3 Bg6 12 Bg5 Re8 13 Rb1 Rb8 14 Qe2 Kh8

The KOTOK/MCCARTHY program is out of ideas, and its king safety algorithm probably sees keeping the king in the corner as improving its safety; other moves evidently make matters worse.

15 d4 Kg8 16 Qc4 Na5 17 B×f6 Q×f6 18 Qd3 c6 19 d×e5 d×e5 20 Bb3 Rbd8
21 Qe3 b6 22 Rbd1 Rd6 23 g5 Qe7 24 Rd3 R×d3 25 c×d3 Rd8 26 Ra1 Qd6
27 d4 e×d4 28 c×d4 N×b3 29 a×b3 a5 30 Ra4 Qe6 31 Ne5 Qe8 32 f4 Rd6
33 f5 Bh5 34 Nc4 Rd8 35 N×b6 Rb8 36 Nc4 Bd1

A human playing at the level of these programs might be a bit reluctant to invade the opponent's camp in this way where a way out is not obvious.

37 Ra3 Bc2 Declared drawn.

White is ahead a pawn and has the better game. In the final position, White would have to continue with 38 Nd2, then chase the bishop to h5 and go on to attack Black's weak queenside pawns.

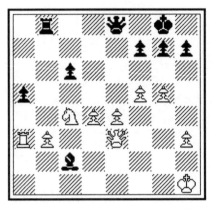

Figure 3.1. Position after 37 . . . Bc2 Declared drawn.

November 22, 1966
Game 2, ITEP program versus KOTOK/MCCARTHY program
four-game match
White: KOTOK/MCCARTHY program   Black: ITEP program
Alekhine's Defense

1 e4 Nf6 2 e5 Nd5 3 Nf3 e6 4 Bb5 a6 5 Ba4 b5 6 Bb3 Bb4 7 Nc3 Nf4 8 O-O Bb7
9 d4 B×c3 10 b×c3 Nd5 11 B×d5 B×d5 12 Ba3 d6 13 e×d6 c×d6 14 Re1 Nc6
15 Re3 O-O 16 Qe2 Bc5 17 Qe1 Qc7 18 Bb4 a5 19 Ba3 Kh8 20 Ng5 h6
21 Ne4 Rfd8 22 Nxd6 Rxd6 23 Bxd6 Qxd6

This shows that the KOTOK/MCCARTHY program believes a bishop and
knight are equal to a rook and pawn.

24 a3 Ne7 25 Re5 Nc6

The ITEP program is consistent in chasing invaders quickly.

26 Rc5 e5 27 Qe4 Ra6 28 Rd1 g6 29 Rd2 g5 30 Rd1 h5

Both sides are out of ideas! Black might have moved its king to the corner,
but it is already there.

31 Rd2 f6 32 Qe3 e×d4 33 c×d4 Ne7 34 Qg3 Q×g3 35 h×g3 Nd5 36 Rc8+ Kh7
37 Rf8 b4 38 a×b4 N×b4 39 c3 Nd5 40 Rc8 Declared drawn.

George Adelson-Velsky of the KAISSA team in Moscow, 1992.

At the level these two are playing, Black should win this endgame. International master Danny Kopec suggested to the author that 40 ... Nb6 41 Rc6 a4 42 d5 a3 43 d6 a2 is winning for Black and if 42 Rb2, then 42 ... Bb3 should still be winning for Black.

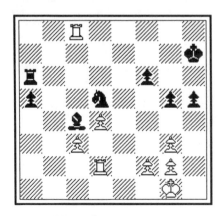

Figure 3.2. Position after 40 Rc8 Declared drawn.

November 22, 1966
Game 3, ITEP program versus KOTOK/McCARTHY program
Four-game match
White: ITEP program   Black: KOTOK/McCARTHY program
Three Knights Game

1 e4 e5 2 Nf3 Nc6 3 Nc3 Bc5 4 Nxe5 Nxe5

Note that in the first game when carrying out a three-ply search in the same position, White played a less venturesome 4 Bc4, unable to see that the six-ply continuation 4 N×e5 N×e5 5 d4 Bd6 6 d×e5 B×e5 doesn't lose material. But White didn't seem to mind Black playing 4 ... B×f2+ K×f2 5 N×e5, which leaves White's king in an awkward position.

5 d4 Bd6 6 d×e5 B×e5 7 f4 B×c3+ 8 b×c3 Nf6

Black invites trouble. After the following five consecutive knight moves, Black will be finished.

9 e5 Ne4 10 Qd3 Nc5 11 Qd5 Ne6

Better for Black is 11 . . . d6, giving his pieces some space.

Figure 3.3. Position after 11 . . . Ne6.

12 f5 Ng5 13 h4 f6 14 h×g5 f×g5 15 R×h7 Rf8 16 R×g7 c6 17 Qd6 R×f5
18 Rg8+ Rf8 19 Q×f8#.

November 22, 1966
Game 4, I<small>TEP</small> program versus K<small>OTOK</small>/M<small>C</small>C<small>ARTHY</small> program
Four-game match
White: K<small>OTOK</small>/M<small>C</small>C<small>ARTHY</small> program   Black: I<small>TEP</small> program
Alekhine's Defense

---

1 e4 Nf6 2 e5 Nd5 3 Nf3 Nb4 4 Bb5 c6

The I<small>TEP</small> program remains consistent in chasing away invaders.

5 Ba4 d6 6 d4

White totally overlooks Black's next move. Its search was too shallow.

6 . . . Qa5 7 c4 Nc2+ 8 Kf1 N×a1

The knight is now trapped, but the K<small>OTOK</small>/M<small>C</small>C<small>ARTHY</small> program does not realize this and will let the opportunity to recover at least some compensation for the captured rook vanish. After just eight moves, Black has a won game.

9 Nc3 Qb4 10 Qe2 d×e5 11 d×e5 Be6 12 Qd1

White is trying to be sure 12 . . . B×c4 does not pin its queen; it should have played 12 Nd2.

12 . . . B×c4+ 13 Ne2 b5 14 Bc2 Nxc2 15 Q×c2

Now, after fifteen moves, Black is ahead a rook and pawn and will have an easy win once it completes developing its pieces.

15 . . . B×a2 16 Ned4 Qc4+

The I<small>TEP</small> program evidently understands that trading queens in this won position is a good idea.

17 Kg1 c5 18 Qd2

This is White's third serious error although it matters little.

18 . . . c×d4 19 N×d4 e6 20 Nf3 Nc6 21 Qg5 Rd8 22 Bd2 Qc1+ 23 Be1 Q×b2
24 Qf4 Bd5 25 Qg3 Qe2 26 Bc3 b4 27 Be1 B×f3 28 g×f3 Q×e1+ 29 Kg2 Q×e5
30 Qh4 a4 31 Rc1 Nd4 32 Rf1 N×f3

Black must see that White cannot play 33 K×f3 because of 33 . . . Rd4, giving Black a queen and pawn in exchange for a rook and knight.

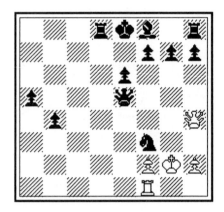

Figure 3.4. Position after 32 . . . N×f3.

33 Qh3 Rd3 34 Qg3 Ne1+ 35 R×e1 R×g3+ 36 Kf1 Qb5+ 37 Re2 Ra3
38 Ke1 Ra1+ 39 Kd2 Qd5+

Black must see mate in three. Otherwise it could have won a rook with
39 . . . Qa2+.

40 Ke3 Ra3+ 41 Kf4 Qf5#.

In 1971, Arlazarov added Moscow State University graduate Mikhail
Donskoy to his group. Several years later, they all moved to the Institute
for Control Science several blocks away. Donskoy rewrote much of the
ITEP program and gave birth to KAISSA. Donskoy was not a strong chess
player, but he was an excellent programmer. He and Arlazarov played
bridge together as a hobby; Donskoy was one of the top players in the former Soviet Union. Whenever they came to chess tournaments, the two
would disappear late in the evening only to be found playing bridge with
colleagues.

KAISSA ran on a British ICL 4/70 and evaluated about 200 positions
per second. In January of 1972, the readers of the Soviet newspaper
Komsomolskaia Pravda invited KAISSA to play a two-game match. Over
the coming weeks, the readers submitted their preferred moves and the
most popular one was selected and given to KAISSA, who in turn calculated a reply that was then published in the newspaper. On each move,
KAISSA searched to a depth of seven plies and deeper along lines that in-

volved captures and forcing moves. KAISSA had a complex scoring function and was designed to search to a depth of thirty plies along highly forced lines. KAISSA drew one game and lost the other. The readers of *Komsomolskaia Pravda* had played Boris Spassky the previous year, losing one game and drawing the other. One can conclude that the readers were a tough lot since they were able to draw with Spassky, and that KAISSA couldn't have been too bad either: it drew with someone who drew with Spassky.

KAISSA introduced the "method of analogies," a technique that attempts to say two positions are sufficiently similar that they can be judged equivalent, making it unnecessary to search the second one. This strategy can be illustrated by the position in Figure 3.5. The moves 1 Qd4 and 1 Qg5 each threaten mate in one and thus superficially seem strong. However, in both cases, the queen can be immediately captured. Now if White were to play 1 a3 followed by Black's 1 ... a5, White would not waste time considering 2 Qd4 or 2 Qg5 because the reasons that these moves were bad before are still present. KAISSA would argue that these positions are analogous, and in this case its analysis is correct. They argued that their method of analogies was quite effective, and that it was similar to the approach of humans, but the technique does not seem to be used in current programs. Deciding whether two positions are analogous is too error prone and requires too much computation.

Figure 3.5. Position illustrating the method of analogies.

1972, Moscow
Game 1, KAISSA versus Komsolmolskaia Pravda readers two-game match
White: KAISSA   Black: Komsolmolskaia Pravda readers
Sicilian Defense

1 e4 c5 2 Nc3

KAISSA was not using a book. It took forty minutes looking at 540,000 positions—225 positions per second —to decide upon this move. It will be seen that twenty-four years later, DEEP BLUE is searching about a million times as fast!

2 ... Nc6 3 Nf3 d6 4 Bb5 Bd7 5 O-O g6 6 d4 c×d4 7 B×c6 d×c3 8 B×b7 Rb8
9 Bd5 Bg7

If 9 ... c×b2, then White forks Black's rooks with 10 B×b2 R×b2 11 Qd4.

10 b3 Nf6 11 Be3 Qc7 12 Qd4 a5 13 Bc4 O-O 14 Rae1 Bc6 15 e5 B×f3
16 e×d6 e×d6 17 g×f3 Nh5 18 Qd3 Be5 19 Bd4 Kg7 20 Re3 f6 21 Rfe1 Nf4
22 Q×c3 Rbc8 23 a4 Qd7 24 B×e5 f×e5 25 Kh1 Qh3 26 Rg1 Nd5 27 Q×a5 Rc5
28 Qa7+ Rc7 29 Qa5 Rc5 30 Qa7+ Rf7

The readers decide not to draw!

31 Q×c5 d×c5 32 B×d5 Rf4 33 R×e5 R×f3 34 B×f3 Q×f3+ 35 Rg2
Declared drawn.

Figure 3.6. Position after 35 Rg2 Declared drawn.

1972, Moscow
Game 2, KAISSA versus Komsolmolskaia Pravda readers two-game match
White: Komsolmolskaia Pravda readers   Black: KAISSA
Larsen's Opening

---

1 b3

This move was selected by the newspaper's chess correspondent. It is one of the first examples of an attempt by humans to throw a computer off stride by playing an unusual move.

1 ... e5 2 Bb2 Nc6 3 c4 f6 4 Nc3 Bb4 5 Nd5 Nge7 6 a3 Bd6 7 g3 O-O 8 Bg2 Ng6
9 e3 f5 10 Ne2 Re8 11 Qc2 e4 12 d3 e×d3 13 Q×d3 Rf8 14 f4 Be7 15 h4 h6
16 h5 Nh8 17 e4 d6 18 O-O-O Rf7 19 N×e7+ Q×e7 20 Nc3 Be6 21 Nd5 Qd7
22 Ne3 f×e4 23 B×e4 Ne7 24 B×b7 Rb8 25 Be4 Nf5 26 Nd5 a5 27 g4 Ne7
28 N×e7+ R×e7 29 g5 h×g5 30 f5 Nf7

KAISSA's analysis concluded that 30 ... Bf7 31 h6 g×h6 32 Qc3 Re5
33 Q×e5 was inferior to the line played.

31 f×e6 Q×e6 32 Bd5 Qe3+ 33 Q×e3 R×e3 34 Rdf1 Black resigns.

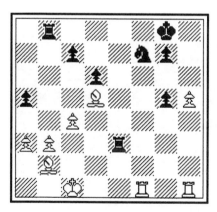

Figure 3.7. Position after 34 Rdf1 Black resigns.

August 1974: Stockholm

Two years later in Stockholm, KAISSA won the first World Computer Chess Championship with a perfect 4-0 score, defeating the author's program OSTRICH in the final round. KAISSA had a perfect score of 3-0 and OSTRICH

had a score of 2-1 going into their encounter. OSTRICH had a forced mate on move 35, but the continuation was nineteen plies long, beyond OS-TRICH's capabilities! Four moves later, OSTRICH has a second chance, but missed again: the continuation, this time eleven plies long, was still too long. However, even a five-ply search would have been enough for OS-TRICH to see that a sacrifice was worthwhile, but the four plies that it was searching was one ply short. KAISSA eventually recovered and went on to win the game and the world championship.

August, 1974, Stockholm
Round 4, first World Computer Chess Championship
White: OSTRICH   Black: KAISSA
*Time control: 40/2, 20/1 thereafter**
Reti Opening

---

1 Nf3 e6 2 d4 Nf6 3 Bg5 d5 4 e3 Be7 5 Nc3 Bb4 6 B×f6 B×c3+ 7 b×c3 Q×f6
8 Bd3 c5 9 O-O O-O 10 Qd2 Nc6 11 d×c5 Qe7 12 c4 d×c4 13 B×c4 Q×c5
14 Qd3 Rd8 15 Qe4 b5 16 Bd3 f5 17 Qh4 e5 18 e4 f4 19 Rfe1 Bb7

KAISSA opens itself up to the loss of an exchange.

20 Ng5 h6 21 Ne6 Qb6 22 N×d8 R×d8 23 a4 b4 24 Bc4+ Kh8 25 Rad1 Nd4
26 Rc1 Bc6 27 c3 b×c3 28 R×c3 B×a4 29 Qe7 Nc6 30 Qf7 Qc5 31 Rd3 Nd4
32 Bd5 Bb5 33 Rh3 Ne2+ 34 Kh1 Q×f2

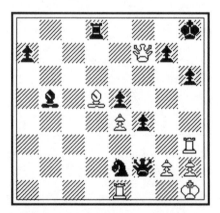

Figure 3.8. Position after 34 . . . Qxf2.

---

*Each side must complete playing 40 moves in the first two hours, and then an additional 20 moves every hour thereafter. Time saved by moving faster than necessary is added to the next time period.

Although facing mate in one itself, OSTRICH has a forced mate here:

35 R×h6+ g×h6 36 Qf6+ Kh7 37 Qe7+. Then if Black plays 37 . . . Kh8, White continues with:

38 Q×d8+ Be8 39 Q×e8+ Kg7 40 Qf7+ Kh8 41 Qg8#
       39 . . . Kh7 40 Qg8#
38 . . . Kg7 39 Qg8+ Kf6 40 Qf7+ Kg5 41 Qg7+ Kh4 42 Q×h6+
  Kg5 43 Be6#
            41 . . . Kh5 42 Bf7+ Kh4
            43 Q×h6+ Kg4 44 Qh5#
38 . . . Kh7 39 Qg8#

If instead, Black plays 37 . . . Kg6, then White mates in five with

38 Qf7+ Kg5 39 Qg7+ Kh4 40 Q×h6+ Kg5 41 Be6#
      39 . . . Kh5 40 Bf7+ Kh4 41 Q×h6+ Kg4 42 Qh5#

For OSTRICH to have seen the mate, it would have had to see the nineteen-ply continuation ending in 44 Qh5#. But a seven-ply search would have revealed the continuation 35 R×h6+ g×h6 36 Qf6+ Kh7 37 Qe7+, followed by capturing Black's rook on d8.

35 Rd1 Qb6 36 Rb1 Rc8 37 Be6 Rd8 38 Qg6 Qb7

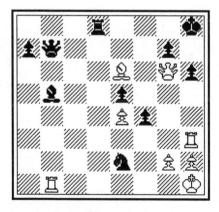

Figure 3.9. Position after 38 . . . Qb7.

OSTRICH has a forced mate with 39 Bf5 and ignoring two fruitless checks by Black, 39 . . . Kg8 40 R×h6 followed by 41 Rh8+ and then mate, or a

winning game after 39 R×h6+ g×h6 40 Q×h6+ Qh7 41 Qf6+ Qg7 42 Q×d8+ Kh7 43 Bf5+ Qg6 44 B×g6+ K×g6 45 R×b5. After surviving this crisis and giving OSTRICH one last chance to draw with 40 R×h6, KAISSA regained its composure and went on to win the game and the first world championship.

39 Qf5 Qc7 40 Rh4 Nd4 41 Qh3 N×e6 42 Q×e6 Bd3 43 Rg1 Bc4 44 Qf5 Be2 45 Ra1 a5

OSTRICH has nudged KAISSA's sleeping passed pawn into action.

46 Qg6 a4 47 Re1 Bc4 48 Ra1 a3 49 Rb1 Qd6 50 Q×d6 R×d6 51 Rh3 a2 52 Rc1 Rd4 53 Rch3 R×e4 54 Ra1 Rd4 55 R×c4 R×c4 56 g3 f3 57 h3 Rc2 58 Rd1 Rd2 59 Rc1 e4 60 g4 e3 61 Kg1 e2 62 Kf2 Rd1 63 Rc8+ Kh7 64 K×f3 e1Q 65 Rc2 Rd3+ 66 Kf4 g5+ 67 Kf5 Rf3#.

The top US program, CHESS 4.0, and KAISSA happened not to meet in the four-round event. The former was defeated by CHAOS in round two and finished with three points. In a friendly one-game match following the final round, the two played to a draw. CHESS 4.0 was running on a CDC 6600.

Samuel Reshevsky, Mikhial Botvinnik and Reuben Fine in New York, 1983.

*Monty Newborn, Mikhial Botvinnik and Mikhail Donskoy
at Botvinnik's summer dacha in 1992.*

Summer dacha of Mikhial Botvinnik near Moscow, 1992.

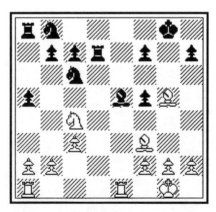

August, 1974, Stockholm
Exhibition game following the first
World Computer Chess Championship
White: CHESS 4.0   *Black:* KAISSA
Time Control: 40/2, 20/1 thereafter
Center Counter Opening

---

1 e4 d5 2 e×d5 Nf6 3 d4 N×d5 4 Nf3 g6 5 Be2 Bg7 6 O-O O-O 7 Re1 Bf5
8 Nh4 e5 9 N×f5 g×f5 10 d×e5 Nb4 11 Q×d8 R×d8 12 Bg5 Rd7 13 Na3 B×e5
14 c3 N4c6 15 Nc4 a5 16 Bf3

White clearly has an advantage with two strong bishops and better pawn placement. It will now go on to win two pawns over the next nine moves and have a won position after 25 R×f5, but it will then find itself on the defensive when it permits Black's rook, and later its knight, to invade its camp. Rather than moving its king to safety with 27 Kg3 or 28 Kg3 or even 33 Kf3, white manages to lose its way. After playing 43 g4, White was fortunate to hang on for a draw.

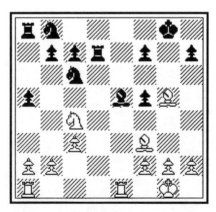

Figure 3.10. Position after 16 Bf3.

16 ... f6 17 Bh6 a4 18 Rad1 R×d1 19 R×d1 Kh8 20 B×c6 N×c6 21 f4 b5
22 f×e5 b×c4 23 e×f6 Rd8 24 Rf1 Kg8 25 R×f5 Rd1+ 26 Kf2 Nd8 27 Bf4 c6

28 Kf3 Rf1+ 29 Ke4 Ra1 30 a3 Re1+ 31 Be3 Re2 32 Rf2 Re1 33 Rd2 Ne6
34 Rd6 Nc5+ 35 Kf3 Nd3 36 Bd4 c5 37 Be3 Kf7 38 Rd7+ Kg6 39 Rg7+ K×f6
40 R×h7 Ne5+ 41 Kf4 Nd3+ 42 Ke4 N×b2 43 g4 Nd1 44 g5+ Kg6
45 Rh6+ Kg7 46 Kd5 R×e3 47 K×c4 R×c3+ 48 Kb5 R×a3 49 h4 Rh3
50 K×c5 Nb2 51 h5 a3 52 Rg6+ Kf7 53 Rf6+ Kg8 54 Rg6+ Kf8 55 Rf6+ Ke7
56 h6 Na4+ 57 Kb4 a2 58 Rf1 Nc3 59 Kb3 a1Q 60 R×a1 Ne4+ 61 Kc4 N×g5
62 Ra6 Nf7 63 Ra7+ Ke6 64 Ra6+ Kf5 65 Kd4 N×h6 Drawn by agreement.

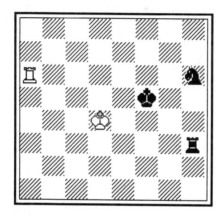

Figure 3.11. Position after 65 . . . N×h6 Drawn by agreement.

August 1977: Toronto

The KAISSA team returned to Moscow with the world championship in hand, but its games with OSTRICH and CHESS 4.0 left some doubts about how far ahead of the other programs it actually was. Three years later, the second world championship was held in Toronto, and KAISSA returned to defend its title. It went into the event as the favorite even though CHESS 4.6 had won almost every other tournament since the 1974 world championship, and KAISSA had done little since then. The rapid progress of the North American programs and the relatively slow progress in the USSR resulted in a sixth place finish for KAISSA, and the end to a strong Soviet presence in computer chess. The following first round game between KAISSA and DUCHESS vividly marked the end of KAISSA's reign.

Mikhail Botvinnik attended as an honored guest of the organizers. This was his first trip to North America. His second trip came in 1983 when he

Tom Truscott, author of the DUCHESS *program, 1977.*

attended the fourth World Computer Chess Championship. Since the late 1960s, he had been working on a program called PIONEER, and we hoped it would participate, but the former world champion decided his program was not ready. In fact, while for many years it looked as though his program would get off the drawing boards, it never played in a tournament. His ideas were very difficult to program and he had somewhat unrealistic expectations about their potential. A number of assistants tried to implement his methods but to no avail. Botvinnik felt the approach of his Soviet rivals was going in the wrong direction, and he hoped to show his approach was correct. Botvinnik, after a long and healthy life, passed away in Moscow in 1995.

♚

August, 1977, Toronto
Round 1, second World Computer Chess Championship
White: DUCHESS   *Black:* KAISSA
Time Control: 40/2, 20/1 thereafter
Center Counter Opening

1 e4 d5 2 e×d5 Nf6 3 d4 N×d5 4 Nf3 g6 5 Be2 Bg7 6 c4 Nb6 7 Nc3 O-O
8 Be3 Bg4 9 c5 Nd5 10 O-O e6 11 Qb3 b6 12 N×d5 e×d5 13 Bg5 Qd7
14 h3 Bf5 15 Qc3 Re8 16 Rfe1 Be4 17 Nd2 Qf5 18 Be3 Qe6 19 N×e4 d×e4

52

20 c×b6 c×b6 21 Rec1 Nd7 22 Bg4 Qd5 23 Qc6 Nf6 24 Be2 Rad8 25 Qa4 Re7
26 Bb5 Qf5 27 Rc2 Nd5 28 Rac1 Bf6 29 Qb3 a5 30 g4 Qe6 31 Rc6 a4

KAISSA falls victim to the horizon effect, putting off playing Rd6.

32 Q×a4 Rd6 33 R×d6 Q×d6

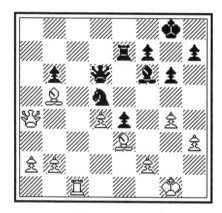

Figure 3.12. Position after 33 . . . Q×d6.

34 Qa8+ Re8

Even Botvinnik, who was sitting in the audience, was surprised by this
move, the first time a world champion missed what was happening in a
game played by computers. Black could not play 34 . . . Kg7 because White
would then mate with 35 Qf8+!! K×f8 36 Bh6+ followed by Rc8. Donskoy and Arlazarov, who were running the program, were sure it was a
programming bug, but after the game, they had time to check it out and
discovered KAISSA understood everything.

35 Q×e8+ Kg7 36 g5 Bd8 37 Bc4 Qe7 38 Q×e7 N×e7 39 Bf4 Nf5 40 Bd5 Kf8
41 Rc8 Ke7 42 Rc4 Ng7 43 B×e4 Ne6 44 Be3 Nc7 45 d5 Nb5 46 Bf3 Kd7
47 a4 Nd6 48 Rc6 Nf5 Black resigns.

Following the last round of the championship, KAISSA and CHESS 4.6
played their second one-game exhibition, again because they hadn't been
paired in the regular competition and because of the wide interest in seeing
them meet. CHESS 4.6 started slowly but obtained a won game on move 25
when KAISSA allowed a Black rook to the seventh rank.

August, 1977, Toronto
Exhibition game following the second
World Computer Chess Championship
White: KAISSA   Black: CHESS 4.6
Time Control: 40/2, 20/1 thereafter
Nimzowitsch's Defense

1 e4 Nc6 2 Nf3 e6 3 d4 d5 4 Bd3 d×e4 5 B×e4 Bd7 6 O-O Nf6 7 Re1 N×e4
8 R×e4 Be7 9 c4 f5 10 Re1 O-O 11 Nc3 f4 12 Qd3 Qe8 13 g3 f×g3
14 h×g3 Qf7 15 Bf4 g5 16 d5

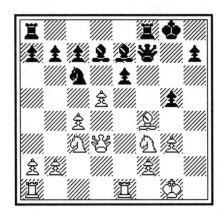

Figure 3.13. Position after 16 d5.

16 . . . e×d5

Black should have played 16 . . . g×f4, where it had the strength to begin
an attack on White's king.

17 N×d5 g×f4 18 N×e7+ N×e7 19 Q×d7 Ng6 20 Q×f7+ R×f7 21 g4 Rd7
22 Rad1 Rad8 23 R×d7 R×d7 24 Kg2 Kg7 25 Ng5

This gives up the seventh rank and Black will now gain a clear upper hand.

25 . . . Rd2 26 Rb1 Rc2 27 b3 Ne5 28 Rh1 R×a2 29 Rh4 Nd3 30 Nh3 Rb2
31 g5 Kg8 32 N×f4 R×f2+ 33 Kg3 R×f4 34 R×f4 N×f4 35 K×f4 Kf7 36 b4 Ke6
37 Ke4 a6 38 Kf4 Kd6 39 Ke4 c5 40 b×c5+ K×c5 41 Kd3 a5 42 Kc3 a4
43 Kd3 Kb4 44 Kc2 K×c4 White resigns.

Kaissa played in the third World Computer Chess Championship in Linz, Austria in 1980 and only was able to score two points. Since Kaissa's demise, there hasn't been a strong program from the former USSR. However, the microcomputer revolution has dawned there and a number of home-grown programs have been developed. Tournaments have taken place and a computer chess organization has been formed, headed by Vladimir Timofeev of the Institute for Physical Culture. But no program is yet on a par with the best from North America and Western Europe.

References

A. Kotok, "A Chess Playing Program for the IBM 7090." B. S. Thesis, MIT, 1962 AI Project Memo 41, Computer Center, MIT, Cambridge, Massachusetts.

G. M. Adelson-Velsky, V. L. Arlazarov, A. R. Bitman, A. A. Zhivotovsky, and A. V. Uskov, "Programming a computer to play chess," *Russian Math. Surveys 25*, (March–April 1970): 221–62.

G. M. Adelson-Velsky, V. L. Arlazarov, and M. V. Donskoy, "Some methods of controlling the tree search in chess programs," *Artificial Intelligence 6*, no. 4 (1975): 361–71.

G. M. Adelson-Velsky, V. L. Arlazarov, and M. V. Donskoy, *Algorithms for Games*. New York: Springer-Verlag, 1988.

M. M. Botvinnik, *Computers, Chess and Long Range Planning*. Berlin and New York: Springer-Verlag, 1970.

M. M. Botvinnik, *Computers in Chess: Solving Inexact Search Problems*. New York: Springer-Verlag, 1984.

"U.S. Computer Battling Soviets' in Chess Game," *New York Times*, November 22, 1966, p. 3.

R. H. Anderson, "Electronic Chess is Won by Soviet," *New York Times*, November 26, 1967.

M. V. Donskoy and J. Schaeffer, "Report on the 1st Soviet Computer-Chess Championship or reawakening a sleeping giant," *ICCA Journal* 11, no. 2/3 (June/September 1988): 111–16.

A. A. Timofeev, "Report on the 1st International Chess-Computer Tournament in the USSR," *ICCA Journal* 12, no. 2 (June 1989): 115–16.

4 MAC HACK
and Transposition Tables

ollowing the success of the KOTOK/MCCARTHY Program at MIT, a new effort was initiated there by undergraduate Richard Greenblatt. When visiting Stanford in late 1966, Greenblatt saw a listing of the moves from one of the games of the match between the KOTOK/MCCARTHY program and the ITEP program and he became inspired to write a program of his own. He had a working program in a month, receiving help from Donald Eastlake and Stephen Crocker. In the spring of 1967, his creation, MAC HACK, participated in several tournaments against humans in the Boston area, earning a rating in the low fifteen-hundreds. In the middle 1960s, time sharing was in its infancy, and MIT had a large government grant to carry on research in this area. It was called "Project MAC," where the MAC stood for "multiple access computing."

MAC HACK ran on a PDP-6 and was programmed in assembly language. The PDP-6 was built of discrete silicon transistors and executed instructions at a rate of one every 6 or 7 microseconds, about 150,000 per second. It cost about $400,000. The chess program took about 16K 36-bit words of memory. It was the first chess program distributed widely, running on many of the PDP-series computers.

MAC HACK was programmed along Shannon's Type B strategy. During tournament play, it searched to a depth of four plies, examining fifteen moves in each position at the first and second plies, nine moves in each position at the third and fourth plies, and seven moves in each position at

deeper plies. Moves beyond the fourth ply were examined if certain tactical problems existed.

MAC HACK was the first program to use an opening book, developed by Larry Kaufman and Alan Baisley. Kaufman, a strong player, has maintained his interest in computer chess and is now involved with the STAR SOCRATES chess program.

The following game was played in the Massachusetts State Championship against a human with a rating of 1510. MAC HACK won a sharp tactical battle in twenty-one moves. Three games played against Bobby Fischer follow.

Spring 1967
Massachusetts State Championship
White: MAC HACK   Black: Human
Sicilian Defense

1 e4 c5 2 d4 c×d4 3 Q×d4 Nc6 4 Qd3 Nf6 5 Nc3 g6 6 Nf3 d6 7 Bf4 e5 8 Bg3 a6
9 O-O-O b5 10 a4 Bh6+

This removes the bishop from defending the pawn on d6.

11 Kb1 b4 12 Q×d6 Bd7

Figure 4.1. Position after 12 . . . Bd7.

Black would have cut its loses with 12 . . . Q×d6, but MAC HACK was probably good enough to win after this move also.

13 Bh4 Bg7 14 Nd5 N×e4 15 Nc7+ Q×c7 16 Q×c7 Nc5 17 Qd6 Bf8 18 Qd5 Rc8
19 N×e5 Be6 20 Q×c6+ R×c6 21 Rd8#.

In 1977, Doug Penrod began the *Computer Chess Newsletter* from his home in California. It was the forerunner of the *ICCA Journal*. Penrod became ill about a year later, and Ben Mittman took over the publication. In 1983, when I was elected president of the ICCA, the current *ICCA Journal* began under the editorship of Jaap van den Herik, who has served in that capacity since the journal's inception. Penrod published three games that Bobby Fischer played against MAC HACK in his second issue. The games were sent to him by Fischer. Fischer toyed with the computer in winning all three games. Exactly when the games were played is not known. In a letter to Penrod published in the first issue of the newsletter, Fischer said he felt he could give the computer a queen and a rook and still win.

Game 1
White: MAC HACK   Black: Bobby Fischer
Sicilian Defense

---

1 e4 c5 2 Nf3 d6 3 d4 c×d4 4 N×d4 Nf6 5 Nc3 a6 6 Be2 e5 7 Nb3 Be7 8 Be3 O-O
9 Qd3 Be6 10 O-O Nbd7 11 Nd5 Rc8 12 N×e7+ Q×e7 13 f3 d5

Fischer has played a quiet game to this point while developing his pieces; this is the first move of the next phase.

14 Nd2 Qb4 15 Nb3 d×e4 16 Qd1 Nd5 17 Ba7 b6 18 c3 Qe7 19 f×e4 Ne3
20 Qd3 N×f1 21 Q×a6 Ne3 22 B×b6 Qg5

Black is up a rook for two pawns and is in total control.

Figure 4.2. Position after 22 . . . Qg5.

23 g3 Ra8 24 Ba7 h5 25 Qb7 h4 26 Kf2 h×g3+ 27 h×g3 f5 28 e×f5 R×f5+
29 Ke1 Raf8 30 Kd2 Nc4+ 31 Kc2 Qg6 32 Qe4 Nd6 33 Qc6 Rf2+ 34 Kd1 Bg4
35 B×f2 Qd3+ 36 Kc1 B×e2 37 Nd2 R×f2 38 Q×d7 Rf1+ 39 N×f1 Qd1#.

Game 2
White: Bobby Fischer   Black: MAC HACK
King's Gambit Accepted

---

1 e4 e5 2 f4 e×f4 3 Bc4 d5 4 B×d5 Nf6 5 Nc3 Bb4 6 Nf3 O-O 7 O-O N×d5
8 N×d5 Bd6 9 d4 g5

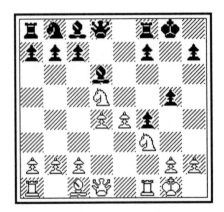

Figure 4.3. Position after 9 . . . g5.

Black's 9 . . . g5 makes life easy for Fischer.

10 N×g5 Q×g5 11 e5 Bh3 12 Rf2 B×e5 13 d×e5 c6 14 B×f4 Qg7 15 Nf6+ Kh8
16 Qh5 Rd8 17 Q×h3 Na6 18 Rf3 Qg6 19 Rc1 Kg7 20 Rg3 Rh8 21 Qh6#.

Game 3
White: MAC HACK   Black: Bobby Fischer
Sicilian Defense

---

1 e4 c5 2 Nf3 g6 3 d4 Bg7 4 Nc3 c×d4 5 N×d4 Nc6 6 Be3 Nf6 7 N×c6 b×c6
8 e5 Ng8 9 f4 f6 10 e×f6 N×f6 11 Bc4 d5 12 Be2 Rb8 13 b3 Ng4 14 Bd4 e5
15 f×e5 O-O 16 B×g4 Qh4+ 17 g3 Q×g4 18 Q×g4 B×g4 19 Rf1 R×f1+ 20 K×f1

Figure 4.4. Position after 20 K×f1.

White's one pawn lead will disappear shortly. From the way Fischer played this game, it seems he wanted to test MAC HACK's endgame abilities.

20 ... c5 21 Bf2 B×e5 22 Be1 Rf8+ 23 Kg2 Rf3 24 h3 R×c3 25 B×c3 B×c3
26 Rf1 Bf5 27 Rf2 h5 28 Re2 Kf7 29 Re3 Bd4 30 Rf3 Ke6 31 c3 Be5 32 Re3 d4
33 c×d4 c×d4 34 Re1 d3 35 h4 d2 36 Rd1 Bc3 37 Kf2 Bg4 38 Rh1 Bd4+
39 Kg2 Kd5 40 a3 Ke4 41 Rf1 Kd3 42 Kh2 Ke2 43 Kg2 Bh3+ 44 K×h3 K×f1
45 b4 d1Q 46 Kh2 Qe2+ 47 Kh3 Qg2#.

MAC HACK never competed in tournament play against other computers. Greenblatt said he had no interest in seeing how MAC HACK would do in such competition. Nevertheless, in the early 1970s most of the other developers of chess programs had access to PDP-series computers and tested their programs against a widely-distributed version of MAC HACK. Prior to the ACM's first tournament in 1970, MAC HACK was recognized by the computer chess community as the strongest program in North America, but by 1971, that was no longer the case.

Transposition tables

Greenblatt introduced the use of a transposition table for storing information about each position as it is searched. If the same position is encounter later, the information in this table might make it unnecessary to search the position further. Extensive work has been done to optimize the use of transposition tables in chess programs. While memory space limited the

size of MAC HACK's transposition table, the current programs have very large transposition tables capable of storing information about millions of positions.

From the initial position, there are many continuations that, through a transposition of moves, lead to the same positions. For example, in Figure 4.5, the continuation 1 e4 d5 2 d4 leads to the same position, denoted *T,* as does 1 d4 d5 2 e4. Identical positions arise at the end of these two continuations due to the transposition of White's two moves, d4 and e4. The continuation 1 d4 d6 2 e4 d5 also leads to the same configuration of pieces, but in this case, it is White's turn and the position cannot be considered the same as *T.* Two positions are identical only if they have identical piece configurations, identical castling rights, identical en passant options, and the same player to move. To be one hundred percent identical, it is also necessary to take into account the number of moves since the last capture or pawn advance although most programs ignore this factor.

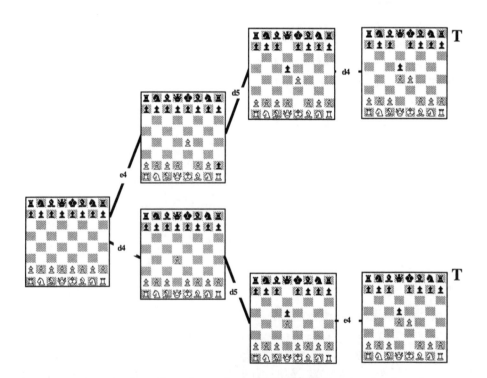

Figure 4.5. Two continuations from the opening position that lead to the same position T through a transposition of moves.

Now suppose position T is first arrived at by the continuation 1 e4 d5 2 d4 and assigned a score either as a result of searching the subtree rooted at T and backing up a score to T or as a result of assigning a score to T by the scoring function. Then when T is arrived at through the transposed continuation 1 d4 d5 2 e4, it is unnecessary to search beyond T or even score T if the results of the first examination were saved. Chess programs use transposition tables, essentially large hash tables, to save this information. When the computer arrives at each position, it probes the transposition table to see whether the position was previously searched. If so and if the information in the transposition table is sufficient—sufficiency will be defined shortly—then this position need not be searched again. It can be considered a terminal position and assigned the score stored in the transposition table. Otherwise, the position must be searched if it not at maximum search depth, or scored if it is at maximum depth. When a score has been assigned to the position, the transposition table is probed for a match. If no match is found, a new table entry is made; if the position is found, the information in the table is updated as appropriate.

In more rigorous terms, when the computer completes the search of some position P, it knows the score of P, denoted SCORE(P), and whether this value is exact (E) or an upper (U) or lower (L) bound, and this information is saved in BOUNDSCORE(P). The computer also knows the depth of the tree rooted at P, denoted by DEPTH(P); the best move to make at P, denoted BESTMOVE(P); and the hash code of P, denoted HASHCODE(P). The hash code of P is an encoding of the information used to describe P. The computer now probes the transposition table to see whether it has previously encountered P. If it has, and if the new information about P is better than that currently stored, the entry in the transposition table is updated. For example, it is possible that BESTMOVE(P) and SCORE(P) change values and that DEPTH(P) increases. In this case the new move and score are more accurate than the old.

When the computer arrives at a position, say Q, the transposition table is probed for a match. If successful and if (1) DEPTH(Q) $\leq$ DEPTH(P) and (2) the score in the table is exact, or if not exact, the bound on the score is sufficient to cause the move leading to Q to be inferior to some other choice, then Q is considered terminal and assigned the score recorded with the entry. If these two conditions are not met, the computer either scores Q or searches its successors. The move found best the last time Q was searched is in the transposition table and should be searched first on this try.

Figure 4.6 illustrates various ways that a transposition table might be used during a search. A four-ply tree is shown in which the side to move has four moves: *s*, *u*, *v*, and *w*. The tree is searched according to the alpha-beta algorithm shown in Figure 2.13. In this contrived example, position *T* appears four times. When the search of the first appearance of *T* is com-

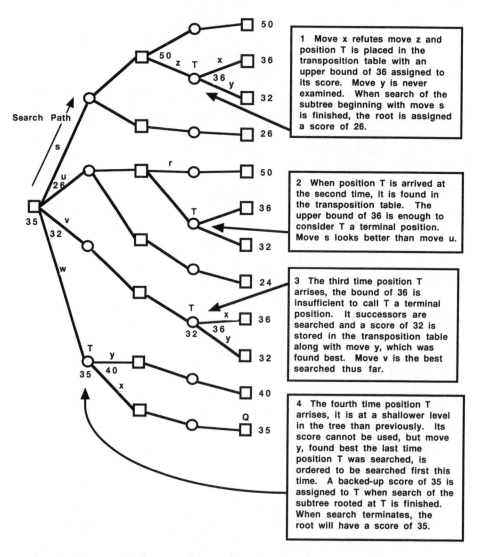

1 Move x refutes move z and position T is placed in the transposition table with an upper bound of 36 assigned to its score. Move y is never examined. When search of the subtree beginning with move s is finished, the root is assigned a score of 26.

2 When position T is arrived at the second time, it is found in the transposition table. The upper bound of 36 is enough to consider T a terminal position. Move s looks better than move u.

3 The third time position T arrises, the bound of 36 is insufficient to call T a terminal position. It successors are searched and a score of 32 is stored in the transposition table along with move y, which was found best. Move v is the best searched thus far.

4 The fourth time position T arrises, it is at a shallower level in the tree than previously. Its score cannot be used, but move y, found best the last time position T was searched, is ordered to be searched first this time. A backed-up score of 35 is assigned to T when search of the subtree rooted at T is finished. When search terminates, the root will have a score of 35.

Figure 4.6. Search of a tree illustrating the use of a transposition table.

plete, the computer finds that SCORE(T) is 36, and since move x refutes move z and move y was not searched, this value is an upper bound on the real value of T that is, that BOUNDSCORE(T) = u, that DEPTH(T) is 1 and that BEST_MOVE(T) is x. When search arrives at T the second time, T is found in the transposition table with an upper bound on its score of 36; since move r leads to a score of 50, search can be terminated at this second appearance. When search arrives at T the third time, the bound of 36 is insufficient to terminate search at T, and this time its successors must be examined. When search of the third T is complete, an exact score of 32 is assigned to it. BEST_MOVE(T), which had been x, is replaced with y, and move v is assigned a score of 32. When search arrives at T the fourth time, the position is at ply 1 in the tree, too shallow to use the information obtained previously to terminate search. If the information were used, not all lines in the tree would have been searched to a depth of 4. In particular, the score of this final occurrence of T would be based on a one-ply search, and thus the score of the root of the tree would be based on only a two-ply search. After the fourth T has been searched, it will be assigned a score of 35 and move w, in turn, will be assigned a score of 35, making it the best move.

The reader might consider what would happen if position Q had a score of 22 instead of the 35 shown. In this case, the search would have found move v best with a score of 32, but move S is in fact the best.

Figure 4.7 shows the effect of using a transposition table on our continuing example. Moves that transpose are assumed to lead to the same position. For example, move sequence a-c-b leads to the same position (D) as does b-c-a (S). Two positions, position L at the end of move sequence a-d-e-c and position S at the end of move sequence b-c-a, were found in the transposition table because scores were previously assigned to them. For position L, information about it, in particular, its score, was entered in the transposition table when the identical position H was scored earlier; the score for L is the same as that of H. For position S, the information was entered in the transposition table when a score was backed up earlier to the identical position D, and that information allowed search to be terminated later at position S. Thus the combination of the alpha-beta algorithm and the use of a transposition table reduced the number of terminal positions necessary to score from twelve to six: positions E, F, H, I, M, and W.

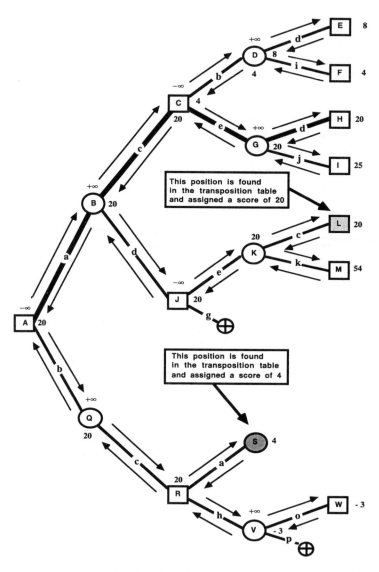

This position is found in the transposition table and assigned a score of 20

This position is found in the transposition table and assigned a score of 4

Figure 4.7. Ongoing example showing the effect of using a transposition table along with alpha-beta search.

While the two contrived examples presented in Figure 4.6 and 4.7 only show several transposition table hits, in the typical chess tree there are many hits, and search is sped up considerably. In deep endgames, transposition tables are extremely effective. The position from Reuben Fine's *Basic Chess Endings* on endgames shown in Figure 4.8 cannot be solved without

Larry Kaufman, currently with the STAR SOCRATES team and formerly with MAC HACK.

transposition tables; a program with transposition tables can find the correct move in a matter of seconds. In this position, White, to move and win, has only three king moves. To each of these moves Black has five replies with its king. A two-ply search will find $3 \times 5 = 15$ different terminal positions. A three-ply search involving only king moves will find ninety terminal positions, although there will be only forty-five different ones. Many moves transpose. An eight-ply search will find only 204 different terminal positions: White's king can move to seventeen squares in the a1-e5 square, and Black's king can move to twelve squares, thus leading to $17 \times 12 = 204$ different positions. The first ten plies of the tree contain only king moves, because until White captures a pawn, only kings can move. To see that Kb1 is the best move, the computer must realize that after 1 Kb1 Kb7 2 Kc1 Kc7 3 Kd1 Kd7 4 Kc2 Kd8 5 Kc3 Kc7 6 Kd3, Black cannot maintain distant opposition. White can eventually capture the pawn on either a5 or f5 and then push a pawn to promotion. To understand this, however, requires a very deep search, way beyond the capabilities of a computer not using a transposition table!

As said previously, the transposition tables of the leading programs have enough space to store several million entries. However, for a program like DEEP BLUE that searches one hundred million positions per second, the transposition table fills up quickly. Various replacement

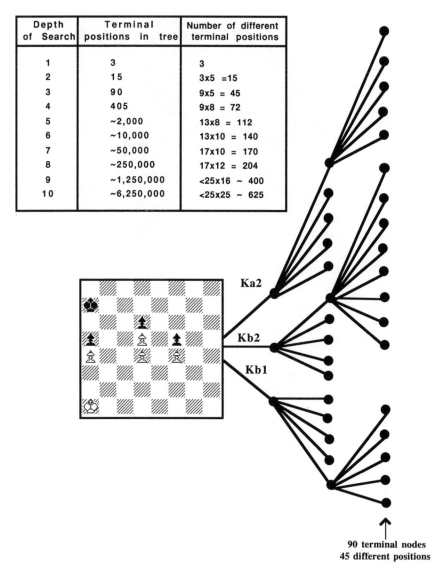

Depth of Search	Terminal positions in tree	Number of different terminal positions
1	3	3
2	15	3x5 =15
3	90	9x5 = 45
4	405	9x8 = 72
5	~2,000	13x8 = 112
6	~10,000	13x10 = 140
7	~50,000	17x10 = 170
8	~250,000	17x12 = 204
9	~1,250,000	<25x16 ~ 400
10	~6,250,000	<25x25 ~ 625

Ka2

Kb2

Kb1

90 terminal nodes
45 different positions

Figure 4.8. Position from Fine's Basic Chess Endings, illustrating the power of transposition tables.

strategies have been developed for handling the table when it is almost full. Usually the depth of the subtree rooted at each position is the determining factor; the greater the depth, the more useful the entry is likely to be. Alternatively, the size of the subtree rooted at each position can be used as the determining factor; the larger the subtree, the more useful the entry. Useful entries are kept in the table, while less useful entries are replaced by new ones.

Machine learning in the context of chess

Steven Skiena, when writing about machine learning in the context of chess, said that learning can occur as a result of memorizing, advice taking, induction, and analogical learning. Memorizing occurs in the area of opening books and endgame databases, where the computer stores vast amounts of information. The computer does no more with this information than produce memorized responses when applicable. An advice-taking chess program was designed by Al Zobrist and Fred Carlson in the early 1970s. Advice was given in the form of patterns that a computer could store and later use to improve its play, but the project never generated a strong chess program. Attempts were made by Ryszard Michalski and Pericles Negri in 1977 to have a computer induce new rules to guide its play in the king-and-pawn versus king (KPK) endgame by training it on several hundred positions, but they indicated that the level of misplay was too high for tournament chess. Later, in 1982, Alan Shapiro and Tim Niblett were able to achieve a perfect decision tree for the KPK endgame by using induction on the KPK endgame database; Max Bramer was able to do the same for KRK and KQK endgames. Learning by analogy is the most difficult learning strategy to implement; Adrian de Groot interviewed grandmasters and found that positions often reminded them of others that they had seen before. The similarities often involved concepts more sophisticated than piece placement. Robert Levinson has designed a self-learning pattern-oriented chess program.

There have been a number of attempts to have chess programs use various optimizing algorithms to self-improve their scoring functions. The earliest such effort was made by Arthur Samuel in the context of checkers. The scoring function of a typical game-playing program assigns weights to various features that it considers when calculating a score. These weights can be adjusted by the program itself as it plays through many games. For example, determining the best value for a bishop can be done by playing several hundred games and varying only the weight for a bishop. There will be some weight that gives the best results. Of course, there are usually many weights to vary. They are often interrelated, and it is quite complex homing in on just the right balance. Andreas Nowatzyk was responsible for tuning the scoring function of DEEP BLUE, using a large set of test positions from nine-hundred

grandmaster- and master-level games. The tuning procedure was aimed at finding the least-squares fit of the machine's evaluation function with respect to the moves actually selected by the human players. An attempt to use neural nets was made by Alex van Tiggelen in 1991. The same year, William Tunstall-Pedoe described how genetic algorithms might be used.

Perhaps the most significant contribution to machine learning in the context of chess is that of David Slate and Tony Scherzer; they experimented with the use of transposition tables to assist in learning. In Slate's experiment, a special "long-term memory (LTM)" hash table was used to store information on root positions found troublesome during the course of a game. This information was retrieved and used when the same position appeared in a future game, although the second time the position might be found deep in the search tree. Troublesome positions were defined as those for which a deep search finds a significantly different score than a shallow one. Only a small percentage of all positions are troublesome. Suppose, now, that a program searches all moves to a depth of eight plies, and on the eighth move of some game, a troublesome position T is found and saved in the LTM hash table, and that the trouble only appeared on the seventh iteration. Suppose later, another game is played that follows the same line of play for the first five moves. Then, on the sixth move, T

Linda and Tony Scherzer watching BEBE *during one of its games.*

will be a position somewhere deep in the search tree. Without the LTM hash table, T would have been assigned an unreliable score. However, using the LTM hash table, T will be given a more reliable score, one based on the previous eight-ply search. The program, then, will less likely make a move leading to the same trouble twice. It will also save some time.

Scherzer extended Slate's idea by storing information on all root positions, not just troublesome ones, in the hash table and using the information when appropriate at a later time. He described his work at the sixth World Computer Chess Championship in Edmonton in May of 1989. He reported that his program learned quite effectively to avoid making the same mistakes. He said this strategy allowed him to come to a tournament and not worry about modifying or correcting his opening book between rounds; his program took care of this all by itself.

References

R. D. Greenblatt, D. E. Eastlake, and S. D. Crocker, "The Greenblatt chess program," *Proceedings of the Fall Joint Computer Conference* (Montvale, NJ: AFIPS Press, 1967), 801–10.

J. Moussouris, J. Holloway, and R. Greenblatt, "CHEOPS: a chess-oriented processing system," in *Machine Intelligence* 9, eds. J. E. Hayes, D. Michie, and L. Mikulich (Chichester: Ellis Horwood, 1979), 351–60.

H. J. van den Herik, "An interview with Richard D. Greenblatt," *ICCA Journal* 15, no. 4 (December 1992): 200–7.

R. D. Greenblatt, "Wedgeitude," *ICCA Journal* 15, no. 4 (December 1992): 192–98.

D. Penrod, ed., *Computer Chess Newsletter,* Issue #1, 1977, p. 3 and Issue #2, 1977, p. 18.

The following papers are concerned with transposition tables

A. L. Zobrist, "A hashing method with applications for game playing," Technical Report 88, Computer Sciences Department, University of Wisconsin, Madison, Wisconsin, 1970. Reprinted in the *ICCA Journal* 13, no. 2 (1990): 69–73.

H. L. Nelson, "Hash tables in CRAY BLITZ," *ICCA Journal* 8, no. 1 (March 1985): 3–13.

D. M. Breuker, J. W. H. M. Uiterwijk, and H. J. van den Herik, "Replacement schemes for transposition tables," *ICCA Journal* 17, no. 4 (December 1994): 183–93.

T. Warnock and B. Wendroff, "Search tables in computer chess," *ICCA Journal* 11, no. 1 (March 1988): 10–13.

The following papers are concerned with machine learning in the context of chess and other games

S. S. Skiena, "An overview of machine learning in the context of chess," *ICCA Journal* 9, no. 1 (March 1986): 20–28.

A. L. Zobrist and F. R. Carlson, "An advice-taking chess computer," *Scientific American* 228, no. 6 (1973): 92–105.

R. S. Michalski and P. G. Negri, "An experiment on inductive learning in chess endgames," in *Machine Intelligence* 8, eds. E. W. Elcock and D. Michie, Ellis Horwood-Wiley, (1977): 175–192.

A. Shapiro and T. Niblett, "Automatic induction of classification rules for a chess endgame," *Advances in Computer Chess 3*, ed. M. R. B. Clarke (New York: Pergamon Press, 1982): 73–92.

M. A. Bramer, "Machine-aided refinement of correct strategies for the endgame in chess," *Advances in Computer Chess 3*, ed. M. R. B. Clarke (New York: Pergamon Press, 1982): 93–112.

A. D. de Groot, *Thought and Choice in Chess*, (The Hague: Mouton, 1965).

R. A. Levinson, "A self-learning pattern-oriented chess program," *ICCA Journal* 12, no. 4 (December 1989): 207–15.

A. L. Samuel, "Some studies in machine learning using the game of checkers," *IBM Journal of Research and Development* 3, no. 3 (1959): 211–29.

A. L. Samuel, "Some studies in machine learning using the game of checkers, II—Recent progress," *IBM Journal of Research and Development* 11, no. 6 (1967): 801–17.

F.-h. Hsu, T. A. Anantharaman, M. S. Campbell, and A. Nowatzyk, "DEEP THOUGHT," in *Computers, Chess and Cognition*, eds. T. A. Marsland and J. Schaeffer (New York: Springer-Verlag, 1990), 55–78.

A. van Tiggelen, "Neural networks as a guide to optimization," *ICCA Journal* 14, no. 3 (September 1991): 115–18.

W. Tunstall-Pedoe, "Genetic algorithms optimizing evaluation functions," *ICCA Journal* 14, no. 3 (September 1991): 119–28.

D. Slate, "A chess program that uses the transposition table to learn from experience," *ICCA Journal* 10, no. 2 (1987): 59–71.

T. Scherzer, L. Scherzer, and D. Tjaden Jr., "Learning in BEBE," *ICCA Journal* 14, no. 4 (December 1991): 183–91.

A reference on endgames

R. Fine, *Basic Chess Endings* (Philadelphia: David McKay, 1941).

5 Northwestern University's Chess Program

In 1968, a team of Northwestern University graduate students, Larry Atkin, Keith Gorlen, and David Slate, began work on a series of chess programs called at first CHESS 2.0, then CHESS 3.0, CHESS 3.5, CHESS 3.6, CHESS 4.0 and on and on. They were supported in their work by Ben Mittman, director of the university's Vogelback Computer Center. Slate and Atkin were good chess players; Slate was an expert while Atkin was a notch weaker. Their succession of programs could be characterized as well debugged with sound heuristics. CHESS 3.0 won the first ACM United States Computer Chess Championship in 1970 and continued to dominate the ACM tournaments until BELLE came along in the late 1970s.

It was in 1976, however, that Slate and company moved their program up from the class B level to the expert level. Northwestern University psychology professor Peter Frey had been working with the team on an informal basis. He suggested that the program modify its search strategy by introducing iteratively-deepening search, a technique that is discussed in the next several pages. Meanwhile, Slate and company had been observing the success of Jim Gillogly's TECH, a program that used no forward pruning at shallow levels in the tree and that was having good success in the ACM tournaments. So the Northwestern University team decided to modify their search strategy to look like Shannon's Type A strategy coupled with Frey's recommended iteratively-deepening search. They found that their program

made a big jump in playing strength, somewhat to their surprise. They had also transferred their program from a CDC 6600 to the CDC Cyber 176, the most advanced supercomputer of its day, creating some doubt about how much of the improvement should be credited to the introduction of iteratively-deepening search, the elimination of forward pruning, or running the program on the new supercomputer.

It was in July 1976 at the Paul Masson American Chess Championship in Saratoga, California, that their program first jolted the chess world. The games were played in a vineyard, outdoors, with lots of fresh air and wine. CHESS 4.5 entered the B section, for players rated under 1800. Slate was prepared to return to Chicago without winning a game, although he was hoping for a respectable performance. He got it. CHESS 4.5 won its first game, then its second, and when the event was over, it remained undefeated with a perfect 5-0 score. It went on to win the 1976 ACM North American Computer Chess Championship in October in Houston and then confirmed to the chess world that its California result was no accident when the following February it won the eighty-fourth Minnesota Open against experts and strong class A players. Finishing the Minnesota tournament with a 5-1 score, it earned a performance rating of 2271. The next week, CHESS 4.5 participated in the Minnesota Closed Championship where the contestants were stronger and had prepared for the computer. The computer finished in last place with a 1.5-5 score.

Iteratively-deepening search is a simple concept. It is, in fact, so simple that at first it didn't seem to offer enough payback to make it worthwhile. It corrected the basic problem computers were having with depth-first search: when carrying out a depth-first search, it is necessary to decide, before beginning the search, exactly how deep to search. It turns out that this is a very difficult decision to make. If the depth is set too large, the search will take too long. If it is set too small, the search will terminate sooner than necessary. Setting it just right is a real trick. If the depth of search was six on one move and that worked fine, it doesn't follow that a depth of six will be appropriate on the next move. For example, if a queen is captured, it is often possible to search deeper on subsequent moves because the average number of branches at each position in the search tree is smaller. Also, there tends to be less extended search when the queen is gone. On the other hand, if a pawn promotes to a queen, the depth of search must be reduced on subsequent moves for the opposite reason. The biggest problem computers were having with depth-first search was that sufficiently often it was necessary to terminate search before all moves at the root of the tree were searched, and one of the unsearched moves was the only move that saved the computer from disaster.

One example of the problem with setting the depth of search was illustrated by TECH at the third ACM U.S. Computer Chess Championship. When playing SCHACH, the position shown in Figure 5.1 was reached after TECH, playing Black, played 50 ... h5. The computer had three minutes, on average, to make a move, but as you will see, some moves took almost no time while others took far too long. Certainly, there was no correlation between the complexity of the position and the time taken to make a move, or perhaps between the problems faced by the computer and the time taken. The game continued as follows; the time, in seconds, taken for each TECH move is shown in parentheses. Keep in mind that it had, on average, 180 seconds to make each move.

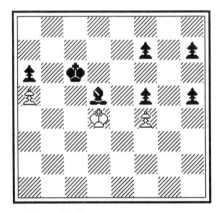

Figure 5.1. Position in SCHACH versus TECH,
ACM U.S. Computer Chess Championship, 1972, Round 1.

51 Ke5 Be4 (1) 52 Kd4 h4 (1) 53 Ke5 h3 (1)

With nothing happening on the board, and no queen in sight, TECH takes one second to search a shallow tree which has only a few bishop and king moves.

54 Kd4 Kb5 (98)

After playing several moves in one second, searching to a depth of four or five levels (there is no record of exactly how deep TECH was searching), it

then takes ninety-eight seconds on this move as queening the pawn starts to sneak into the search tree.

55 Ke5 K×a5 (175)

TECH sees that it can grab a pawn and then queen a pawn. The queening remains and the time increases to 175 seconds.

56 Kd4 h2 (54)

This move took slightly less time, perhaps because the depth was decreased based on the time consumed on the previous move, or possibly there was less extended search, with the king capture on a5 now gone.

57 Ke5 h1Q (764) 58 Kd4 h6 (1,265)

These two moves took far longer than the previous ones, showing how difficult it is to control the search time. Gillogly sat waiting at the board for his computer to reply, knowing that it would take a while, but nevertheless concerned that it may have broken down.

59 Ke5 Qh4(2)

Now TECH is back to moving in two seconds. The search depth must have been decreased possibly to meet the approaching time control. White resigned several moves later. The current programs control the use of time very effectively, in part because iteratively-deepening search makes this easy to do.

Iteratively-deepening depth-first search works as follows: Rather than initially deciding a depth of search, the computer carries out a sequence of deeper and deeper depth-first searches for as long as time permits. The first "iteration" carries out a depth-first search to a depth of one level and finds the best continuation based on this shallow search. Then a second iteration is carried out looking at all two-move continuations for the best continuation. If time permits, a third depth-first search is carried out looking at all three-move continuations, this time for the best three-move continuation, and so on. When time runs out, the search stops, and whatever is found to be the best continuation thus far is the one selected for play. At first, it sounds like a waste of time to carry out all these shallow searches, but that turns out not to be the case. Because of the exponential rate of growth of the chess tree, the shallow searches take relatively no time at all. Only the last one or two iterations take a significant amount of the total search time.

An analogy is how a person might search for a lost diamond ring. A search of the house would be carried out first. If the ring is not found, the yard around the house would be searched, then the neighborhood. The city police might be called next, then the federal law enforcement agency, and so on—assuming the ring was sufficiently valuable. It wouldn't make sense to call the police before at least searching the house. This sequence of deeper and deeper searches is an iteratively-deepening search. Of course, when carrying out this procedure, clues found regarding the ring on one iteration are used on the next to speed up that iteration, to make it more effective. For example, if tire tracks were found in the yard, that information would be given to the police to aid them in their search.

When chess programs carry out an iteratively-deepening search, they too find information on one iteration that makes the next iteration proceed more effectively. Each iteration returns a principal continuation and that sequence of moves is searched first on the next iteration. Searching this continuation first usually gives an effective ordering of moves and speeds up the search. Further, if search must be stopped at any time, the best continuation found thus far by the search is always available to be played. Each iteration also places many positions in the transposition table with information about them that is useful on the next iteration; in particular, the best move to make in each position is recorded in the table.

Iteratively-deepening depth-first search was recognized by researchers in automated theorem proving as a technique also useful in their domain. In the middle 1980s, ten years after the success of this technique was recognized in the computer chess world, the first papers appeared in the general AI literature suggesting that proofs of theorems could be found using iteratively-deepening search. Essentially a proof in one step was first sought, then two steps, and so on. Figure 5.2 illustrates the use of iteratively-deepening search in the domains of finding diamond rings, chess, and theorem proving. Of course there are some differences between these problems. In chess, there is a time limit imposed, and while more time would lead to a better move being found, the search must terminate with the best move found in the allotted time. In theorem proving, one either finds a proof or does not, and there is no sense stopping the search unless the proof is found or the computer becomes unavailable.

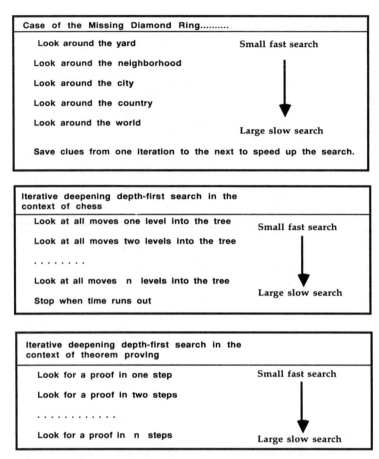

Figure 5.2. Iteratively-deepening search.

The importance of computer speed was shown earlier in the match between the KOTOK/MCCARTHY Program and the ITEP Program, but it was shown again when CHESS 4.4 played a game against TREEFROG, a program developed at Waterloo University by Ron Hansen, Russell Crook, and Jim Parry. In that game, CHESS 4.4 started on a superfast Cyber 175; faced machine problems; switched to an old, slow CDC 6400 on move 4; back to the 175 on move 8; to the 6400 on move 14; to the 175 on move 23, where the power of the supercomputer began to wear on TREEFROG; and finally back to the 6400 on move 35. Three moves later, TREEFROG's programmers resigned when they realized they had entered an incorrect move into their computer several moves earlier and felt it wasn't worth replaying another losing line.

Round 4, sixth North American Computer Chess Championship
Minneapolis, 1975
White: CHESS 4.4   Black: TREEFROG
Time control: 40/2, 20/1 thereafter
Center Counter Opening

---

1 e4 d5 2 e×d5 Nf6 3 d4 N×d5 4 Nf3 Bg4 5 Be2 e6 6 O-O Nc6 7 c4 Nf6 8 Nc3 Bb4

CHESS 4.4 returns to the 175 after having played the last four moves on the slower 6400. Thus far, the difference between the two computers is not visible.

9 d5 B×c3 10 d×c6 Q×d1 11 R×d1 Bb4 12 c×b7 Rb8 13 h3 Bf5

Now it's back to the 6400. For the last several moves, CHESS 4.4 has played aggressively and has obtained a clear advantage, although at the level the programs are playing, the game is still wide open. The pawn on b7 will go in six moves when the slower 6400 fails to find a way to save it.

14 a3 Bc5 15 g4 Bc2 16 Rd2 Bb3 17 Nd4 B×d4 18 R×d4 e5 19 Rd2 R×b7 20 g5 Ne4 21 Rd5 f6 22 Bh5+ Ke7

White's position has weakened while trying to push the loss of the advanced pawn over its search horizon. The 175 will take over now and clinch the game in the next dozen moves.

23 Bf3 c6 24 Ra5 Bc2 25 b4 Rhb8 26 Be3 N×g5 27 B×g5 f×g5 28 R×e5+ Kd6 29 Rae1

CHESS 4.4 is now in a position to apply winning pressure.

Figure 5.3. Position after 29 Rae1.

Max Euwe, former world champion, commentating on the CHESS *4.7 and David Slate versus David Levy one-game match in Detroit in 1979.*

29 ... Rf7 30 Re6+ Kc7 31 R×c6+ Kd8 32 Rce6 Rb6 33 Re8+ Kd7 34 Bd5 Rf5

The finishing touches, when there was little chance for anything to go wrong, came on the 6400.

35 R1e7+ Kd6 36 Be6 Rc6 37 B×f5 B×f5 38 c5+ Black resigns.

David Slate of the Northwestern University's computer chess team, 1978.

August 8–12, 1977: Toronto

The second World Computer Chess Championship was held at the Triennial International Federation for Information Processing Congress 77 in Toronto. As we saw in the previous chapter, until then, KAISSA was officially the best of the chess programs, although because of its lack of a track record since capturing the title in 1974, there were many doubts about the reality of this status. More likely, CHESS 4.5 had passed KAISSA in 1976, when iteratively-deepening search was added. When KAISSA lost to DUCHESS in the first round of this second world championship, CHESS 4.6 became the clear favorite to win. However, it did have to win or draw its game against BELLE in the final round. BELLE was improving fast, and as will be seen in the next chapter, surpassed CHESS 4.6 the following year.

August 12, 1977, Toronto
Round 4, second World Computer Chess Championship
White: BELLE   Black: CHESS 4.6
Time Control: 40/2, 20/1 thereafter
French Defense

---

1 e4 Nc6 2 Nf3 e6 3 d4 d5 4 Nc3 Bb4 5 e5 Nge7 6 a3 B×c3+ 7 b×c3 Na5 8 Bb5+ Bd7 9 Bd3 Rc8 10 Ng5 h6 11 Nf3 c5 12 d×c5

BELLE isn't sufficiently concerned about its pawn structure yet.

12 . . . R×c5 13 Be3 R×c3 14 B×a7 Nc4 15 O-O R×a3 16 R×a3 N×a3 17 Bc5

This is necessary to avoid getting the bishop trapped with 17 . . . b6.

17 . . . Qa5 18 Bd6 Nc4

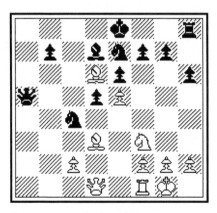

Figure 5.4. Position after 18 . . . Nc4.

19 Qa1

BELLE should have played 19 B×c4, and then if 19 ... d×c4 20 B×e7 K×e7, 21 Qd6+, forcing the king to block the rook from developing and giving White pressure on the d-file.

19 ... Nc6 20 Q×a5 N6×a5 21 Ra1 Bc8 22 c3 Nc6 23 Ra4

CHESS 4.6 can now coast to a victory.

23 ... N×d6 24 e×d6 Kd7 25 Rg4 g5 26 Bc2 K×d6 27 Ra4 b5 28 Ra1 b4
29 c×b4 N×b4 30 Bb1 Bd7 31 Kh1 f5 32 Nd4 Rc8 33 Ne2 Bb5 34 Ng1 Rc1 35 Ra5 R×b1

White cannot play 36 R×b5 because of the mate threat 36 ... Nd3 followed by 37 ... N×f2#!

36 f3 Bf1 37 h4 Rb2 38 h×g5 B×g2+ 39 Kh2 h×g5 40 Ra4 B×f3+ 41 Kg3 Bh5
42 Kh3 f4 43 Ra8 Bg6 44 Kg4 Rg2+ 45 Kh3 R×g1 46 Kh2 Rg4 47 Rd8+ Ke5
48 Rg8 Be4 49 Rg7 Bf3 50 Rh7 Nd3 51 Rh3 Rg2+ 52 Kh1 Nf2#.

August 26–September 4, 1978: The Levy Challenge, Toronto

In 1968, David Levy wagered $10,000 with a group of leading computer scientists that no computer would defeat him in a match during the coming decade. Levy was one of the top players in Great Britain. During the 1970s, he served as the tournament director at the ACM championships, and consequently was well tuned into the abilities and peculiarities of the programs. There were four challenges during that period, the first coming from CHESS 4.5, the second from KAISSA, and the third from CHEOPS, a descendent of MAC HACK that included a fast move-generator that searched 150,000 positions per second. Each of these matches was two games, and each time after Levy won the first game, the second wasn't played. The fourth and final challenge came from CHESS 4.7 and resulted in a six-game match held in late August, 1978, at the Canadian National Exhibition in Toronto. Levy, dressed in a tuxedo, and CHESS 4.7 played in a glass-enclosed booth, with the audience gathered around on the outside. Levy drew the first game, won the second and third, lost the fourth and won the fifth. The sixth game was not played.

After the third game, Levy needed only a draw in the remaining three games to win the bet. For the first three games he had played closed, quiet games, waiting for the computer to lose its way. In the fourth game, he decided to beat the computer at its own game. His experiment failed, and he returned to his winning conservative style for the fifth game. These two games follow.

September 3, 1978, Toronto
Game 4, CHESS 4.7 versus Levy Challenge Match
White: CHESS 4.7   Black: David Levy
Time Control: 40/2, 20/1 thereafter
Latvian Gambit

1 e4 e5 2 Nf3 f5

This took CHESS 4.7 out of book.

3 e×f5 e4 4 Ne5 Nf6 5 Ng4 d5 6 N×f6+ Q×f6 7 Qh5+ Qf7 8 Q×f7+ K×f7 9 Nc3 c6 10 d3 e×d3 11 B×d3 Nd7 12 Bf4 Nc5 13 g4 N×d3+ 14 c×d3 Bc5 15 O-O h5 16 Na4 Bd4 17 Be3

CHESS 4.7 invites Levy to exchange bishops and to improve its own pawn structure in the process.

17 . . . Be5 18 d4 Bd6 19 h3 b6 20 Rfe1 Bd7 21 Nc3 h×g4 22 h×g4 Rh4 23 f3 Rah8 24 Kf1

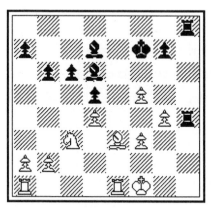

Figure 5.5. Position after 24 Kf1.

24 . . . Bg3

Levy felt in retrospect that 24 . . . Bc8 would result in an overwhelming position for Black. CHESS 4.7 has been searching anywhere from about 150,000 positions to 750,000 positions on each move, looking seven or eight plies deep. It has evaluated the game as about one-half to one pawn in its favor for most of the game thus far.

25 Re2 Bc8 26 Kg2 Bd6 27 Bg1 Rh3 28 Rae1 Rg3+ 29 Kf2 Rhh3 30 Re3 Ba6
31 Ne2 B×e2 32 R1×e2 c5

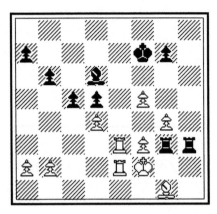

Figure 5.6. Position after 32 . . . c5.

33 f4

Levy overlooked this strong move.

33 . . . R×e3 34 R×e3

CHESS 4.7 searched to a depth of ten plies on this move now that the amount of material on the board is dropping.

34 . . . Rh4 35 Kg3 Rh1 36 Bf2 Rd1 37 Ra3 c×d4 38 R×a7+ Kf8

Afterward, Levy felt 38 . . . Ke8 39 R×g7 d3 40 Kf3 Rb1 would have been sufficient to win.

39 Rd7 Rd3+

Another mistake by Levy. Playing instead 39 . . . Bc5 followed by 40 R×d5 d3 41 B×c5+ b×c5 would have given White little chance to win and maybe even some ways to lose because of the passed d-pawn.

40 Kg2

CHESS 4.7 is looking nine and ten plies deep on every move at this stage in the game. Here it evaluates the position as 1.61 pawns in White's favor.

40 . . . Bc5 41 R×d5 Rd2 42 b4 B×b4 43 Rd8+ Kf7 44 Rd7+ Kf8 45 R×d4

CHESS 4.7 calculates that it is ahead by three pawns.

45 ... Rb2 46 Kf3 Bc5 47 Rd8+ Ke7

The final blunder by Levy. He overlooked White's next move, a visual error. The author has observed over the years that moves to the side of the board account for a disproportionate number of blunders. In this case, Levy was focusing on White continuing with what he saw as its only move, 48 B×c5.

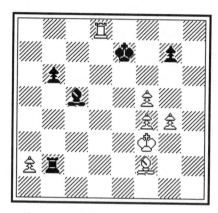

Figure 5.7. Position after 47 ... Ke7.

48 Bh4+ Kf7 49 g5 g6 50 Rd7+ Kf8 51 f×g6 R×a2 52 f5 Ra3+ 53 Kg4 Ra4+ 54 Kh5 Rd4 55 Rc7 Be7 56 f6 Black resigns.

CHESS 4.7 saw 56 ... Bd8 57 g7+ Kg8 58 Kg6 B×f6 59 g×f6 Rg4+ 60 Bg5 with a +8.43 score for White.

After this fiasco, Levy had to get back to serious business. He had to draw at least one of the next two games.

September 4, 1978, Toronto
Game 5, CHESS 4.7 versus Levy Challenge Match
White: David Levy   Black: CHESS 4.7
Time Control: 40/2, 20/1 thereafter
English Opening

1 c4 Nf6 2 a3 c6 3 d3 d5 4 Qc2

Black's first three moves were from its book, the second and third added by Slate after CHESS 4.7's loss in the third round. Levy was enticing CHESS 4.7 to expend its valuable d5 pawn for his less valuable c4 pawn.

4 ... d×c4 5 Q×c4 e5 6 Nf3 Bd6 7 g3 Be6 8 Qc2 Nbd7 9 Bg2 O-O 10 O-O Qb6
11 Nbd2 Qc5 12 Qb1

CHESS 4.7 has been carrying out only six-ply searches on most moves, the
game being conducive to inefficient alpha-beta searches because of a lack
of obvious, or forced, moves. Levy realized this and avoids simplifying the
position here with a queen trade.

12 ... h6 13 b4 Qb5 14 Qc2 Nb6 15 Bb2 a5 16 a4 Qa6 17 b×a5 Q×a5 18 Bc3 Qc5
19 Rfc1 Nbd7 20 a5 Qa7 21 Qb2 Ng4

The game has become so difficult for CHESS 4.7's search that it is only carrying out five-ply searches. For most of the game thus far, the computer felt
it was ahead by about a quarter of a pawn.

22 Ne4 Bc7 23 h3 f5

The game has reached maximum complexity.

Figure 5.8. Position after 23 ... f5.

24 h×g4 f×e4 25 d×e4 B×g4 26 Be1 Nc5 27 Rcb1

At this point the computer mysteriously went silent. It was revived after 25
minutes of first aid by its programmers, but that left CHESS 4.7 only twenty
minutes to make the next thirteen moves.

27 ... Rae8 28 Bd2 Rf7 29 Be3 Bd6 30 Qc2 B×f3

For the first time, CHESS 4.7 gives Levy credit for being ahead by 0.12
points.

31 B×f3 Ra8

For the next several moves CHESS 4.7 evaluates the game as being in White's favor by somewhere between a pawn and a pawn and a half.

32 Rc1 b6 33 Kg2 Qb7 34 a×b6 R×a1 35 R×a1 Ne6 36 Ra7 Qc8

CHESS 4.7 goes down quickly here. The shallow searches of the last fifteen moves or so have not been enough.

37 Qa2 Rf6 38 Ra8 Bb8 39 Bg4 Kf7 40 Qa7+ B×a7 41 R×c8 B×b6 42 B×e6+ R×e6 43 B×b6 Black resigns.

The computer broke down again and Slate decided enough is enough. Thus, as of 1978, the best chess playing computer was not on a par with a British international master. Nevertheless, CHESS 4.7 put on a good show, although Levy might have won the match in four games if there had been some incentive for him to polish off the computer quickly.

February 1980: The United States Amateur Team Championship, Somerset, New Jersey

One of the highlights of CHESS 4.9's career came at the 1980 United States Amateur Team Championship in Somerset, New Jersey, in 1980 when it drew with Larry Evans, rated 2393 at the time. It was Evans's only non-victory in the event. He became the highest-rated player to do no better than draw against a computer in a regular tournament game.

♚

February 1980, Somerset, New Jersey
United States Amateur Team Championship
White: CHESS 4.9   Black: Larry Evans
Time Control: 40/2, 20/1 thereafter
Sicilian Defense

---

1 e4 c5 2 Nf3 d6 3 d4 c×d4 4 N×d4 Nf6 5 Nc3 a6 6 Be2 e6 7 O-O Be7 8 Be3 O-O
9 f4 Nc6 10 e5 d×e5 11 N×c6 b×c6 12 Q×d8 R×d8 13 f×e5 Nd5 14 N×d5 c×d5
15 Bb6 Rd7 16 Rad1 Rb8 17 Bd4 Rc7 18 Bd3 Rb4 19 Bc3 Ra4 20 Ra1 Bb7 21 b3 Rg4
22 h3

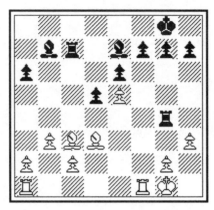

Figure 5.9. Position after 22 h3.

22 . . . R×g2+

Evans trades a rook for a bishop and pawn and obtains a king-side pawn advantage, offsetting the computer's pawn advantage on the other side of the board.

23 K×g2 R×c3 24 Rae1 a5 25 Kg3 Bg5 26 h4 Bh6 27 Rf3 Rc7 28 a4 d4 29 Be4 B×e4 30 R×e4 Be3

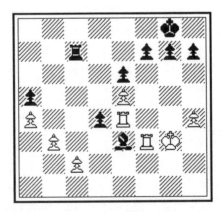

Figure 5.10. Position after 30 . . . Be3.

31 Rf×e3

White has little choice but to trade its rook for a bishop and pawn.

31 . . . d×e3 32 c4 Kf8 33 R×e3 Ke7 34 Kf4 f6 35 Rg3 Kf7 36 Rd3 Rc5 37 Rd7+ Kg6 38 h5+ K×h5 39 e×f6 g×f6 40 R×h7+ Kg6 41 Rb7 Rh5 42 Ke4 Rh4+ 43 Kd3 Rh3+

44 Kc2 Rh2+ 45 Kc3 Rh3+ 46 Kc2 Rh2+ 47 Kc3 f5 48 Rb6 Kf6 49 Ra6 f4 50 R×a5 f3
51 Ra8 Kf7 52 Rd8 e5 53 Rd1 Ke6 54 c5 e4 55 c6 Rh8 56 c7 Rc8 57 Kd4 R×c7
58 K×e4 Rb7 59 K×f3 R×b3+ 60 Ke4 Rb4+ 61 Rd4 R×d4+ 62 K×d4 Drawn.

References

D. A. Cahlander, "The Computer is a Fish, or is it?" *SIGART Newsletter* of the ACM (April 1977): 8–11.

D. Levy, "Invasion from Cyberland," *Chess Life and Review* (June 1977): 312–14.

K. Thompson, "United States Amateur Team Championship," *ICCA Newsletter* 3, no. 1 (July 1980): 7–12.

D. J. Slate and L. R. Atkin, "CHESS 4.5—The Northwestern University Chess Program," in *Chess Skill in Man and Machine* ed. P. Frey (New York: Springer-Verlag, 1977), 82–118.

The following papers are concerned with iteratively-deepening depth-first search applied to problems other than chess

R. E. Korf, "Iteratively-Deepening-A*: An optimal admissible tree search," *Proceedings of the Ninth International Joint Conference on Artificial Intelligence,* Los Angeles, California (1985): 1034–36.

M. E. Stickel and W. M. Tyson, "An analysis of consecutively bounded depth-first search with applications in automated deduction," *Proc. of the Ninth International Joint Conference on Artificial Intelligence,* Los Angeles, California (1985): 1073–75.

6 BELLE and High-Speed Chess Circuitry

After completing his work on the UNIX operating system, an incredible accomplishment in itself and sufficient on which to rest one's laurels, Ken Thompson turned to developing a chess program. Thompson has a tremendous amount of energy, and when he becomes interested in something, exciting things happen. In addition to his work on computers, Thompson had other strong interests, including traveling to the South Pole, restoring antique autos, and, well, flying, about which a story cannot go unrecorded.

Thompson learned to fly in the late 1970s and flew one of his early solo flights to Montreal in a small two-passenger, single-winged plane to attend a conference on computer chess at McGill University. David Slate came too from Chicago, and when Thompson found out that both Slate and he were going on from Montreal to Carnegie Mellon University, Thompson invited Slate to fly there with him. Well, Slate has always been a very cautious person, someone who feels he is risking his life every time he boards a commercial airliner, and here Thompson wants him to go up in the sky on a plane that looks like it fought in the Battle of Normandy. Slate initially declined, but Thompson's charm eventually wore him down, and Slate finally accepted, much against his better judgment. Thompson was delighted with Slate's change of mind. Tony Marsland, who also attended the conference, drove with Thompson and Slate and me to the airport to send the fliers on

their way. Thompson's small plane was wheeled nearby to have gas put in and then pulled over to where we were waiting. The flyers got in; Thompson turned the key to start the engine, but the battery was dead as a doornail. Slate was overjoyed. Maybe the mission was off! But no such luck. Thompson simply got out, cranked the propeller a few times, and the engine caught. Slate swallowed hard! We waved as they flew off, imagining Slate's knees knocking in the rear seat. This is not the end of the story. When Thompson finally arrived in Pittsburgh, the airport landing was very difficult. It was one of Thompson's first solo landings, a fact Slate probably didn't know. Thompson did his best, but somehow the plane wound up next to the runway on the grass but with everybody safe and sound. Rumor has it that Slate has stuck to commercial airlines ever since.

A decade after Thompson started his work on BELLE, his protégé became the first program crowned a master by the U.S. Chess Federation. He also was awarded the $5,000 Fredkin Prize for having BELLE achieve this level of play before any other computer. This prize was established by Ed Fredkin's Fredkin Foundation of Cambridge, Massachusetts, in 1980. Fredkin also established a prize of $100,000 to be awarded to the developers of the first program to defeat the human world champion in a regulation match. A $10,000 prize was established for the developers of the first grandmaster-level computer, and as will be seen, this prize was picked up in 1989 by DEEP THOUGHT's team. Thompson began work on BELLE in 1973 and quickly came to the conclusion that his program could move to the head of the field if it could search much larger trees than the competition. At that time BELLE was searching about two hundred positions per second.

BELLE and special-purpose circuitry

Having the facilities of Bell Laboratories at his disposal, Thompson turned his energy toward developing special-purpose, high-speed circuitry for chess. Move generation is the most time-consuming process in chess programs and it was primarily this part of the code that he transformed into hardware. Working with design specialist Joe Condon, Thompson built three circuits: the first in 1977 with twenty-five chips, which gave virtually no speedup over the software version; the second a year or so later with 325 chips, which searched 5,000 positions per second; and a third shortly thereafter with 1,700 chips, which searched 120,000 positions per second.

BELLE won the third world championship in Linz, Austria, in 1980 with this version.

December 3, 1978: Washington

It was in 1978 at the ninth ACM North American Computer Chess Championship that the 325-chip version of BELLE replaced CHESS 4.7 as the best program, when BELLE upset the former champion in a real slugfest. BELLE dominated computer chess for the following five years. CHESS 4.7 did not immediately disappear, however, and it continued to remain one of the stronger programs until the mid-1980s. It won the tenth ACM North American championship in Detroit the following year, drawing with BELLE in the final round. In February of 1980, CHESS 4.9 played first board, followed by DUCHESS, BELLE, and CHAOS, at the United States Amateur Team Championship in Somerset, New Jersey, where as we saw in the previous chapter, CHESS 4.9 drew a game with Larry Evans.

In the crucial game when BELLE defeated CHESS 4.7, Thompson's new hardware was searching about 5,000 positions per second; CHESS 4.7, running on a CDC Cyber 176, was searching about 3,500 positions per second. BELLE had lost to CHESS 4.7 the previous year at the second world championship, as was shown in the previous chapter. But this time it was different.

Ken Thompson, Claude Shannon, and David Slate in Edmonton, 1989.

December 3, 1978, Washington
Round 2, ninth ACM North American Computer Chess Championship
White: BELLE   Black: CHESS 4.7
Time Control: 40/2, 20/1 thereafter
French Defense

---

1 e4 Nc6 2 d4 d5 3 Nc3 e6 4 Nf3 Bb4 5 e5 Nge7

Although moves were transposed a bit, this game has reached the same position as was reached by these two in Toronto the previous year. In that game, BELLE played 6 a3. This time it tries something else.

6 Bd2 Nf5 7 Ne2 Be7 8 c3 O-O 9 Nf4 f6 10 Bd3 f×e5 11 d×e5 g5

This threatens to win the pawn on e5 but also weakens the defenses around the king. White sees all this coming, and being also a materialist, weakens its own king's safety in return!

12 g4 Ng7 13 Ng2

Figure 6.1. Position after 13 Ng2.

13 ... b6

CHESS 4.7 wants to develop the bishop on the a8-h1 diagonal. Hans Berliner suggested that 13 ... R×f3 14 Q×f3 N×e5 15 Qe2 N×d3t 16 Q×d3 e5 would give Black a strong center and active pieces, which he felt compensated for the material sacrifice. The eight-ply sequence described by Berliner leaves CHESS 4.7 down one point in material, and the positional pluses would not have led the computer to make the material sacrifice.

14 Qe2 Bb7 15 Rg1

White may not have castled here because it didn't like the pawns defending the king on either side. Placing the rook on the same column as its opponent's king along with having the advanced pawn may have motivated 15 Rg1. The sacrifice on f3 still looks good.

15 . . . a5 16 a4 Kh8 17 h3 Kg8

Neither side can see how to improve its position, and they resorted to the typical pawn advances along with king and rook shuffling that typically characterized even the strong programs of that period.

18 Rh1 h6 19 h4 d4

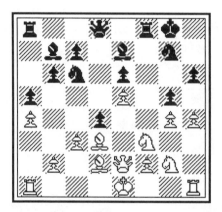

Figure 6.2. Position after 19 . . . d4.

After having advanced their pawns about as far as they can go, both sides now see tactical possibilities. The sacrifice on f3 could still be played, but 19 . . . d4 is a mistake, giving White an opportunity to win with 20 Qe4 R×f3 21 Qh7+ Kf8 22 Bg6. CHESS 4.7 must not have seen the consequences of this line, and evidently BELLE didn't either.

20 h×g5 Nb4

An exciting move, in which CHESS 4.7 effectively tells BELLE that it is ready to start the big battle.

21 g×h6

BELLE's scoring function liked undoubling its pawns and having one of them deep in its opponent's territory, but this gives up the strength it had

on the h-file. BELLE predicted 21 ... N×d3+ 22 Q×d3 R×f3 23 h7+ Kf7 24 Q×d4 with a small advantage for Black. The battle continues.

21 ... N×d3+

Black would have done better with 21 ... d×c3. White is ahead two pawns going into this rumble, and unless Black can improve its position, it will not have enough material to hang on in the endgame.

22 Q×d3 d×c3 23 Qg6

Threatening mate in one!

23 ... c×d2+ 24 N×d2 Rf7 25 h×g7 R×g7 26 Q×e6+ Rf7 27 Qh6 Rg7 28 Qh8+ Kf7 29 e6+ K×e6 30 Q×g7 B×g2 31 Rh6+ Kd7 32 O-O-O Bd5 33 Ne4

Black's king is under tremendous pressure, and BELLE is on the verge of being crowned the king of the chess computers, although this game will continue another fifteen moves.

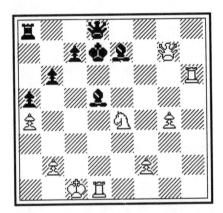

Figure 6.3. Position after 33 Ne4.

33 ... Kc8 34 Rh8 B×e4 35 Rd×d8+ B×d8 36 Qe7 Kb7 37 Q×e4+ Ka7 38 Rg8 Rb8 39 g5 Be7 40 R×b8 B×g5+ 41 f4 B×f4+ 42 Q×f4 K×b8 43 Kd2 Kb7 44 Kd3 Kc8 45 b4 a×b4 46 Q×b4 Kd7 47 Qb5+ Kd8 48 Ke4 Black resigns.

October 30, 1979: Detroit

In 1979, BELLE failed to win the tenth ACM championship when it drew with CHAOS in the second round and later with CHESS 4.9 in the final round. CHESS 4.9 finished with 3.5/4, while BELLE was a half point behind.

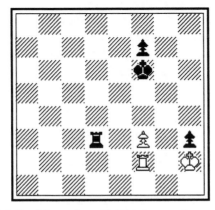

October 30, 1979, Detroit
Round 4, tenth ACM North American Computer Chess Championship
White: BELLE   Black: CHESS 4.9
Time Control: 40/2, 20/1 thereafter
Benoni Defense

1 d4

BELLE had played 1 e4 in its last two encounters with CHESS 4.9.

1 ... Nf6 2 c4 c5 3 d5 e6 4 Nc3 e×d5 5 c×d5 d6 6 e4 g6 7 Nf3 Bg7 8 Be2 O-O
9 O-O Re8 10 Nd2 Na6 11 f3 Nc7 12 a4 b6 13 Nc4 Ba6 14 Bg5 h6 15 Bh4 g5
16 Bf2 Nh5 17 Ne3 Bc8 18 Qc2 Nf4 19 Bc4 Bd7 20 Rfd1 Qf6 21 Bg3 Nh5 22 Be1 Nf4
23 Kh1 a6 24 Bg3 b5 25 a×b5 a×b5 26 R×a8 R×a8 27 Bf1 b4 28 Ne2 b3 29 Qb1 Nh5
30 Bf2 Nf4 31 Nc4 N×e2 32 B×e2 Bb5 33 Bg3 Ra4 34 Qc1 Bf8 35 Rd2 Qd8 36 Qf1 h5
37 Kg1 h4 38 Bf2 Bg7 39 Ne3 B×e2 40 Q×e2 Ra1+ 41 Rd1 Ra2 42 Qd3 R×b2
43 Nc4 Rc2 44 e5 B×e5 45 N×e5 d×e5 46 Q×b3 Re2 47 Kf1 c4

White has difficulties staying focused. It can now play 48 Qb1 and win the
rook for a bishop, but it gets distracted by the knight on c7 while underes-
timating the danger of 49 ... h3.

48 Qb7 Ra2 49 Bb6 h3 50 Q×c7 Qf6 51 Qd8+ Q×d8 52 B×d8 R×g2 53 Re1 c3
54 R×e5 c2 55 Re8+ Kg7 56 B×g5 R×g5 57 Rc8 Rg2 58 d6 R×h2 59 d7 Rd2
60 Kg1 R×d7 61 R×c2 Rd3 62 Rf2 Kf6 63 Kh2 Drawn by agreement.

Figure 6.4. Position after 63 Kh2 Drawn by agreement.

September 25-29, 1980

BELLE went on the win the third World Computer Chess Championship in Linz, Austria, in 1980. It finished the four-round event with 3.5/4, tied with CHAOS, but won a one-game playoff for the title.

Ben Mittman, Monty Newborn, Tony Marsland, David Slate, David Levy, Claude Shannon, Ken Thompson, Betty Shannon, and Tom Truscott in Vienna following the third World Championship in Linz, Austria, 1980.

September 29, 1980
Third World Computer Chess Championship, Linz, Austria
Playoff for world champion title
White: BELLE   Black: CHAOS
Time Control: 40/2, 20/1 thereafter
Alekhine's Defense

---

1 e4 Nf6 2 e5 Nd5 3 d4 d6 4 Nf3 d×e5 5 N×e5 g6 6 g3 Bf5 7 c4 Nb4 8 Qa4+ N4c6
9 d5 Bc2

Over the years, this kind of bishop move has been one characteristic of computer play.

10 Qb5

Black is in a real bind after just ten moves by White.

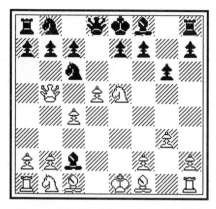

Figure 6.5. Position after 10 Qb5.

10 . . . Qd6

Black might better play 10 . . . a6, and then 11 Q×b7 N×e5 12 Q×a8
Nf3+ 13 Ke2 Nd4+, where Black has better chances than in the line that
the game follows.

11 N×c6 N×c6 12 Nc3 Bg7 13 Q×b7 O-O 14 Q×c6 Qb4 15 Kd2 Be4 16 Rg1 Rfb8
17 Bh3 Bh6+ 18 f4 Qa5 19 Re1 f5 20 Qe6+ Kf8 21 b3 Bg7 22 Bb2 Bd4 23 g4 Rb6
24 Qd7 Rd6 25 Qa4 Qb6 26 Ba3 B×c3+ 27 K×c3 Rdd8 28 Rad1 Qf2

Although White is a piece up, Black's active pieces hold off its opponent
for a while longer.

29 g×f5 Qc2+ 30 Kd4 g×f5 31 Qc6 Qf2+ 32 Ke5

Black is finally out of tricks!

32 . . . Kg8 33 Rg1+ Kh8

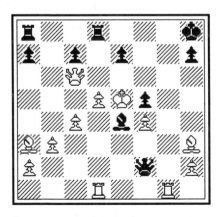

Figure 6.6. Position after 33 . . . Kh8.

Fred Swartz, one of the programmers of CHAOS, *1980.*

34 B×e7

BELLE announces mate in eight! It always gives chess programmers great joy announcing mate in any number of moves on behalf of their programs! Announcing mate in eight is very impressive.

34 . . . Qb2+ 35 Rd4 Qg2 36 Qf6+ Kg8 37 B×g2 R×d5+ 38 Ke6 h6 39 Q×h6 Re5+ 40 f×e5 Rf8 41 Bf3#.

October 26-28, 1980: Nashville

Several months after winning the world championship, BELLE won the eleventh ACM North American championship with a perfect score, although CHESS CHALLENGER, its opponent in the last round, could have drawn the game. CHESS CHALLENGER was running on a 4-MHz 6502 processor. Its programmers, Dan and Kathe Spracklen, were responsible for developing the SARGON chess program. This game is one of the most exciting games in the history of computer chess.

♚

October 28, 1980, Nashville
Round 4, eleventh ACM North American Computer Chess Championship
White: Chess Challenger   Black: Belle
Time Control: 40/2, 20/1 thereafter
Ruy Lopez

———

1 e4 e5 2 Nf3 Nc6 3 Bb5 a6 4 Ba4 Nf6 5 O-O N×e4 6 d4 b5 7 Bb3 d5 8 d×e5 Be6
9 c3 Bc5 10 Be3

This gives Black the opportunity to give White doubled, isolated pawns on the e-file.

10 . . . B×e3 11 f×e3 Rb8 12 Nbd2 Nc5 13 Qe1 Nd3 14 Qg3 O-O 15 Rab1 Qe7
16 Bc2 Qc5

Belle was carrying out eight-ply searches on most moves. It predicted that White would play 17 Ng5.

17 Ng5

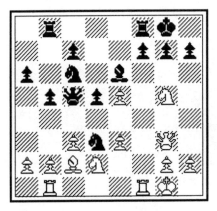

Figure 6.7. Position after 17 Ng5.

17 . . . Nc×e5 18 N×h7 Rfd8

Based on an eight-ply search, Belle anticipated 19 Nf6+ and judged the position as being 0.4 pawns to White's advantage.

19 Nf6+ Kf8 20 B×d3 N×d3 21 Nh5 g6 22 Nf6 Bf5 23 Qg5 b4 24 Nh7+ Ke8
25 Nf6+ Kf8

White can draw but will choose not to.

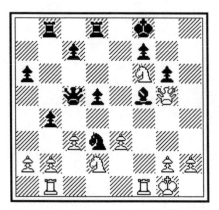

Figure 6.8. Position after 25 . . . Kf8.

26 Nb3 Qc4 27 Nh7+ Ke8 28 c×b4 R×b4 29 Nf6+ Kf8 30 Ng4 Rd6 31 Nh6 Qe4

Black is down a pawn but its pieces are on active squares. White's position will deteriorate after a sacrifice fails to work.

32 R×f5 g×f5 33 Qg8+ Ke7 34 Q×f7+ Kd8 35 N×f5 Rc6 36 h4 Rc2

BELLE judges the position as even.

37 Qf8+ Kd7 38 Qf7+ Kc8 39 Qg6 Kb7 40 Na5+ Ka8 41 Q×a6+ Kb8 42 Qg6 Ne5

BELLE judged the position as a three pawn advantage for Black.

43 Qg8+ Ka7 44 Rf1 Rb×b2 45 Kh1 R×g2 46 Nc6+ N×c6 47 Qa8+ K×a8 48 a4

At this point, BELLE exhibited a strange bug.

48 . . . Kb8 49 a5 Ka8 50 a6 Ka7 51 h5 Kb6 52 a7 Rg1+

White's 52 a7 must have brought BELLE to its senses.

53 K×g1 Qg2#.

November 8-10, 1981: Los Angeles

In 1981, BELLE won the twelfth ACM championship, held in Los Angeles, scoring 3.5/4. It drew with NUCHESS (David Slate's rewrite of CHESS 4.9, done in 1980 with Northwestern University student William Blanchard) in the third round and then had to defeat CRAY BLITZ in the final round. CRAY BLITZ had won its first three games and would have won the championship if it had obtained a draw with BELLE.

Fidelity's experimental Chess Challenger, *1979.*

Kathe and Dan Spracklen facing each other across the board, creators of Chess Challenger *and* Sargon, *in Detroit, 1979.*

November 10, 1981, Los Angeles
Round 4, twelfth ACM North American Computer Chess Championship
White: CRAY BLITZ   Black: BELLE
Time Control: 40/2, 20/1 thereafter
Two Knights Game

---

1 e4 e5 2 Nf3 Nc6 3 Bc4 Nf6 4 Ng5 d5 5 e×d5 Na5 6 Bb5+ c6 7 d×c6 b×c6 8 Qf3 Rb8
9 B×c6+ N×c6 10 Q×c6+ Nd7 11 d3 Be7 12 Ne4 Bb7

The last moves by White and Black were their first out of book.

13 Qa4 Qc7 14 Nbc3 Bc6 15 Qc4 Qc8 16 Nd5 B×d5 17 Q×d5 Q×c2 18 O-O f6

Figure 6.9. Position after 18 ... f6.

Black is a pawn down and White will soon have two passed pawns on the queen-side.

19 f4 Nb6 20 Qa5 Q×d3 21 Q×a7 O-O 22 Q×e7 Q×e4 23 Qe6+ Kh8 24 f×e5 f×e5
25 R×f8+ R×f8 26 h3 Qe1+

Black's pieces are active and well placed. White is playing without a rook.

27 Kh2 h6 28 Q×b6

White bites!

28 ... Rf1 29 Qd8+ Kh7 30 Qd3+ e4 31 Q×f1 Q×f1 32 a3 e3 33 B×e3 Q×a1
34 Bd4 h5 35 Bc3 g5 36 Be5 Qe1 37 Bc3 Qf2 38 Kh1 g4 39 h×g4 h×g4 40 Kh2 Qh4+
41 Kg1 g3 42 Kf1 Kg6 White resigns.

October 24-26, 1982: Dallas.

Having won the world championship in 1980 and the ACM championships in 1980 and in 1981, BELLE seemed invincible. However, in the thirteenth ACM championship, BELLE showed some cracks in its armor. In the first round it drew with OSTRICH when the dying bird played the best game of its career. In the final round, BELLE drew with CRAY BLITZ, winding up with three points out of a possible four and winning the championship on tie-break points over CRAY BLITZ, NUCHESS, and CHAOS, all also finishing with three points.

October 24, 1982, Dallas
Round 1, thirteenth ACM North American
Computer Chess Championship
White: BELLE   Black: OSTRICH
Time Control: 40/2, 20/1 thereafter
Center Counter

---

1 e4 d5 2 e×d5 Nf6 3 d4 N×d5 4 Nf3 Bg4 5 Be2 Nc6 6 c4 Nf6 7 d5 B×f3 8 B×f3 Ne5
9 Bg5 e6 10 O-O Bc5 11 Re1 N×f3+ 12 Q×f3 Bb4 13 Re4 Qe7 14 d×e6 O-O-O

A great disappearing act by Black's king! In addition, the rooks are now connected and become a force in the game. Black's pieces find themselves on good squares all of a sudden and by coincidence. White needed to develop its knight but may have been concerned that Black would wreck its queen-side pawns if it did.

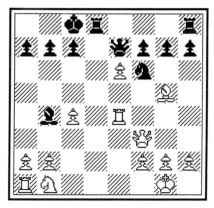

Figure 6.10. Position after 14 . . . O-O-O.

15 Qe2 h6 16 B×f6 Q×f6 17 g3 Rhe8 18 e×f7 R×e4 19 Q×e4 Q×b2 20 c5 B×c5
21 Qf5+ Rd7 22 Q×c5 R×f7 23 Q×a7 Q×a1 24 Qa8+ Kd7 25 Q×b7 Q×a2
26 Qb5+ c6 27 Qb7+ Kd6 28 Qb4+ Kc7 29 Nd2 Qa7 30 Ne4 Qa1+ 31 Kg2 Qe5
32 Qa4 Re7 33 Qa7+ Kd8 34 Qa8+ Kd7 35 Qb7+ Qc7 36 Qb3

BELLE smartly avoids trading queens, while OSTRICH can see no way to
make progress.

36 . . . Qe5 37 Qb7+ Qc7 38 Qb3 Qe5 39 Qb7+ Drawn by repetition.

October 26, 1982, Dallas
Round 4, thirteenth ACM North American
Computer Chess Championship
White: CRAY BLITZ   Black: BELLE
Time Control: 40/2, 20/1 thereafter
Vienna Game

---

1 e4 e5 2 Nc3 Nf6 3 Bc4 Nc6 4 d3 Bc5 5 Nf3 d6 6 Bg5 Na5 7 B×f6 Q×f6 8 Nd5 Qd8
9 b4 N×c4 10 b×c5 c6 11 d×c4 c×d5 12 c×d5 Qa5+ 13 Qd2 Q×c5 14 O-O O-O

A little breather after the storm.

15 Rab1 b6 16 Qb4 f5 17 Q×c5 b×c5 18 Nd2 f×e4 19 N×e4 Ba6 20 Rfc1 Bc4
21 N×d6 B×d5 22 c4 Bc6 23 Nb7 B×b7 24 R×b7 Rf7 25 Rb5 Rc8 26 f3 Kf8 27 Re1 Re7
28 Kf2 g6 29 Rd1 e4 30 Re1 e×f3 31 R×e7 K×e7 32 Rb7+ Ke6 33 g×f3 Rd8

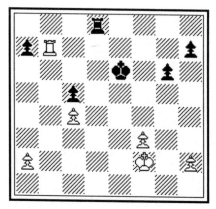

Figure 6.11. Position after 33 . . . Rd8.

White's rook has been able to hold the seventh rank and now can pick up a pawn. On move 43, it will pick up a second pawn but, in spite of a two-pawn advantage, it will have to settle for a draw.

34 R×a7 Rd4 35 R×h7 R×c4 36 Rc7 Kd5 37 a3 Rc2+ 38 Kg3 c4 39 Rd7+ Ke6
40 Rg7 Kf5 41 Rc7 Ke6 42 Rc6+ Kd5 43 R×g6 c3 44 Rg7 Kc4 45 h4 Rc1 46 Rc7+ Kb3
47 Rb7+ Ka2 48 Kf4 c2 49 Rc7 Kb1 50 Rb7+ Ka2 51 Rc7 Kb1 52 Rb7+ Ka2
Drawn by repetition.

The end of Belle's reign

BELLE ruled the world of chess programs until late in 1983. It reached new levels of excellence during August of 1983 when it finished the twelve-round United States Open with eight and one-half points and a performance rating of 2363. BELLE defeated Mitchel Saltzberg (2310), Leslie Au (2228), Harry Radke (2313), William Wharton (2236), and drew with Craig Mar (2403). Two weeks later BELLE participated in the Fredkin Incentive Match, winning all three of its games against humans with United States Chess Federation ratings within a few points of 2,000. It came to the fourth world championship in New York as the clear favorite to repeat. It won its first two games and was paired against NUCHESS in the third round. A ceremony at which the United States Chess Federation would award BELLE the title of U.S. master was arranged to take place during that game. At the very moment when the award was being made, BELLE's fate took a dramatic turn for the worse: the program lost to NUCHESS. Later in the final round, it lost a second game to CRAY BLITZ. It finished in sixth place, and CRAY BLITZ became the new king.

October 23, 1983, New York
Round 3, fourth World Computer Chess Championship
White: NUCHESS   Black: BELLE
Time Control: 40/2, 20/1 thereafter
Ruy Lopez

1 e4 e5 2 Nf3 Nc6 3 Bb5 a6 4 Ba4 Nf6 5 d4 e×d4 6 O-O Be7 7 e5 Ne4 8 N×d4 O-O
9 Nf5 d5 10 e×d6 B×f5 11 d×e7 N×e7 12 Be3 Nd5 13 Qf3 N×e3 14 f×e3 Bg6
15 Qf4 b5 16 Bb3 c5 17 c4 Qf6 18 Q×f6 N×f6 19 Rc1 b4 20 Nd2 Rfe8 21 Re1 Rad8
22 Nf1 Bd3

Black's bishop enters a spidor's trap, causing great grief for its other pieces. It is not until 30 . . . f4 that Black understands its difficulties.

23 Rad1 Ng4 24 Ba4 Rf8 25 Nd2 Ne5 26 Bb3 Rd6 27 Nf3 N×f3+ 28 g×f3 f5
29 Rd2 Re8 30 Kf2 f4 31 e×f4 R×e1 32 K×e1 Rd4 33 Kf2 Kf7 34 Ke3 B×c4
35 R×d4 c×d4+ 36 K×d4 B×b3 37 a×b3

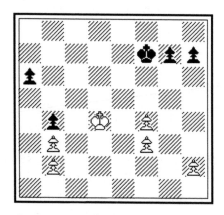

Figure 6.12. Position after 37 a×b3.

White will go on to win this game because its king is better placed—and its king is better placed because the relatively shortsighted searches encouraged the king to pursue the pinned bishop which happened to be in the middle of the board.

37 . . . Kf6 38 Ke4 g6 39 h4 Ke6 40 f5+ g×f5+ 41 Kd4 Kd6 42 f4 Ke6 43 Kc5 a5
44 h5 Kf7 45 Kd5 Kf6 46 Kd6 Kf7 47 Ke5 Ke8 48 K×f5 Black resigns.

Thompson, as good a sport as there is, was approached after this game by Zuck the Book—Bernie Zuckerman, that is—a New York City master. Zuck wanted to play BELLE some speed chess. He asked Thompson, who had already had a difficult evening suffering with his program, whether he would own BELLE's soul if he defeated it ten in a row. Thompson kept quiet and the first game began—at 3:00 A.M. The Book resigned in a lost position some ten minutes later, and struggled in the remaining games to finish with a nearly equal score. He shook Thompson's hand and left the room.

BELLE went into the final round in second place and with three of four points. It was paired with CRAY BLITZ, who led the field with three and one-half points. BELLE could have kept its title with a victory over CRAY BLITZ, but that wasn't in the cards.

October 25, 1983, New York
Round 5, fourth World Computer Chess Championship
White: BELLE   Black: CRAY BLITZ
Time Control: 40/2, 20/1 thereafter
Sicilian Defense

1 e4 c5 2 c3 d5 3 e×d5 Q×d5 4 Nf3 e6 5 d4 Nf6 6 Bd3 Nc6 7 O-O Be7 8 Be3 O-O
9 d×c5 Rd8 10 Nd4 B×c5 11 c4 Qd6 12 N×c6 b×c6 13 B×c5 Q×d3 14 Qa4 Ne4
15 Bb6 Rd7 16 Ba5 Bb7 17 Nc3 Nc5 18 Qb4 Qd4 19 Rad1 Nd3 20 Qa4 Qg4 21 c5 Qf5
22 b4

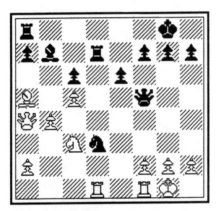

Figure 6.13. Position after 22 b4.

Black will now capture White's queen in exchange for a rook and knight.
White would have had an even game after 22 Qe4 Q×c5 23 R×d3 R×d3
24 Q×d3 Q×a5 25 Qd7.

22 . . . Nb2 23 R×d7 N×a4 24 N×a4 Qc2 25 R×b7 Q×a4 26 Ra1 e5 27 f3 Qc2
28 Rc7 Qd3 29 Rf1 Qd5 30 a3 g5 31 Re7 f6 32 Rc7 h5 33 h3 Kh8 34 Kh2 a6 35 Re1 Re8
36 Re4 f5 37 Re2 g4 38 h×g4 f×g4 39 f×g4 h×g4 40 Rf2 e4 41 Rff7 Qe5+ 42 g3 e3
43 Rh7+ Kg8 44 b5 c×b5 45 Be1 Qb2+ 46 Kg1 Qa1 47 Kg2 Qf6 48 Kh2 Rd8
49 Rhd7 Rf8 50 Rd6 Qb2+ 51 Kg1 Qb1 52 Kh2 Qc2+ 53 Kg1 Qf5 White resigns.

Thus five years after having established itself as the best chess program,
BELLE found itself replaced by one of its long-time rivals. In 1984, BELLE
could do no better than fifth place in the fifteenth ACM championship,

and the following year, 1985, it skipped the event altogether. Then in 1986, it came out of retirement for the seventeenth ACM championship and finished first in the softest field in a number of years. CRAY BLITZ and HITECH passed up the event, as it was only several months after the world championship in Cologne and neither was particularly ready to do battle again and so shortly.

Opening databases

During the same period of time, Thompson was developing a large database of opening positions. Most programs had opening databases ranging from several hundred lines to several thousand. Thompson took it to a new level with a book containing a half-million positions and all of *Modern Chess Openings*. In developing his database, he found many errors in the books and learned to take what he read with a bit of skepticism.

Endgame databases

Early in his work on chess, Thompson constructed databases for many endgames. He currently has databases for all three-, four-, and five-piece endgames without pawns on the board as well as databases for some endgames with pawns present. These databases are available to other chess programmers and are a part of DEEP BLUE. In DEEP BLUE, they can be accessed during the search and they provide optimal play for all positions found. Each position in a database is assigned a score that depends on the minimum number of moves to force that particular endgame to a simpler won endgame or mate. If there are pawns, the score also depends on the number of moves until a pawn advance can be forced that leads to another won endgame. Databases for the KQPKQ, KRPKR, KNPKB, and KNPKN endgames were also developed by Thompson.* Larry Stiller obtained data for the same 5-piece nonpawn endgames using a 32K-processor Connection Machine CM-2. There are eighty such endgames (see Figure 6.14) and Stiller's computer found databases for them all in 227 minutes.

---

*Names for endgame databases are determined as follows. First, list White's pieces and then Black's. Next, if the database includes any pawns, indicate the squares of the pawns in parentheses. Lastly, if the database includes a bishop and the color of the squares on which the bishop moves is pertinent, precede the bishop with a b (indicating black-squared bishop) or a w (indicating a white-squared bishop).

With all five-piece endgames solved, the effort now has turned to six-piece endgames. There are many more of these, of course, but it is likely that they will all be constructed in the next ten years. Stiller has developed databases for the KQRKQN, KRBKNN, and KQNKRR endgames. For the KRBKNN endgame, he found there were two positions that required 223 moves, without a capture or pawn advance, to win. Jaap van den Herik, Bob Herschberg, and Najid Nakad have developed a database for a KRP(a2)KbBP(a3) endgame.

In the 1980s, when it was found that many endgames require more than fifty moves without a capture or pawn advance to win, the rules of chess, which until then considered these games as drawn, were modified. Exceptions had previously been made for KRBKR and KNNKP endgames as it was known for some time that these endgames could required more than fifty consecutive noncapturing and nonpawn moves to win. New exceptions were made for other endgames and as more and more databases were built, still more exceptions were made. Then, in 1992, the old fifty-move rule was re-established. In Figure 6.14, the reader can see that six five-piece endgames with no pawns on the board may require more than fifty moves without a capture to force a win. Figures 6.15 and 6.16 show two examples where White can win but if Black plays perfectly, it takes considerably more than 50 moves without a capture or a pawn advance to do so.

White: King, bishop, and knight
Black: King and bishop
White to win from the position shown in Figure 6.15.

In the following, equally good alternatives are shown in parentheses.

1 Bg3 Nc4 2 Kd1 Ne3+ 3 Ke2 Nf5 4 Bf2 Ne7 5 Kf3 Nc6 6 Kg3 Nd4 7 Kg4 Nc6 (7 . . . Nb3) 8 Kh3 Nb4 (8 . . . Ne5) 9 Bb6 Nd3 10 Nc2 Nf2+ 11 Kg3 Ne4+ 12 Kf4 Nd2 13 Ne3 Kh2 14 Kg4 Nb3 15 Ba7 Nc1 16 Bd4 Nd3 17 Kh4 Nf2 18 Be5+ (18 Bc5 or 18 Bb6) Kg1 19 Bc3 (19 Bg3) Ne4 (19 . . . Nh1) 20 Be1 Nf6 (20 . . . Nd6 or 20 . . . Nc5 or 20 . . . Nf2 or 20 . . . Kh1 or 20 . . . Kh2) 21 Kg5 (21 Kg3 or 21 Kh3) Nd7 (21 . . . Ne4+) 22 Kf4 (22 Kg4) Nc5 23 Kf3 Ne6 (23 . . . Kh2) 24 Bc3 Kh2 25 Kg4 Nd8 (25 . . . Nc5) 26 Be5+ (26 Ba5) Kg1 27 Kg3 Ne6 28 Bf6 (28 Bh8 or 28 Bc3 or 28 Bb2 or 28 Ba1) Nc5 29 Bd4 Nb3 30 Ba7 Nd2 31 Nc4+ Kh1 32 Ne5 (32 Nb2) Nc4 33 Nd3 (33 Ng4) Nd6 (33 . . . Nd2) 34 Kh3 Nf7 35 Be3 Ne5 36 Nf4 (36 Nf2+) Nc4

Three Pieces		Four Pieces	
Endgame	**Maximum number of moves to win**	**Endgame**	**Maximum number of moves to win**
KQK	10 to mate	KQKR	31 to conversion of KQK
KRK	16 to mate	KRKB	18 to conversion of KRK
		KRKN	27 to conversion of KRK
		KBBK	19 to mate
		KBNK	33 to mate

Five Pieces

Endgame	Maximum number of moves to a win (mate or conversion)	Endgame	Maximum number of moves to a win (mate or conversion)	Endgame	Maximum number of moves to a win (mate or conversion)
KNNNK	21	KBBKQ	4	KRKNR	5
KNNBK	14	KBRKN	21	KRKNQ	3
KNNRK	11	KBRKB	25	KRKBB	9
KNNQK	7	KBRKR	59	KRKBR	4
KNNKN	7	KBRKQ	7	KRKBQ	2
KNNKB	4	KBQKN	7	KRKRR	2
KNNKR	3	KBQKB	8	KRKRQ	2
KNNKQ	1	KBQKR	19	KRKQQ	2
KNBKN	77	KBQKQ	30	KQQNK	4
KNBKB	13	KNBRK	8	KQQBK	4
KNBKR	6	KNBQK	5	KQQRK	4
KNBKQ	5	KNRQK	5	KQQQK	3
KNRKN	24	KBRQK	5	KQQKN	5
KNRKB	25	KRRNK	6	KQQKB	4
KNRKR	33	KRRBK	6	KQQKR	14
KNRKQ	9	KRRRK	5	KQQKQ	25
KNQKN	9	KRRQK	4	KQKNN	63
KNQKB	9	KRRKN	8	KQKNB	42
KNQKR	22	KRRKB	10	KQKNR	46
KNQKQ	35	KRRKR	25	KQKNQ	14
KBBNK	14	KRRKQ	16	KQKBB	71
KBBBK	11	KRQKN	5	KQKBR	42
KBBRK	11	KRQKB	5	KQKBQ	17
KBBQK	6	KRQKR	16	KQKRR	20
KBBKN	66	KRQKQ	60	KQKRQ	9
KBBKB	6	KRKNN	11	KQKQQ	7
KBBKR	7	KRKNB	13		

Figure 6.14. On the maximum number of moves to force a win in endgames with no more than five pieces other than pawns.

Figure 6.15. A KBNKN endgame with White to play and win in seventy-seven moves.

37 Bd4 (37 Bc5 or 37 Ba7 or 37 Bf2) Nd6 (37 . . . Nd2) 38 Nh5 (38 . . . Nd3) Ne4
39 Be3 Nf2+ 40 Kg3 Ne4+ (40 . . . Nd3) 41 Kf3 Nd6 42 Bf4 Nc4 43 Kf2 Na5 44 Nf6 Nb7
45 Kf3 Nd8 (45 . . . Na5) 46 Bd6 (46 Ne4) Kg1 47 Ne4 Nc6 (47 . . . Ne6) 48 Nd2 Nd4+
49 Ke4 Ne2 50 Ke3 Nc3 51 Be5 Na2 52 Kf3 Nb4 53 Kg3 Kh1 54 Bd4 Nc6 55 Bc5 Nd8
56 Ne4 Nb7 57 Bb4 Nd8 58 Ba5 Ne6 59 Bb6 Ng5 60 Nf2+ Kg1 61 Kf4 Nf7 62 Ng4+ Kg2
63 Ne3+ Kh3 64 Nf5 Kg2 (64 . . . Kh2) 65 Bc5 Nh8 (65 . . . Nd8 or 65 . . . Kh2)
66 Nd4 Kh3 67 Kf5 Kh4 68 Ne6 Kh5 69 Be3 Nf7 70 Ng7+ Kh4 71 Bf4 Nh8 (71 . . . Kh3)
72 Ne6 (72 Kf6) Nf7 73 Kg6 (73 Kf6) Nh8+ 74 Kg7 Kg4 75 Bh6 (75 Bd6 or 75 Bc7 or
75 Bb8 or 75 Bd2 or 75 Bc1 or 75 Bh2) Kh5 (75 . . . Kf5) 76 Nf4+ Kh4 (76 . . . Kf4)
77 K×h8 with conversion to KBNK endgame.

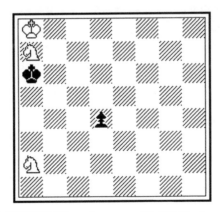

Figure 6.16. KNNKP(d4) endgame with White to play and win in eighty-four moves.

White: King and two knights
Black: King and pawn
White to win in eighty-four moves from the position shown in Figure 6.16.

1 Nb4+ Kb6 2 Nd3 Kc7 3 Nb5+ Kc6 4 Na3 Kb6 5 Kb8 (5 Nc4+ or 5 Nc2) Kc6
6 Nc4 (6 Nc2) Kb5 7 Nce5 Kb6 8 Kc8 Ka6 (8 . . . Ka5 or 8 . . . Kb5) 9 Kc7 (9 Kd7) Kb5
10 Kd6 Ka4 11 Kc5 Kb3 12 Kb5 Kc3 13 Ka4 Kc2 14 Kb4 Kd1 15 Kb3 Kd2 16 Kb2 Kd1
17 Nc4 Ke2 18 Kc2 Kf3 19 Kd2 (19 Kd1) Kg3 (19 . . . Ke4) 20 Ke2 (20 Nce5) Kg2
21 Nce5 Kg3 22 Kf1 Kh4 23 Kg2 (23 Kf2) Kg5 24 Kf3 Kf5 25 Nc4 Kf6 26 Kf4 Ke6
27 Ke4 Kf6 28 Kd5 Ke7 29 Ke5 Kf7 30 Kd6 Kf6 31 Nd2 Kf5 32 Ke7 Kg6 33 Ke6 Kg7
(33 . . . Kg5) 34 Ne4 Kg6 35 Ke5 Kg7 36 Kd6 Kh7 (36 . . . Kh6) 37 Nd2 (37 Nef2) Kg7
38 Ke6 Kf8 39 Ne4 (39 Nc4) Ke8 40 Nf6+ (40 Nd6+) Kf8 (40 . . . Kd8) 41 Nh5 Ke8
42 Ng7+ Kd8 43 Kd6 Kc8 44 Ne6 Kb8 (44 . . . Kb7) 45 Kc5 Ka7 46 Kc6 Ka6 47 Nec5+
(47 Ng5) Ka5 48 Nb3+ (48 Ne4) Ka4 49 Nd2 Ka5 50 Kc5 Ka6 51 Nc4 Kb7 52 Kd6 Kc8
53 Na5 Kd8 54 Nb7+ Ke8 55 Ke6 Kf8 56 Nd6 Kg7 57 Kf5 Kh6 58 Kf6 Kh5 59 Nf7
(59 Ne4) Kg4 60 Ng5 Kh4 61 Kf5 Kg3 62 Ke4 Kg4 63 Nf7 Kh5 (63 . . . Kg3) 64 Kf5 Kh4
65 Nfe5 Kh5 66 Ng4 Kh4 67 Nf6 Kh3 68 Ke5 Kg3 69 Ke4 Kh3 70 Kf3 Kh4 71 Kf4 Kh3
72 Ne8 (72 Ne4 or 72 Nh5) Kh4 73 Ng7 Kh3 74 Nf5 Kg2 (74 . . . Kh2) 75 Kg4 Kh2
(75 . . . Kf1 or 75 . . . Kg1 or 75 . . . Kh1) 76 Nd6 (76 Ng3) Kg2 (76 . . . Kg1 or 76 . . . Kh1)
77 Nc4 (77 Ne4) Kh2 (77 . . . Kg1) 78 Nd2 Kg2 79 Kh4 Kh2 (79 . . . Kg1) 80 Nf4
(80 Ne1) Kg1 81 Kg3 Kh1 82 Nf3 (82 Ne2 or 82 Nh3) d3 followed by 83 Nh3 d2
84 Nf2#.

In 1977, Thompson came to the World Computer Chess Championship in Toronto with his KQKR database and gave those masters in attendance an opportunity to challenge it. Those that did were surprised at how badly they performed, often unable to win when they were sure they could. Several months later, Walter Browne challenged the database. He had two and one-half hours to play fifty moves in each of two won positions, while BELLE, the defender, played instantaneously. Browne was forced to accept a draw in the first game. The second game, played the following week and after he had practiced intensively, was won by Browne on the fiftieth move. The two KQKR positions selected are wins for White in thirty moves by either mating or safely capturing the rook. All other KQKR wins take fewer moves.

1977

Game 1

White: *Walter Browne* Black: *BELLE*

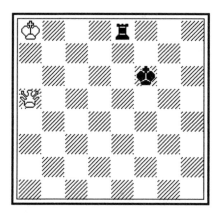

**Figure 6.17. Position from BELLE's database:
White to play and win in thirty moves.**

1 Kb7 Re7+ 2 Kc6 Re6+ 3 Kd7 Re7+ 4 Kd8

Browne properly found a way to get his king out of endless checking moves. These moves weren't particularly hard to find.

4 . . . Re4 5 Qcs Re5 6 Qd4

Browne's last move set him back one move and a win is now twenty-five moves away; correct is 6 Qc3, 6 Qc4, 6 Qf8+, or 6 Qg1.

6 . . . Kf5 7 Kd7 Re4 8 Qd3 Kf4 9 Kd6 Re3 10 Qd4+ Re4 11 Qf2+ Kg4 12 Kd5 Re8
13 Qf6 Re3 14 Kd4 Rf3 15 Qg6+ Kf4 16 Qg2

Browne has made ten consecutive correct moves and a win is now fifteen moves away.

16 . . . Ra3 17 Qc6

Browne is now seventeen moves away from a win and will still be that far away after his twenty-sixth move!

17 . . . Ra1 18 Qc7+ Kf5 19 Qc2+ Ke6 20 Qd2 Ra7 21 Qb4 Re7 22 Ke4 Kf6+
23 Kf4 Ke6 24 Qd4 Rf7+ 25 Ke4 Rf6 26 Qd5+

Browne is still 17 moves away from a win; BELLE's database gives 26 Qd8
Rf7 27 Qd5+ Kf6 28 Kf4.

26 . . . Ke7 27 Ke5 Rh6 28 Qb7+ Kd8 29 Qf7 Rc6 30 Kd5 Rb6 31 Kc5

After four correct moves, Browne's last move leaves him 13 moves away
from a win; correct is 31 Qf4.

31 . . . Ra6 32 Qc4

A win is now 16 moves away; BELLE indicates 32 Qd5+ Kc7 33 Qe4 Ra5+
34 Kb4 Ra6 35 Qe7+ Kc6 36 Qe6+ Kb7 37 Qd7+.

32 . . . Rf6 33 Qh4

A win is now seventeen moves away and Browne can no longer meet the
50-move limit. On move 16, Browne was fifteen moves away from a win;
now after sixteen more moves, he is 17 moves away. He played on for another twelve moves before accepting a draw.

1977
Game 2
White: Walter Browne   Black: BELLE

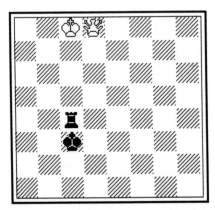

**Figure 6.18. A second position from BELLE's database:
White to play and win in thirty moves.**

1 Kb7 Rb4+ 2 Kc6 Rc4+ 3 Kb5 Rb4+ 4 Ka5

Browne follows the same opening strategy of Game 1, playing these moves correctly.

4 . . . Re4 5 Qd6 Rd4 6 Qe5

Browne's first incorrect move; a win is now twenty-five moves away; correct is 6 Qa3+

6 . . . Kd3 7 Kb5 Re4 8 Qf6 Ke3 9 Kc5 Rf4 10 Qg6 Ra4 11 Qg3+ Ke2 12 Qc3 Rf4
13 Kd5 Rh4 14 Qc2+ Ke3 15 Qd1 Kf2 16 Qd2+

This last move was incorrect and a win is now sixteen moves away; correct is 16 Qd3

16 . . . Kf3 17 Qe1

An incorrect move leaving a win eighteen moves away; correct is 17 Qd3+.

17 . . . Rg4 18 Qd1+ Kf4 19 Qe2

An incorrect move leaving a win twenty moves away; correct is 19 Qc1+.

19 . . . Rg5+ 20 Kd4 Rf5 21 Qe3+ Kg4 22 Ke4 Rf7 23 Qg1+ Kh5 24 Qg3 Rf8
25 Ke5 Rf7 26 Ke6

An incorrect move leaving a win fourteen moves away; correct is 26 Qg2.

26 . . . Rf8 27 Qa3 Rf4 28 Qh3+ Kg5 29 Qg3+ Rg4 30 Qe5+ Kh4 31 Qh2+ Kg5
32 Ke5 Kg6 33 Qh8 Rg5+ 34 Ke6 Rg4 35 Qg8+

Browne has made no progress for the last nine moves! He remains fourteen moves from victory; correct is 35 Qe5.

35 . . . Kh5 36 Qh7+ Kg5 37 Ke5 Rg3 38 Qg7+

Note the pattern!

38 . . . Kh4 39 Qh6+ Kg4 40 Ke4 Rg2 41 Qg6+

And again!

41 . . . Kh3 42 Qh5+ Kg3 43 Ke3 Rg1 44 Qg5+

Browne's first error since move 35. A win is six moves away and there is no room for error! Correct is 44 Qf3+.

44 . . . Kh2 45 Qh4+ Kg2 46 Ke2 Ra1 47 Qe4+ Kh3 48 Qh7+ Kg3 49 Qg7+ Kh3
50 Q×a1 Black resigns.

Creating an endgame database

Consider the simple endgame of king and queen versus king (KQK endgame). The number of positions in the database is determined as follows: First, Black's king can be placed on the board on any of sixty-four squares, although from the standpoint of symmetry, there are only the ten shown in Figure 6.19 that need be considered. Once Black's king has been placed, there are 64 × 64 different ways to place white's two pieces legally, illegally or even on top of one-another. The KQK database must thus contain information on no more than 10 × 64 × 64 = 40,960 positions; for each position, the database must specify whether White wins and, if so, in how many moves.

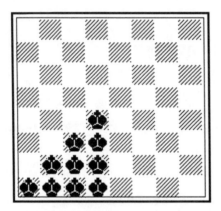

Figure 6.19. Squares for Black's king that must be considered in KRK database.

When creating a database, information must be placed in it for each of these positions by using retrograde analysis, as the following illustrates. This was effectively Thompson's approach and that of others who have tried. Each of the 40,960 entries is initially set to zero (see Figure 6.20a). The first entry corresponds to the position BK (black king) on a1, WK on a1, and WQ on a1, denoted <a1–a1–a1> and the second entry corresponds to the position BK on a1, WK on a1, and WQ on b1, denoted <a1–a1–b1>. The 129th entry corresponds to the position <a1–c1–a1>, the 130th entry to the position <a1–c1–b1>, and the last entry to the position <d4–h8–h8>. Retrograde analysis then performs the following three steps until the table is complete:

Position	Information on position		Position	Information on position
\<a1-a1-a1\>	0		\<a1-a1-a1\>	Illegitimate
\<a1-a1-b1\>	0		\<a1-a1-b1\>	Illegitimate
...	...		...	...
...	...		...	...
\<a1-a1-h8\>	0		\<a1-a1-h8\>	Illegitimate
\<a1-b1-a1\>	0		\<a1-b1-a1\>	Illegitimate
\<a1-b1-b1\>	0		\<a1-b1-b1\>	Illegitimate
...	...		...	...
...	...		...	...
\<a1-c1-a1\>	0		\<a1-c1-a1\>	Illegitimate
\<a1-c1-b1\>	0		\<a1-c1-b1\>	In check
...	...		...	...
...	...		.. .	...
\<a1-c1-h8\>	0		\<a1-c1-h8\>	In check
...	...		.. .	...
...	...		...	...
\<d4-h8-h8\>	0		\<d4-h8-h8\>	In check
(a)			(b)	

Figure 6.20. Building a KQK database: (a) initial contents of database, and (b) contents after performing the first step.

1. Determine all positions with Black's king in check and all positions that are illegitimate. Illegitimate positions are those in which the two kings occupy the same square or are adjacent to one another. Positions with Black's king and White's queen occupying the same square are not illegitimate because they turn out to be necessary to determine those positions in which Black's king must capture White's queen. [The first 128 positions in the table are found to be illegitimate because the two kings either occupy the same square or are on adjacent squares. The 129th position finds Black's king in check. At the end of this step, the database appears as in Figure 6.20b.]

2. Next, all mate-in-one positions are determined as follows: For each of the positions with Black's king in check, see whether Black has a safe move. If there is none, mark all positions in which White can move to the checking position as a mate-in-one for White, excluding positions that are themselves checking positions (since Black can't have moved into check) or illegitimate, and record these in the table. [Position 129 is the first position in the table with Black's king in check. Black has three possible moves, Kb1 (illegitimate position), Kb2 (illegitimate position), or Ka2 (still in check), and thus Black has no safe move. Now

White's positions that are not checking or illegitimate and that have moves that lead to this position are determined and indicated in the table as such. They are the twelve positions <a1–c1–b3., <a1–c1–b4., . . . , <a1–c1–b8> and <a1–c1–c2>, <a1–c1–d3>, . . . , <a1–c1–h7>, and they are all mate-in-one.]

3. Starting with N equal to 1, recursively determine all positions that are mate-in-(N + 1) from positions that are mate-in-N. [The first mate-in-two position on the list is <a1–d1–b4>. In this position, White plays Kc1 and then mates on the next move.] When there is no mate-in-N for some N, stop.

White mates in at most ten moves in any KQK endgame. There is only one such position, shown in Figure 6.21, apart from symmetry, that attains this maximum. This means that the KQK endgame database requires only four bits per position for a total of 20,480 bytes for the entire database.

Building a database for an endgame with pawns on the board turns out to have some added subtleties. In particular, games do not all end directly in mates or draws but transform themselves into other endgames. A KPK endgame transforms itself into a KQK game, for example, when the pawn promotes to a queen. Thus to build a database for a KPK endgame, the KQK database must be used. Michael R. B. Clarke first used retrograde analysis on KPK endgames, reporting his work in 1977. Clarke's results differed slightly from those of individuals who tried to repeat his procedure. The conflicting results seem to have been straightened out in 1989 by Hans Zellner of Mallersdorf, West Germany, in an article in the *ICCA Journal*.

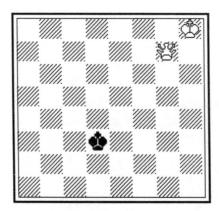

Figure 6.21. Worst-case position of KQK database: White mates in ten moves.

Of the $64 \times 64 \times 24 = 98,304$ ways to place the two kings on a board while restricting the pawn to one side, 62,480 are wins for White. Of these, 12,749 are wins in one—that is, the game can be transformed in one move to a won KQK or KRK endgame—for White. Earlier work had failed to realize that in the position shown in Figure 6.22, a move by White's king is necessary; promoting to a queen leads to a draw while promoting to a rook does no better. In any case, no victory requires more than nineteen moves to queen the pawn, and since the worst-case position for the KQK endgame (Figure 6.21) could not possibly arise as the result of a promotion, no won game requires more than $19 + 9 = 28$ moves to mate.

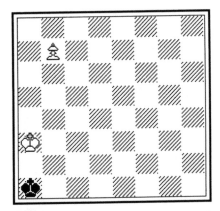

Figure 6.22. A KPK endgame with White to play and win.

On the relation between computer speed and program performance

That there is a relation between the speed of a computer and the strength of a chess program made itself obvious when the ITEP program resoundingly defeated the KOTOK/MCCARTHY program in two games when searching five plies and settled for draws in two games when searching three plies. In the late 1970s, when more data was available, performance ratings of the programs were plotted by the author as a function of the number of positions searched. Over the range of ratings for which results were available—from about a USCF rating of 1000 to one of 2000—doubling computer speed seemed to improve play by about one hundred points, although there were many other improvements that were made to the programs that were also responsible for their stronger performance. At higher ratings and in more recent years, the improvement continues, although at a slower rate, as shown in Figure 6.23.

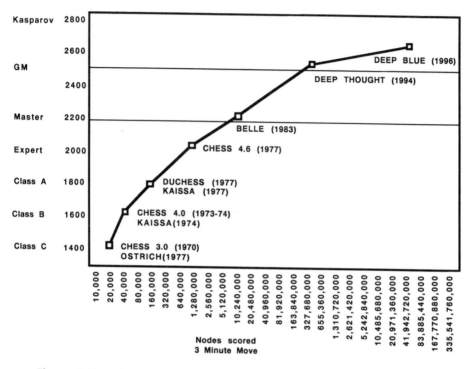

Figure 6.23. Relationship between the level of play by chess programs and the size of the tree searched during a three minute move.

Thompson conducted two experiments in the late 1970s to study this issue. In his first experiment, he had one version of BELLE play a series of twenty games against an identical second version, except that one version, call it BELLE(P), searched to a depth of, say, P levels while the other, BELLE($P + 1$), searched to a depth of $P + 1$ levels. The results of this experiment are presented in Figure 6.24a for $3 \leq P \leq 8$. It shows, for example, that BELLE(3) won four of the twenty points against BELLE(4), and that BELLE(4) won five and a half of twenty points against BELLE(5). His second experiment, carried out shortly thereafter, was more extensive: for $4 \leq P$, $Q \leq 9$ and for $P \neq Q$, BELLE(P) played a twenty-game series against BELLE(Q). The results are presented in Figure 6.24b. Rather than relating rating improvement to the number of positions searched, Thompson related rating improvement to the depth of search, pointing out that an improvement of one hundred points for each doubling of speed was approximately equivalent to an improvement of 250 points for each additional level of search.

(a)

	BELLE (3)	BELLE (4)	BELLE (5)	BELLE (6)	BELLE (7)	BELLE (8)	
BELLE (3)		4					1091
BELLE (4)	16		5.5				1332
BELLE (5)		14.5		4.5			1500
BELLE (6)			15.5		2.5		1714
BELLE (7)				17.5		3.5	2052
BELLE (8)					16.5		2320

(b)

	BELLE (4)	BELLE (5)	BELLE (6)	BELLE (7)	BELLE (8)	BELLE (9)	
BELLE (4)		5	.5	0	0	0	1235
BELLE (5)	15		3.5	3	.5	0	1570
BELLE (6)	19.5	16.5		4	1.5	1.5	1826
BELLE (7)	20	17	16		5	4	2031
BELLE (8)	20	19.5	18.5	15		5.5	2208
BELLE (9)	20	20	18.5	16	14.5		2328

Figure 6.24. Results of Thompson's two experiments: (a) first experiment, (b) second experiment. Entries in the tables indicate the number of games won by the program heading the row against the program heading the column.

The main difference between the curve of ratings shown in Figure 6.23 and Thompson's results is that the relation between ratings and search depth appears to be almost linear to about 2500 while Thompson found that rating improvement drops off from linear at ratings above 2000 points. Certainly, eventually the curve approaches the limit imposed by perfect play but the question is how fast. Thompson evidently did not study deeper search depths because of the large amount of time required to obtain results.

In 1985, the author suggested that one could calculate ratings by a different approach. It was based on the fact that all chess programs of note carry out an iteratively-deepening search when trying to come up with a move. It required knowing the principal continuation found by each iteration of an iteratively-deepening search in a random assortment of game positions. One could then observe how often the i-th iteration picked a

different move from the (i-1)-th iteration. How often this happened could then be used to help calculate the rating that different search depths might be assigned.

Consider the following hypothetical situation: Suppose a program that carries out an iteratively-deepening search to a depth of four levels, called P(4), has a rating of 1300, and the same program when carrying out an iteratively-deepening search to a depth of five levels, called P(5), has a rating of 1550. Now suppose one observes that when making moves in a large number of random game positions, P(5) picks different moves from those picked by P(4) thirty percent of the time. Further, suppose P(6) picks the same move as P(5) one hundred percent of the time. From this information, the rating of P(6) should be the same as the rating of P(5); that is, the rating of P(6) should be 1550. Instead now, suppose P(6) picks moves different from those picked by P(5) exactly thirty percent of the time. In this case, it seems reasonable to conclude that the rating of P(6) should exceed that of P(5) by the same amount as P(5) exceeded that of P(4). That is, the rating of P(6) should be 1800.

More generally, if programs P(i) and P(i + 1) have ratings of R(i) and R(i + 1) respectively, and if P(i + 1) picks a different move from P(i) F(i) percent of the time and P(i + 2) picks a different move from P(i + 1) F(i + 1) percent of the time, then it seems reasonable to assign P(i + 2) a rating of R(i + 2), where

$$R(i + 2) = R(i + 1) + [R(i + 1) - R(i)]\frac{F(i + 1)}{F(i)} \tag{1}$$

The data of many moves made by BELLE were analyzed, and it was found that for $4 \le i \le 11$, the percent of time BELLE(i) picked a different move from BELLE(i − 1) was as shown in column 2 of Figure 6.25. Given these percentages and the values for R(4) and R(5), the values for the remaining R(i)'s can be recursively calculated using expression (1). Thompson, based on his own observations, assigned to P(5) a rating of 1500 in his first paper and a rating of 1570 in his second. Because the second paper was written after the first, the value of 1570 is probably more accurate than 1500 and this figure is used in the analysis that follows. That is, R(5) = 1570. Based on the results of his first experiment (that is, based on the results of the twenty-game matches) a rating of 1332 was assigned to P(4) and based on the results of his second experiment, a rating of 1235 was assigned to P(4). Thompson's first experiment found a 168-point difference between R(4)

i	F(i) % of time Belle(i) picked moves different from Belle(i − 1)	R(i) Rating of Belle(i) if R(4) = 1320 and R(5) = 1570	R(i) Rating of Belle(i) if R(4) = 1300 and R(5) = 1570
4	33.1	1320	1300
5	33.1	1570	1570
6	27.7	1779	1796
7	29.5	2002	2037
8	26.0	2198	2249
9	22.6	2369	2433
10	17.7	2503	2577
11	18.1	2639	2725

Figure 6.25. Percentage of time Belle(i) picked different moves from Belle(i − 1) and the corresponding predicted ratings based on expression (1) for two cases: (1) R(4) = 1320 and R(5) = 1570, and (2) R(4) = 1300 and R(5) = 1570.

and R(5) and his second found a 335-point difference. Averaging these two figures suggests that a difference of 250 points is a reasonable compromise. Moreover, given that his second experiment may be more valid than his first, the difference is more likely to be 270 than 250. Column 3 thus shows the ratings R(6) through R(11) that follow using a rating of 1320 for P(4), a rating of 1570 for P(5), the percentages in column 2 and expression (1). Similarly, column 4 shows the ratings R(6) through R(11) that follow using a rating of 1300 for P(4), a rating of 1570 for P(5), the percentages in column 2, and expression (1).

References

J. H. Condon and K. Thompson, "Belle chess hardware," in *Advances in Computer Chess* 3, ed. M. R. B. Clarke (Oxford: Pergamon Press, 1982), 45–54.

J. H. Condon and K. Thompson, "Belle," in *Chess Skill in Man and Machine*, 2nd edition, ed. P. Frey, (Springer-Verlag, 1983), 201–10.

The following papers are concerned with endgame databases

T. Ströhlein, "Untersuchungen über kombinatorische Spiele," Dissertation, Fakultät für Allgemaine Wissenschaften der Technischen Hochschule München, 1970.

D. E. Knuth, *The Art of Computer Programming* 1, *Fundamental Algorithms,* 2nd ed., (Addison-Wesley, 1975). [See pages 270 and 546 for a discussion on retrograde analysis.]

M. R. B. Clarke, "A quantitative study of king and pawn against king," *Advances in Computer Chess 1,* ed. M. R. B. Clarke (Edinburgh University Press, 1977): 108–118.

M. A. Bramer, "Computer-generated databases for the endgame in chess," Mathematics Faculty Technical Report, The Open University (1978).

V. L. Arlazarov and A. L. Futer, "Computer analysis of a rook endgame," *Machine Intelligence 9,* eds. J. E. Hayes, D. Michie, and L. J. Mikulich (Ellis Horwood Limited, Chichester, England, 1984): 361–371.

J. Roycroft, "A proposed revision of the '50-move rule'," *ICCA Journal* 7, no. 3 (September 1984): 164–170.

H. J. van den Herik and I. S. Herschberg, "The construction of an omniscient endgame data base," *ICCA Journal* 8, no. 2 (June 1985): 66–87.

H. J. van den Herik and I. S. Herschberg, "Elementary theory improved, a conjecture refuted," *ICCA Journal* 8, no. 3 (September 1985): 141–149.

Ard van Bergen, "An ultimate look at the KPK data base," *ICCA Journal* 8, no. 4 (December 1985): 216–218.

H. J. J. Nefkens, "Constructing databases to fit a microcomputer," *ICCA Journal* 8, no. 4 (December 1985): 219–224.

I. S. Herschberg and H. J. van den Herik, "A gauge of endgames," *ICCA Journal* 8, no. 4 (December 1985): 225–229.

H. J. van den Herik and I. S. Herschberg, "A data base on databases," *ICCA Journal* 9, no. 1 (March 1986): 29–34.

A. van Bergen and T. van der Storm, "The KPK endgame: a unit correction," *ICCA Journal* 9, no. 1 (March 1986): 35–36.

I. S. Herschberg and H. J. van den Herik, "Thompson's new data-base results," *ICCA Journal* 9, no. 1 (March 1986): 45–49.

K. Thompson, "Retrograde analysis of certain endgames," *ICCA Journal* 9, no. 3, (September 1986): 131–139.

E. A. Komissarchik and A. L. Futer, "Computer analysis of a queen endgame," *ICCA Journal* 9, no. 4 (1986): 189–199.

H. J. van den Herik and I. S. Herschberg, "The KBBKN statistics: new data from Ken Thompson," *ICCA Journal* 10, no. 1 (March 1987): 39–40.

S. T. Dekker, H. J. van den Herik, and I. S. Herschberg, "Complexity starts at five," *ICCA Journal* 10, no. 3 (September 1987): 125–138.

H. J. van den Herik, I. S. Herschberg, and N. Nakad, "A six-men-endgame database: KRP(a2)KbBP(a3)," *ICCA Journal* 10, no. 4 (December 1987): 163–180.

L. Rasmussen, "Ultimates in KQKR and KRKN," *ICCA Journal* 11, no. 1 (March 1988): 21–25.

R. Sattler, "Further to the KRP(a2)KbBP(a3)," *ICCA Journal* 11, no. 2/3 (June/September 1988): 82–87.

H. J. van den Herik, I. S. Herschberg, and N. Nakad, "A reply to R. Sattler's remarks on the KRP(a2)KbBP(a3) database," *ICCA Journal* 11, no. 2/3 (June/September 1988): 88–91.

L. Rasmussen, "A database for KRKP," *ICCA Journal* 11, no. 4 (December 1988): 144–150.

D. Forthoffer, L. Rasmussen, and S. Dekker, "A correction to some KRKB-database results," *ICCA Journal* 12, no. 1 (March 1989): 25–27.

L. Stiller, "Parallel analysis of certain endgames," *ICCA Journal* 12, no. 3 (June 1989): 55–64.

H. Zellner, "The KPK database revisited," *ICCA Journal* 12, no. 2 (June 1989): 78–82.

K. Thompson, "KQPKQ and KRPKR endings," *ICCA Journal* 13, no. 4 (December 1990): 196–199.

K. Thompson, "New results for KNPKB and KNPKN," *ICCA Journal* 14, no. 1 (March 1991): 17.

L. Stiller, "Some results from a massively parallel retrograde analysis," *ICCA Journal* 14, no. 3 (September 1991): 129–134.

L. Stiller, "KQNKRR," *ICCA Journal* 15, no. 1 (March 1992): 16–18.

The Editors, "Thompson: all about five men," *ICCA Journal* 15, no. 3 (September 1992): 140–143.

I. S. Herschberg and H. J. van den Herik, "Back to fifty," *ICCA Journal* 16, no. 1 (March 1993): 1–2.

The Editors, "Thompson: quintets with variations," *ICCA Journal* 16, no. 2 (June 1993): 86–90.

S. J. Edwards and the Editorial Board, "An examination of the endgame KBNKN," *ICCA Journal* 18, no. 3 (September 1995): 160–167.

S. J. Edwards, "An examination of the endgame KBBKN," *ICCA Journal* 19, no. 1 (March 1996): 24–32.

The following papers are concerned with the relation between computer speed and chess program performance.

K. Thompson, "Computer chess strength," *Advances in Computer Chess 3*, ed. M. R. B. Clarke (Oxford: Pergamon Press, 1982), 55–56.

M. Newborn, "Computer chess: recent progress and future expectations," *Proc. Jerusalem Conference on Information Technology* (North-Holland, 1978): 189–92.

M. Newborn, "A hypothesis concerning the strength of chess programs," *ICCA Journal* 8, no. 4 (December 1985): 209–15.

7 CRAY BLITZ and HITECH: Parallel Search and Parallel Evaluation

n 1975, Robert Hyatt was an undergraduate at the University of Southern Mississippi when he began work on BLITZ. Early on, he teamed up with Bert Gower, a fellow member of the USM Chess Club and a professor of music at the university; Gower worked primarily on book openings. The program slowly improved during the late 1970s and by 1979 had earned a USCF rating of 1690. The next year, Hyatt had the opportunity to install his program on a Cray-1 computer, renaming the program CRAY BLITZ. At the 1980 ACM championship, a special speed-chess tournament was held, and CRAY BLITZ captured first place, going undefeated in nine games. This gave notice to the computer chess community that CRAY BLITZ was going to be a serious contender in the coming years. In 1982, Harry Nelson, a Cray assembly language specialist joined the team and helped optimize the code; the program went on to finish equal in points with the winning program BELLE at that year's ACM championship. It was awarded second place based on tie-break points.

The following year, CRAY BLITZ moved to the top of the computer chess world when it won the fourth world championship in New York City, defeating BELLE in the final round. For this event, CRAY BLITZ ran on a two-processor Cray XMP and searched approximately 20,000 positions per second. Its victory over BELLE was presented in the previous chapter.

April 1984: London

When David Levy defeated CHESS 4.7 in 1978 to win his famous $10,000 wager, *Omni* magazine and David put up another $5,000 to the first program that defeated him in a match. After CRAY BLITZ's success in the world championship, Hyatt thought his program was ready to take a shot at the British master. So in 1984, a four-game match was arranged. Using the same two-processor Cray XMP that was used in New York, CRAY BLITZ lost all four games to a well-prepared and cagey human opponent. In two of its games, serious technical problems doomed the computer, although Hyatt observed after the match that his program wouldn't have won even without the technical problems.

CRAY BLITZ's best game was the first one. It was carrying out eight- and nine-ply searches on most moves. However, communication between the game board in London and the computer in Minnesota was consuming a minute on each move, and the computer was out of sync with the actual time it had to make its moves. At move 30, it found it had no time left and began to play in a speed chess mode and went downhill fast.

April 14, 1984, London
Omni Challenge Match
White: CRAY BLITZ   Black: David Levy
Time Control: 40/2, 20/1 thereafter
Irregular King's Pawn Opening

1 e4 a6 2 d4 g6

Levy has taken CRAY BLITZ out of its opening book as he planned.

3 Nf3 Bg7 4 Nc3 b5 5 Bd3 Bb7 6 O-O d6 7 Bf4 e6 8 e5 d5 9 b4

White's position isn't too bad. Its pieces are well developed and the last move threatens to expand its control of the queen-side.

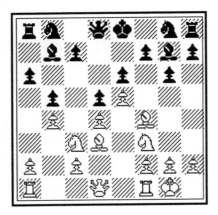

Figure 7.1. Position after 9 b4.

9 ... Nd7 10 Qd2 Ne7 11 a4 c6 12 a×b5 c×b5 13 Bh6 O-O 14 Bg5 Re8
15 Ra3 Nb6 16 Nd1 Nc4 17 B×c4 d×c4 18 Nb2 Qc7 19 Rfa1 Rec8

At this point CRAY BLITZ finds out that it has consumed ninety minutes of its first two hours, leaving fifteen minutes for the twenty-one moves that remain to the first time control. A fifteen-minute safety factor was used by CRAY BLITZ. From here until move 30, the program plays more quickly, searching one or two plies fewer than on earlier moves. Its position weakens dramatically over the next six moves.

20 c3 B×f3 21 g×f3 Nf5 22 R×a6 R×a6 23 R×a6 Qb7 24 Ra5 Q×f3 25 R×b5

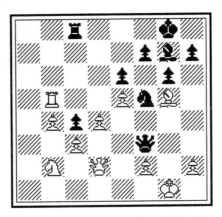

Figure 7.2. Position after 25 R×b5.

CRAY BLITZ may be ahead a pawn but its king-side is too weak to hold out for very long.

Burt Gower and Robert Hyatt watching their program CRAY BLITZ compete in Reno, 1989.

25 ... h6 26 Bf4 Qh3 27 Bg3 h5 28 Rc5 Ra8 29 Qc1 h4 30 Bf4 Qf3 31 h3 Q×h3
32 R×c4 Qf3 33 Bh2 h3 34 Qf1 Ra1 35 Nd1 R×d1 White resigns.

October 7–9, 1984: San Francisco

Later that year, CRAY BLITZ captured the fifteenth ACM North American Computer Chess Championship, held in San Francisco, with a perfect 4-0 score. BELLE finished fifth with 2.5 points. CRAY BLITZ was dead lost in its fourth-round game with NUCHESS but good fortune smiled on it: NUCHESS passed up capturing a CRAY BLITZ passed pawn and then several moves later traded off the only piece that could catch it, resulting in an easy win for CRAY BLITZ.

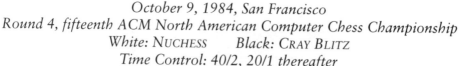

October 9, 1984, San Francisco
Round 4, fifteenth ACM North American Computer Chess Championship
White: NUCHESS   Black: CRAY BLITZ
Time Control: 40/2, 20/1 thereafter
English Opening

1 c4 e5 2 Nc3 Bb4 3 a3 B×c3 4 d×c3 Ne7 5 g3 d5 6 c×d5 Q×d5 7 Q×d5 N×d5
8 Bg2 Nb6 9 a4 O-O 10 a5 Nc4 11 Ra4 Nd6 12 a6 Nd7 13 Be3 Nb6 14 Rh4 Rd8

15 a×b7 B×b7 16 B×b7 N×b7 17 Nf3 Rd5 18 c4 Ra5 19 O-O Ra2 20 Rd1 R×b2
21 c5 Nc8 22 Rd7 f6 23 Rg4 g6 24 Rh4 h5 25 R×c7 Nd8 26 Ra4 Rb7
27 R×b7 N×b7 28 Ra6 Kf7 29 Nd2 Nd8 30 Ne4 f5 31 Ng5+ Kg7 32 Nf3 Nf7
33 N×e5 N×e5 34 Bd4 Kg8 35 B×e5 Ne7 36 e3 Kf7 37 Rf6+ Kg8 38 Kg2 Rc8
39 Kf3 Re8 40 Ra6 Ra8 41 Kf4 Kf7 42 Kg5 Rg8

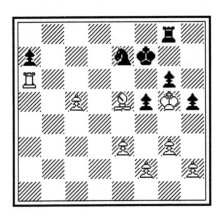

Figure 7.3. Position after 42 . . . Rg8.

43 Rf6+

White passes on capturing the poison pawn. CRAY BLITZ will now escape
the jaws of certain death and reign on as the champion! Over the next few
moves, White essentially commits suicide.

43 . . . Ke8 44 Bd6 Nc8 45 R×g6 R×g6+ 46 K×g6 N×d6 47 c×d6 a5 48 g4 h×g4
49 K×f5 a4 50 e4 a3 51 K×g4 a2 52 e5 a1Q 53 f4 Qg1+ 54 Kf5 Q×h2 55 e6 Qc2+
White resigns.

October 13–15, 1985: Denver

In 1985, Hans Berliner brought his new creation, HITECH, to the ACM
tournament in Denver. HITECH was designed around a sixty-four-chip very
large scale integrated (VLSI) circuit that functioned as a move generator
and searched 200,000 positions per second. HITECH was a team effort,
with Berliner the head and mainly concerned with the scoring function.
The others were Carl Ebeling—hardware design and construction, Gordon Goetsch—system software, Andy Palay—initial concept and search

strategies, Larry Slomer—hardware construction, and Murray Campbell—
openings and testing. Unique to HITECH was its scoring function. It was designed to evaluate in parallel the various factors that were used to assign a
score. New factors could be added to the function and computed in parallel
with the existing ones, resulting in a smarter program that ran no slower.
HITECH had played in human competition in the months leading up to Denver and had established a rating of 2255, about fifty points higher than any
other computer to date. Just before Denver, HITECH won the Gateway
Open, a tournament held in Pittsburgh, in which four masters participated.
HITECH won the ACM event with a perfect 4-0 score, defeating CRAY BLITZ
in the final round, and clearly establishing itself as the top program—even
though CRAY BLITZ would remain world champion for four more years.

♚

October 15, 1985, Denver
Round 4, sixteenth ACM North American
Computer Chess Championship
White: HITECH   Black: CRAY BLITZ
Time Control: 40/2, 20/1 thereafter
Scotch Game

───────────────

1 e4 e5 2 Nf3 Nc6 3 d4 e×d4 4 N×d4 Nf6 5 N×c6 b×c6 6 Bd3 d5 7 Qe2 Bg4
8 f3 Be6 9 e×d5 N×d5 10 Bf5 Qh4+ 11 Kf1 Qf6 12 B×e6 Q×e6 13 c4 Q×e2+
14 K×e2 Nb6 15 b3 Bd6 16 Nc3 O-O 17 Be3 Be5 18 Rac1 Rfe8 19 Kf2 Rad8
20 f4 Bf6 21 Rhd1 R×d1 22 N×d1 h5 23 Nc3 Kh7 24 Ne2 Rd8 25 Kf3 Kg6 26 Ng3 h4

Figure 7.4. Position after 39 . . . B×d8.

27 f5+ Kh7 28 Ne4 Be7 29 Kg4 Re8 30 Bf2 Nd7 31 Kh3 a6 32 Rd1 Nf6 33 Re1 N×e4
34 R×e4 Kg8 35 Bd4 Kf8 36 c5 f6 37 R×h4 Rd8 38 Rh8+ Kf7 39 R×d8 B×d8

HITECH enters the final stage with a pawn advantage and presses its advantage perfectly.

40 Kg4 Be7 41 h4 Ke8 42 Kf4 Bd8 43 g4 Be7 44 Ke4 Bd8 45 Be3 Be7 46 a4 Kd8
47 Kd4 Kc8 48 g5 f×g5 49 h×g5 Kd8 50 Ke5 Kd7 51 f6 Bf8 52 a5 g6

Black is now out of moves and faces a classic zugzwang position after White's next move.

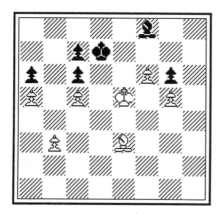

Figure 7.5. Position after 52 . . . g6.

53 Bd4 Black resigns.

June 12–15, 1986: Cologne

The following year, the fifth world championship was held in Cologne, West Germany. HITECH continued to improve and went into the tournament rated 2352 by the USCF. HITECH and CRAY BLITZ met again in the final round, with CRAY BLITZ gaining the victory. Overall, HITECH had the better tournament, winning its other four games, while CRAY BLITZ dropped a game to BOBBY, who finished with three points. HITECH and CRAY BLITZ finished tied for first with four points, along with BEBE and SUN PHOENIX, but CRAY BLITZ was awarded the title based on tie-break points. HITECH finished second.

After CRAY BLITZ lost to BOBBY, Hyatt realized that a bug in his program was causing problems. It turned out that code added just prior to the

1985 ACM tournament was incorrectly discouraging pawns from advancing. In the games at the 1985 ACM championship and in its game with BOBBY, CRAY BLITZ rarely advanced its pawns. The bug was eliminated before its next game.

June 15, 1986, Cologne
Round 5, fifth World Computer Chess Championship
White: CRAY BLITZ   Black: HITECH
Time Control: 40/2, 20/1 thereafter
Queen's Gambit Accepted

1 d4 d5 2 c4 d×c4 3 Nf3 Nf6 4 e3 e6 5 B×c4 c5 6 Qe2 a6 7 d×c5 B×c5 8 O-O b5
9 Rd1 Qe7 10 Bd3 e5 11 e4 Nc6 12 Nc3 Bg4 13 Be3 Rd8 14 h3 B×e3
15 Q×e3 B×f3 16 Q×f3 Nd4 17 Qg3 O-O 18 a4 b4 19 Nd5 N×d5 20 e×d5 R×d5
21 B×a6 b3 22 Qe3 Rfd8 23 Bc4 Nc2 24 Qe2 Rc5 25 R×d8+ Q×d8 26 Rb1 Nd4

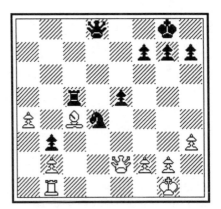

Figure 7.6. Position after 26 . . . Nd4.

Black has more active pieces but must be careful of White's extra pawn on the queen-side.

27 Qf1 Qd7 28 Ra1 Qc6 29 Bb5 N×b5 30 a×b5 Qb7 31 Ra3 g6 32 R×b3 Qd5
33 Rb4 Rc2 34 b3 Qd2 35 Rc4 Rb2 36 Re4 Qd5 37 Qc4 Qd1+ 38 Kh2 R×f2
39 R×e5 Qd6 40 Qc8+ Kg7 41 Qc5 Qd2 42 Rg5 Re2 43 Rg4 Qa2

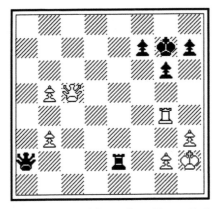

Figure 7.7. Position after 43 . . . Qa2.

Black's last move gives White an easy road to victory.

44 Qc3+ Kg8 45 b6 Qa8 46 Qc7 Qf8 47 b7 Re8 48 Rc4 Kg7 49 Rc6 Rb8 50 Qc8 R×c8
51 b×c8Q Qb4 52 Qc7 Q×b3 53 Qe5+ Kh6 54 Qf4+ Kg7 55 Qd4+ Kh6 56 Rb6 Qc2
57 Qf4+ Kg7 58 Qf6+ Kh6 59 Q×f7 Qc8 60 Rd6 Black resigns.

Following the world championship, HITECH continued to improve while competing in human tournament play in the eastern United States. Among its successes, the program won the Pennsylvania State Championship in August 1987 and again the following year. After its 1988 victory, its rating climbed to over 2400, making it the first program to reach the level of a U.S. Senior Master. Below is HITECH's victory over Allan Savage, rated 2412 by the USCF, at the 1987 tournament.

August 30, 1987, State College, Pennsylvania
Pennsylvania State Championship
White: Allan Savage   Black: HITECH
Time Control: 40/2, 20/1 thereafter
Ruy Lopez

---

1 e4 e5 2 Nf3 Nc6 3 Bb5 a6 4 B×c6 d×c6 5 O-O f6 6 d4 Bg4 7 c3 Bd6
8 d×e5 f×e5 9 Qb3 B×f3 10 g×f3 Ne7 11 Be3 Qd7 12 Q×b7 O-O
13 Qb3+ Kh8 14 Nd2

Berliner, in his analysis of the game, indicates the game thus far can be found in the *Encyclopedia of Chess Openings*, with White being credited as having a definite advantage. Berliner, however, programmed HITECH to see one move further, grabbing a pawn while daring its opponent to recapture:

14 ... R×f3 15 Kh1 Rff8 16 Rg1 Ng6 17 Qc4 Nf4 18 Rg3 a5 19 b3 Be7 20 Rag1 Nh3
21 R×h3 Q×h3 22 Q×c6 Rad8 23 Rg3 Qd7 24 Q×d7 R×d7 25 Nc4

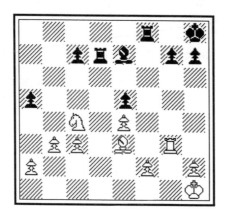

Figure 7.8. Position after 25 Nc4.

White, though down an exchange, has an extra pawn and active pieces. For Black to win this game, it must not to trade away too much material and find itself with no means to press for victory.

25 ... Rd3 26 N×e5 R×c3 27 Bd4 Rc2 28 Nd7 Rf7 29 Ne5 Rf4 30 Nd3 R×e4
31 B×g7+ Kg8 32 Bc3+ Kf8 33 B×a5 Ba3

Black has only two pawns remaining—to White's four—and is running out of scenarios that might yield a win.

34 b4 Re7 35 Rf3+ Kg7 36 Nc5 R×a2 37 Na6 Ree2 38 N×c7 R×f2 39 Ne6+ Kg6
40 R×f2 R×f2

Though Black is almost out of ammunition, what remains turns out to be just enough.

41 Kg1 Rb2 42 Nf4+ Kf5 43 Nd3 Rd2 44 Nf2 Kf4 45 Kg2 Rb2 46 Bc7+ Kf5
47 Bd6 B×b4

White must not trade away its bishop here, but Black will give it no alternative in several moves.

48 Bg3 Bc5 49 Kf3 Rb3+ 50 Kg2 Bd4 51 Bd6 Be5 52 Bc5 Rb2 53 Be3 h5 54 Bc5 Kf4 55 Ba7 Rd2 56 Bb6 Bd4 57 B×d4 R×d4 58 Nh1 Rd2+ 59 Nf2 White resigns.

Parallel search

Parallel search is a very difficult programming problem with many possible approaches. Consider the problem of the missing diamond introduced in Chapter 4. If a team of two people went looking for the missing diamond, one might initially go looking in the front yard while the other went looking in the back. In theory, with two people searching, the diamond should be found twice as quickly on average as with one person. But there are some problems that must be ironed out to do that. The two people must divide up the search space in proportion to their ability to search it; the faster searcher should be given more space. What happens when one finishes and the other still has some space to search? The first one done should go assist the other. Not much communication is necessary when they are searching. They must agree on where they will search, and if one succeeds, that person must tell the other to stop. The complication with chess is that the size of the yard, so to speak, is unknown when the search begins, so the rule for dividing up the search must be done on the fly.

Suppose now a small army of a thousand soldiers showed up to search this yard of unknown size. How could they be used to gain a thousand-fold speedup over one person? Unless they were organized very cleverly, they would probably be stepping on each other's feet, getting communications all garbled up, and might not even be as effective as a single person in looking for the diamond.

With these problems in mind, various parallel search algorithms have slowly evolved for searching chess trees. Their objective has been to attain an N-fold speedup when using N processors. This has proved to be a very difficult goal to reach.

The first systems used only a handful of computers while the more recent ones are using up to a thousand. The most effective parallel search algorithms are called tree decomposition algorithms; in one way or other, they divide up the search tree among the processors. One processor is usually

selected as "master" while the others are considered "slaves." The master assigns work to the slaves, attempting to keep them all busy doing useful work.

Debugging parallel chess programs presents special problems, the main one being the problem of repeating a move. It is very difficult to get a number of computers to go through exactly the same computation more than once because interprocessor communication is not synchronized with the search. A message arriving one millionth of a second late may affect the computation. When a program running on one computer crashes, there is only one computer on which the bug exists. But when a program is running on more than one, it must first be determined on which computer the problem exists. Sometimes it is in the chess program itself, and at other times it may be in the communication software.

Figure 7.9 lists the names of computing systems that have used parallel search. The first to compete in tournament play was OSTRICH, in 1981, when it used a five-processor Data General system with five Nova 3 computers. The computers were connected by a high-speed bus. One year later, the system was expanded to eight computers. A speedup of five was obtained on the eight computers. OSTRICH used what has been called the principal variation splitting algorithm for controlling the parallel search. This

Name	Year	Description of System
OSTRICH	1981	5-processor Data General system
OSTRICH	1982	8-processor Data General system
CRAY BLITZ	1983	2-processor Cray XMP
CRAY BLITZ	1984	4-processor Cray XMP
SUN PHOENIX	1986	Network of 20 VAXs and SUNs
CHESS CHALLENGER	1986	20 8086 microprocessors
WAYCOOL	1986	64-processor N/CUBE system
WAYCOOL	1988	256-processor N/CUBE system
DEEP THOUGHT	1989	3 2-processor VLSI chess circuits
STAR TECH	1993	512-processor Connection Machine
STAR SOCRATES	1995	1,824-processor Intel Paragon, Sandia National Labs
ZUGZWANG	1995	96-processor GC-Powerplus distributed system (based on the PowerPC)
DEEP BLUE	1996	32-processor IBM RS/6000 SP with 6 VLSI chess circuits per processor

Figure 7.9. Multiprocessing systems that have participated in major chess tournaments.

algorithm divides up the search of moves along the principal continuation that was found best on one iteration when carrying out the next iteration. This has the effect of returning a score to the root of the tree for the first move as quickly as possible so that it can be used to help refute other moves. However, when dividing up moves at the root, where the chunks of the tree searched by each processor are fairly large, there is a wide difference in the finishing times of each processor, resulting in a loss in efficiency.

Eight-screen terminal used by OSTRICH. *Each of the eight Data General comput-*
ers was connected to a screen.

Hyatt first used parallel search in 1983 on a two-processor Cray XMP/24. In his first version, each processor took one of the moves at the root of the tree, searched it, and then went on to see whether another move remained. Such an algorithm is relatively simple to implement, but comes far from doubling the overall speed of the search. The drawback, according to Hyatt, was that "the entire move list is not examined twice as fast due to the first two moves taking a substantial amount of time." With good move ordering in a serial version, only the first move takes a lot of time to search. The following year, when Cray introduced the four-processor

XMP/48, Hyatt moved to the principal variation splitting algorithm and found the same problems faced by Ostrich.

Jonathan Schaeffer found that he had more computers than he could effectively use for parallel tree decomposition. In 1986, his program Sun Phoenix used a network of twenty VAXs and SUNs when it participated in the seventeenth ACM tournament. Six processors were set aside to search exclusively for material gains. Schaeffer felt this was a better use of his computing power than having them all carry out the principal variation splitting algorithm. The processors concerned exclusively with material were typically able to search two plies deeper than the rest of the parallel program. When they found that their material evaluation differed from the main parallel search program, a re-search was carried out. The success that Schaeffer had with Sun Phoenix raises the question of whether a parallel search in which processors are assigned to search for specific goals is a good idea. One processor could be set aside to look for mates, for example.

Ron Nelson was in charge of research at Fidelity Electronics, a Florida-based company that produced the Chess Challenger. In 1986, Nelson came to the seventeenth ACM tournament with a parallel version of Chess Challenger. It used twenty 8086 processors. Nelson thought it would be fun for his system to think on its opponent's time by having each processor guess a different move by the opponent and go on to calculate a reply. In that way, it would always have a reply ready when the opponent moved.

Waycool, developed at Cal Tech by Ed Felton, Steve Otto, and Rod Morison, also appeared for the first time at the seventeenth ACM tournament with a sixty-four-processor N/CUBE. The following year, Waycool participated in the eighteenth ACM tournament using a 256-processor N/CUBE. Its programmers claim a speedup factor of 101. One year later, Waycool came to the nineteenth ACM competition prepared to use a 512-processor N/CUBE, claiming that they were able to achieve a speedup of approximately 170. However, they were unable to use all 512 processors during the tournament, using 256 instead. Each processor ran at 7 MHz and contained 512 kilobytes of memory.

Star Socrates competed in the eighth world championship in Hong Kong in 1995 on a 1,824-processor Intel Paragon computer located at Sandia National Laboratories. Developed at MIT by Bradley Kaszmaul and Charles Leiserson, it is essentially a parallel implementation of Don Dailey and Larry Kaufman's Socrates. The Paragon is about fifty feet long and weighs fifteen tons. Each processor consists of two 50-MHz 1860 processors with either sixteen or thirty-two megabytes of memory.

ZUGZWANG, developed by Rainer Feldmann and Peter Mysliwietz at Paderborn University in Germany, also participated in Hong Kong on a multiprocessing system, a ninety-six-processor GC-Powerplus distributed system, based on the PowerPC. Each processor had a one megabyte transposition table and searched about three thousand positions per second. The parallel search algorithm was based on the "young-brothers-wait" concept, which the programmers indicate gives good speedups on as many as one thousand processors. They indicated that on one thousand processors it was possible to obtain a speedup of four hundred.

DEEP THOUGHT, when playing Garry Kasparov in 1989, used a SUN computer that housed three specially-designed dual-processor VLSI chess circuits. The dual-processor circuits shared the search of branches at positions deep in the tree, while the SUN divided up the search using a variation of the principal variation splitting algorithm. Each circuit searched approximately 720,000 chess positions per second, resulting in an overall rate of approximately 2,000,000 positions per second by the three-processor systems.

DEEP BLUE, when playing Kasparov in 1996, used a thirty-two-node IBM RS/6000 SP high-performance computer. Each node of the SP contained six dedicated VLSI chess processors, for a total of 192 processors working in tandem. DEEP BLUE's programming code was developed in C and ran under the AIX operating system. The highly parallel system was capable of searching one hundred billion chess positions on each move.

Ken Thompson and Hans Berliner discussing a game in Edmonton, 1989.

References

R. M. Hyatt, "CRAY BLITZ: A Computer Chess Playing Program" (M. Sc. thesis, University of Southern Mississippi, Hattiesburg, 1983).

R. M. Hyatt, "Using time wisely," *ICCA Journal* 7, no. 1 (March 1984): 4–9.

R. M. Hyatt, "CRAY BLITZ versus David Levy," *ICCA Journal* 7, no. 2 (June 1984): 102–5 [Levy's version of the match appears on pages 106–17.]

H. L. Nelson, "Hash tables in CRAY BLITZ," *ICCA Journal* 8, no. 1 (March 1985): 3–13.

R. M. Hyatt, "Parallel search on the Cray XMP/48," *ICCA Journal* 8, no. 2 (June 1985): 90–99.

R. M. Hyatt, B. E. Gower, and H. L. Nelson, "CRAY BLITZ," *Advances in Computer Chess 4*, ed. D. Beal (Oxford: Pergamon Press, 1985), 8–18.

H. L. Nelson and R. M. Hyatt, "The draw heuristic of CRAY BLITZ," *ICCA Journal* 11, no. 1 (March 1988): 3–9.

R. M. Hyatt, "A High-Performance Parallel Algorithm to Search Depth-First Game Trees," (Ph.D. thesis, Department of Computer Science, University of Alabama, Birmingham, 1988).

R. M. Hyatt, B. W. Suter, and H. L. Nelson, "A parallel alpha-beta tree searching algorithm," *Parallel Computing* 10, no. 3 (1989): 299–308.

The following papers are about HITECH

C. Ebeling and A. Palay, "The design and implementation of a VLSI move generator," *IEEE 11th Annual International Symposium on Computer Architecture* (Ann Arbor, 1984): 74–80.

H. J. Berliner, "The 1985 Fredkin competition," *ICCA Journal* 8, no. 4 (December 1985): 253–259.

H. J. Berliner, "HITECH wins North American Computer-Chess Championship," *ICCA Journal* 8, no. 4 (December 1985): 146–147.

H. J. Berliner, "HITECH Update," *ICCA Journal* 9, no. 2 (June 1986): 111–112.

H. J. Berliner and C. Ebeling, "The SUPREM architecture: a new intelligent paradigm," *Artificial Intelligence* 28 (1986): 3–8.

H. J. Berliner, "Computer chess at Carnegie Mellon University," *Advances in Computer Chess 4*, ed. D. Beal (Oxford: Pergamon Press, 1986), 166–180.

H. J. Berliner, "Some innovations introduced by HITECH," *ICCA Journal* 10, no. 3 (September 1987): 111–117.

H. J. Berliner, "HITECH wins Pennsylvania State Chess-Championship Tourney," *ICCA Journal* 10, no. 3 (September 1987): 155–156.

H. J. Berliner, "A new HITECH computer chess success," *ICCA Journal* 11, no. 2/3 (June/September 1988): 24.

H. J. Berliner, "HITECH again wins Pennsylvania Chess Championship: becomes first Senior Master," *ICCA Journal* 11, no. 2/3 (June/September 1988): 125–126.

The following papers are concerned with parallel search.

S. G. Akl, D. T. Barnard, and R. J. Doran, "Design, analysis, and implementation of a parallel tree search algorithm," *IEEE Transactions on Pattern Analysis and Machine Intelligence* 4, no. 2 (1982): 192–203.

T. A. Marsland and M. S. Campbell, "Parallel search of strongly ordered game trees," *ACM Computing Surveys* 14, no. 4 (1982): 533–551.

M. Newborn, "A parallel search chess program," *Proc. of the 1985 ACM Annual Conference* (1985): 272–277.

T. A. Marsland, M. Olafsson, and J. Schaeffer, "Multiprocessor tree-search experiments," *Advances in Computer Chess 4*, ed. D. F. Beal (Oxford: Pergamon Press, 1985), 37–51.

T. A. Marsland and F. Popowich, "Parallel game-tree search," *IEEE Transactions on Pattern Analysis and Machine Intelligence* 7 (1985): 442–452.

J. Schaeffer, "Improved parallel alpha-beta search," *1986 Proc. of the FJCC* (1986): 519–527.

M. Newborn, "Unsynchronized iteratively deepening parallel alpha-beta search," *IEEE Transactions on Pattern Analysis and Machine Intelligence* 10, no. 5 (1988): 687–694.

F.-h. Hsu, "Large-Scale Parallelization of Alpha-Beta Search: An Algorithmic and Architectural Study with Computer Chess," Technical Report CMU-CS-90-108, Computer Science Department, Carnegie Mellon University, Pittsburgh, Pa., 1990.

R. Feldmann, P. Mysliwietz, and B. Monien, "Game tree search on a massively parallel system," *Advances in Computer Chess 7*, eds. H. J. van den Herik, I. S. Herschberg, and J. W. H. M. Uiterwijk (Maastricht, the Netherlands, University of Limburg, 1993): 203–19.

B. C. Kuszmaul, "The STAR TECH massively-parallel chess program," *ICCA Journal* 18, no. 1 (March 1995): 3–19.

8 CHIPTEST, DEEP THOUGHT, and DEEP BLUE—and Garry Kasparov

The story of DEEP BLUE begins in 1985 at Carnegie Mellon University (CMU). At that time, Feng-hsiung Hsu—CB to his friends—was a doctoral student in the Department of Computer Science. He had received his undergraduate degree in electrical engineering from Taiwan National University. His interest in computer chess had been fermenting for some time, but it was triggered into action when he heard Hans Berliner lecture on the subject.

Hsu was motivated to design and implement a single-chip chess move generator using 3-micron VLSI technology. His CMU advisor was H. T. Kung, well known for his work on systolic arrays. Hsu's move generator was designed along the lines of BELLE rather than HITECH, although instead of using discrete logic circuits as Ken Thompson had, it was designed using VLSI technology. Hsu had concluded after comparing the circuits of BELLE and HITECH that Thompson's had greater potential for speed than the bulkier HITECH circuit. Hsu's circuit was ready for testing in mid-1986; it was connected to a toy chess program, developed by Thomas Anantharaman earlier in the year. Anantharaman, also a doctoral student at CMU, had completed his undergraduate studies at Benares Hindu University in India. The two soon teamed up, combining Hsu's VLSI circuit for generating moves with Anantharaman's program. Their creation was initially searching approximately fifty thousand positions per second, controlled by a SUN

3/160 workstation. After some testing, Hsu and Anantharaman decided to make their first major modification, adding search capabilities to the hardware. Essentially, Anantharaman's program explored the shallow levels in the tree, sending positions at deep levels to Hsu's hardware search engine.

In the autumn of 1996, Murray Campbell joined the team. Campbell is a strong expert-level player, having played in a number of tournaments in Alberta when he was younger. Neither Hsu nor Anantharaman ever played much chess. Even today, after a decade of intensive work on his chess program, Hsu rarely plays, although he understands the game quite well. Campbell received his bachelor's and master's degrees from the University of Alberta, where he studied parallel search in the context of chess with Tony Marsland. Campbell prepared the opening book and assisted with the scoring function and the testing.

November 2–5, 1986: Dallas

Hsu, Campbell, and Anantharaman entered CHIPTEST in the 1986 ACM North American Computer Chess Championship in Dallas. This was seven weeks after it had played its first test game at CMU; Gordon Goetsch, of the HITECH team, had seen it scrimmaging, and at a "Thank God It's Friday" party of the graduate students suggested to Hsu that he should put it to a serious test. It had a rather mediocre coming-out party, plagued by bugs in the management of its transposition table and in its hardware. Nevertheless, it showed some promise. It managed to win 2.5/5.0 points losing to BEBE and OSTRICH, drawing with RECOM, and defeating REX and MERLIN. The career of OSTRICH was coming to an end, and this was one of its last victories. It was the second public game of CHIPTEST's career.

November 3, 1986, Dallas, Texas
Round 2, seventeenth ACM North American
Computer Chess Championship
White: CHIPTEST   Black: OSTRICH
Time Control: 40/2, 20/1 thereafter
Bird's Opening

---

1 f4 d5 2 e3 Nf6 3 Nf3 Bg4 4 b3 Nbd7 5 Bb2 Ne4 6 Be2 B×f3 7 B×f3 e6 8 B×e4 d×e4
9 O-O Qh4 10 g4 O-O-O 11 Nc3 f5 12 g×f5 e×f5 13 Kh1 Nc5 14 Nb5 a6 15 Nd4 Qh3
16 Rg1 Rd5 17 N×f5 R×f5 18 B×g7 B×g7 19 R×g7 Qf3+ 20 Q×f3 e×f3

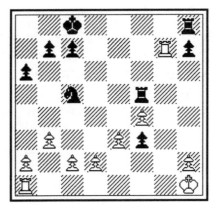

Figure 8.1. Position after 20 . . . e×f3.

21 R×c7+

Not too many people will ever see CHIPTEST's descendants play like this!

21 . . . K×c7 22 Rf1 Ne4 23 d3 Nd2 24 Rf2 Re8

OSTRICH sees that 24 . . . Nb1 25 Rf1 Nc3 26 R×f3 loses one point, while so does the line played; but the latter keeps the passed pawn on the board.

25 R×d2 R×e3 26 Kg1 R×f4 27 Kf2 Re5 28 c3 Rh5 29 Kf1 f2 White resigns.

October 25–27, 1987: Dallas

Upon returning to Carnegie Mellon, CHIPTEST was debugged further and renamed CHIPTEST-M. The "M" stood for "microcode" version: the search engine had been rewritten in microcode and the new version was searching about five hundred thousand chess positions per second, or typically about eighty million positions in the typical three-minute move—more than CRAY BLITZ! CRAY BLITZ, the world champion at the time, ran on a four-processor Cray XMP, searching ten to fifteen million chess positions per three-minute move.

In late October of 1987, CHIPTEST-M participated in the eighteenth ACM North American Computer Chess Championship in Dallas, finishing in first place with a perfect 4-0 score. The bugs that had plagued it the previous year were all gone. Ken Thompson's rating program assigned it a rating of 2584 for its performance. It defeated David Levy and Mark Taylor's

CYRUS in round 1; Burt Wendroff and Tony Warnock's LACHEX in the second round; CRAY BLITZ in the third round; and polished off SUN PHOENIX in the final round. The victory over CRAY BLITZ was the greatest success by Hsu and company to that time. In spite of the fact that CRAY BLITZ held the title of world champion for two more years, this game clearly established that not only HITECH but CHIPTEST-M as well were now stronger that Hyatt's program. Whether CHIPTEST-M was stronger than HITECH was not clear, although by May of 1988, CHIPTEST's successor DEEP THOUGHT 0.01 led the field.

October 26, 1987, Dallas
Round 3, eighteenth ACM North American
Computer Chess Championship
White: CRAY BLITZ   Black: CHIPTEST-M
Time Control: 40/2, 20/1 thereafter
Center Counter Defense

1 e4 d5 2 e×d5 Q×d5 3 Nc3 Qa5 4 d4 c6 5 Nf3 Nf6 6 Bc4 Bg4 7 h3 Bh5 8 Qe2 Nbd7 9 Bd2 Qc7 10 g4 Bg6 11 O-O-O O-O-O 12 Ng5 e5

The beginning of Black's attack!

Figure 8.2. Position after 12 . . . e5.

13 B×f7 e×d4 14 Na4 Ne5 15 B×g6 N×g6 16 Ne6 Re8 17 Rhe1 Qd6 18 g5 Nd7
19 Qg4 b5 20 Nac5 Nge5

White goes down fast from here on in a brilliant attack by Black.

21 N×f8

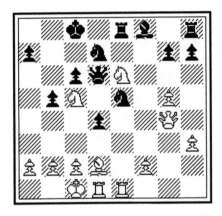

Figure 8.3. Position after 21 N×f8.

21 ... Rh×f8

Black cannot play 21 ... N×g4 because 22 R×e8+ Kc7 23 Ba5#.

22 Ne4 Qd5 23 Qg2 Re6 24 Kb1 Nf3 25 Qg4 N×e1 26 R×e1 Ne5 27 Qd1 Nf3
White resigns.

May 28–30, 1988: Pittsburgh

In 1985 at the Fredkin Masters Invitational, HITECH had established that it
could compete against tough master-level competition. Now, three years
later, four programs were invited to participate in the Fredkin Masters
Open with twenty-nine humans—three with ratings over 2400 and ten
with ratings over 2300. Both CHIPTEST-M and the new DEEP THOUGHT 0.01
participated, as did HITECH and Don Beal's BP. HITECH finished with a
score of 3.5/6 and a performance rating of 2318; BP finished with a score
of 3/6 and a performance rating of 2185.

Andreas Nowatzyk joined the team at this time. Nowatzyk worked on
the scoring function of DEEP THOUGHT 0.01 along with Campbell; his main
contribution was software he developed to optimize the coefficients of the

terms of the scoring function based on a set of nine hundred test positions. He had received his undergraduate degree from Hamburg University in Germany.

CHIPTEST-M was searching about five hundred thousand positions per second and running on a SUN 4. DEEP THOUGHT 0.01 was not fully debugged before the tournament, according to Hsu, with wire-wrapping of the circuitry taking place the day before the event, and was running at about half speed—about five to seven hundred thousand positions per second—and also on a SUN 4. Even so, DEEP THOUGHT 0.01 finished in a tie for second place behind the winner, Alexander Ivanov (2415), with 4.5/6 points and a performance rating of 2571. After four rounds, DEEP THOUGHT 0.01 was tied for first with Ivanov, with a score of 3.5/4. It then lost to Ivanov and defeated Vivek Rao (2491) in the final round. CHIPTEST-M finished with 4/6 points placing 4-7 and with a performance rating of 2505. According to Hsu, because DEEP THOUGHT 0.01 was not fully debugged, some typically weak computer-recognizable rook pawn moves were made. Let's see.

May 30, 1988, Carnegie Mellon University
Round 5, Fredkin Masters Open
White: Alexander Ivanov   Black: DEEP THOUGHT 0.01
Time Control: 40/2, 20/1 thereafter
Center Counter Defense

---

1 e4 d5 2 e×d5 Q×d5 3 Nc3 Qa5 4 Nf3 Nf6 5 d4 c6 6 Bc4 Bg4 7 h3 Bh5 8 Qe2 Nbd7
9 Bd2 Qc7

With a transposition of moves, this position is identical to the one reached in the previous game between CRAY BLITZ and CHIPTEST-M, but with colors reversed. In that game CRAY BLITZ played 10 g4 and went on to lose. Here Ivanov castles and winds up having his king exactly where it is needed.

10 O-O-O B×f3 11 Q×f3 e6 12 g4 Bd6 13 g5 Nd5 14 Ne4 O-O 15 N×d6 Q×d6
16 Qg3 Q×g3 17 f×g3 a5 18 Be2 b5 19 c4 b×c4 20 B×c4 N7b6 21 Be2 Rfb8
22 Kc2 c5 23 d×c5 Na4 24 b3 N×c5 25 Bf3

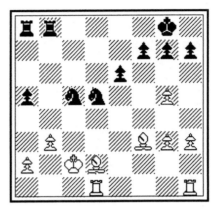

Figure 8.4. Position after 25 Bf3.

White's king and strong bishops are positioned perfectly for what is to follow. With its own king out of play, Black is unable to prevent White's queen-side pawn majority from translating into the winning margin. The rooks, bishops, and knights will come off shortly, leaving White with an easy way to victory.

25 ... Rb5 26 Rc1 Rc8 27 Kb1 a4 28 B×d5 e×d5 29 Be3 Rc6 30 R×c5 Rb×c5 31 B×c5 R×c5 32 Rc1 R×c1+ 33 K×c1 a3 34 Kc2 Kf8 35 Kc3 Ke7 36 Kb4 Ke6 37 K×a3 Ke5 38 Kb2 d4 39 Kc2 Ke4 40 Kd2 Black resigns.

May 30, 1988, Carnegie Mellon University
Round 6, Fredkin Masters Open
White: DEEP THOUGHT 0.01   Black: Vivek Rao
Time Control: 40/2, 20/1 thereafter
Sicilian Defense

1 e4 c5 2 c3 d5 3 e×d5 Q×d5 4 d4 Nf6 5 Nf3 Nc6 6 Be2 c×d4 7 c×d4 e6 8 O-O Be7 9 Nc3 Qd8 10 Be3 O-O 11 Bc4 b6 12 a4 Bb7 13 Ne5 Rc8 14 Bb3 Nb4 15 Rc1 Nbd5 16 N×d5 B×d5 17 Qd3 Bb7 18 R×c8 Q×c8 19 Rc1 Qa8 20 f3 Nd5 21 Bd2 Rc8 22 Bc4 Rc7 23 f4 Qc8 24 b3 f6 25 Ng4 Ba6 26 g3 Bb7

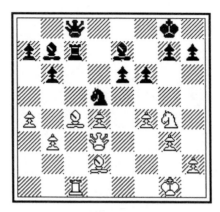

Figure 8.5. Position after 26 . . . Bb7.

27 f5

A great move by White. Black finds itself on the defensive for the remainder of the game, resigning after another thirteen moves.

27 . . . a6 28 Rf1 Kh8 29 f×e6 Q×e6 30 Ne3 b5 31 a×b5 a×b5 32 N×d5 B×d5
33 B×d5 Q×d5 34 Rf5 Qa8 35 R×b5 Ra7 36 d5 Ra1+ 37 Kg2 Ra2 38 b4 Qc8
39 Ra5 Rb2 40 Qc3 Black resigns.

August 7–19, 1988: Boston

The twelve-round U.S. Open was won by Dmitry Gurevich who finished with ten points while Deep Thought 0.01 finished with a respectable score despite one bug that caused it to enjoy being checkmated, another that caused it not to generate en passant moves, and a third that caused problems with its draw detection routines! Its shining moment, however, was its triumph over international master Igor Ivanov in round nine. Ivanov was so upset after the game that he withdrew from the tournament. This victory was the first victory in tournament play by a computer against someone with such a high rating.

August 16, 1988, Boston
Round 9, U.S. Open
White: DEEP THOUGHT 0.01   Black: Igor Ivanov
Time Control: 40/2, 20/1 thereafter
Center Counter Defense

1 e4 d5 2 e×d5 Nf6 3 d4 N×d5 4 c4 Nf6 5 Nf3 Bg4 6 Be2 e6 7 Be3 Bb4+ 8 Nbd2 O-O
9 a3 Be7 10 h3 Bh5 11 O-O c6 12 g4 Bg6 13 Nh4 Nbd7 14 N×g6 h×g6 15 f4 c5
16 g5 Ne8 17 Ne4 Nd6 18 N×d6 B×d6 19 b4 c×b4 20 c5 Bc7 21 a×b4 a6 22 Qc2 Qe7

Figure 8.6. Position after 22 . . . Qe7.

23 Qe4

White's pieces all now come to life, while Black's scurry to buy time but to
no avail! White's last move threatens 24 Q×b7 and 24 d5.

23 . . . b6 24 Qb7 Rfc8 25 B×a6 e5 26 f×e5 b×c5 27 Bc4 Rab8 28 R×f7 R×b7 29 Rf4+
Black resigns.

November 13–15, 1988: Orlando

In 1986, it was called CHIPTEST, a year later CHIPTEST-M, then DEEP
THOUGHT 0.01. This time it came to the nineteenth ACM championship

as Deep Thought 0.02. Hsu enjoyed spoofing the computer world with the names he gave to his programs. Carnegie Mellon University graduate student Mike Browne worked with the team for one year around this time and developed utility programs associated with the opening book.

The new program used two custom VLSI chess processors and searched positions at a rate of 720,000 per second. The program searched to a depth of ten plies in typical middle-game positions. It ran on a SUN 4 workstation using the high-speed custom processors to evaluate the last three plies of the search tree. Many lines were searched to a depth of fifteen plies and on rare occasions, forty-ply searches occurred. Deep Thought 0.02's opening book contained about five thousand positions, small relative to other programs playing strong chess.

In the first round, Deep Thought 0.02 was behind in most of the game against Chess Challenger and settled for a draw after fifty moves. It easily defeated Sun Phoenix in the second round, played one of its best games against Hitech in the third round, and overcame Mephisto in the final round. Mephisto had become the best of the commercial programs, although Chess Challenger was not far off. Cray Blitz finished in third place but did not play Deep Thought 0.02.

Deep Thought 0.02's game with Hitech figured to be a dramatic encounter. Hitech had won the Pennsylvania State Championship two years running and was rated over 2400 by the United States Chess Federation. Expecting to be pitted against Deep Thought 0.02 during the event, Berliner had prepared a special opening line that he hoped would do in his arch rival. The line involved White (Deep Thought 0.02) making a pawn sacrifice in return for attacking opportunities. The opening went as Berliner planned, but when Hitech left book, it made several passive moves and quickly found itself in trouble.

This was the first battle between these two competitors. They met again five more times, and each game was surrounded by an aura of drama. Berliner carefully prepared his opening book for each game, but his program was unable to follow through in the complex middle-games that followed. Hitech managed to win only one of the games, and that happened in 1991 when Hsu and company had to use an old version of their program. They last played in 1995 in Hong Kong. The six games are included in this chapter.

November 14, 1988, Orlando
Round 3, nineteenth ACM North American
Computer Chess Championship
White: Deep Thought 0.02   Black: Hitech
Time Control: 40/2, 20/1 thereafter
Alekhine's Defense

Deep Thought 0.02's analysis was made available to your author when he reported on this event in the ACM *Communications*.

1 e4 Nf6 2 e5 Nd5 3 d4 d6 4 Nf3 Nc6

Berliner had prepared this line just for Deep Thought 0.02, believing his opponent would make the coming pawn sacrifice, but that Hitech would be the one to obtain a positional advantage.

5 c4 Nb6 6 e6 f×e6 7 Ng5

This is the best move here, threatening Bd3.

7 . . . g6

Deep Thought 0.02 is out of book with this move.

8 Bd3

Deep Thought 0.02 sees that 8 . . . N×d4 9 N×h7 Nf5 10 N×f8 R×f8 11 Nd2 e5 leads to a score of −0.77 pawns.

8 . . . N×d4 9 N×h7 Nf5 10 N×f8 K×f8

Black's move exposes the king. Although Black has an extra pawn, his king is vulnerable due to the awkward king-side pawns. Better was 10 . . . R×f8.

11 O-O c5 12 b3

Deep Thought 0.02's scoring function anticipates that Bb2 is coming.

12 . . . d5 13 Nd2 Qd6 14 Nf3 Nd7 15 Re1

White is concentrating its strength on the e-file.

15 . . . d4 16 Ne5

This may look like a sacrifice, but it isn't.

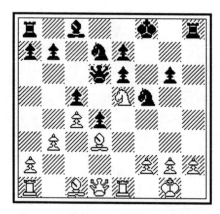

Figure 8.7. Position after 16 Ne5.

16 . . . N×e5 17 Bf4 Rh7

Black could have tried 17 . . . N×d3 18 B×d6 N×e1, getting reasonable compensation for the queen.

18 R×e5

DEEP THOUGHT 0.02's scoring function returns a positive value for the first time, anticipating 18 . . . Qb6 19 g4 Nh4 20 Bg3 Bd7 21 Rh5 R×h5.

18 . . . Qb6 19 g4 Nh4 20 Bg3

White has a won position after just twenty moves.

20 . . . Bd7 21 Rh5

This move surprised everyone who was watching. DEEP THOUGHT 0.02 believes that this leads to an advantage of a pawn. More simply, White could have captured the knight.

21 . . . g×h5 22 B×h7

DEEP THOUGHT 0.02 anticipates 22 . . . Kg7 23 Qd3 e5 24 B×h4 Rh8 25 Bf5 e6 with a 2.69 pawn advantage.

22 . . . e5 23 B×h4 B×g4 24 Qd3 Rc8 25 Re1 Qe6 26 f3 Bh3 27 Qg6

DEEP THOUGHT 0.02 might better hold on to its queen for a little longer. It might better have played 27 Bg3.

27 . . . Q×g6 28 B×g6 Rc6 29 B×h5 Re6 30 Bg3 Ra6

This is a real fishing expedition, but it doesn't ruffle Deep Thought 0.02.

31 a4 d3 32 R×e5 Rd6 33 Re1 Rb6 34 Bf4 a5 35 Be3 R×b3 36 B×c5 d2 37 B×e7+ Kg7
38 Rd1 Re3 39 Bh4 Ra3 40 Be8 R×f3 41 Bg5 Rf8 42 Bb5 Kg6 43 Be3 Rf3 44 B×d2 Rd3
45 c5 Rd5 46 c6 b×c6 47 B×c6 Rd6 48 Bf3 Rd4 49 B×a5 R×a4 50 Rd6+ Kf5 51 Bc3 Ra2
52 Rh6 Bg4 53 Bd5 Rc2 54 Rc6 Re2 55 h4 Kf4 56 Rc4+ Kg3 57 Ba5 Black resigns.

November 24–27, 1988: Long Beach

Over the long Thanksgiving weekend, the $130,000 Software Toolworks Chess Championship was held in Long Beach, California. Deep Thought 0.02 was invited to participate and surprised everyone when it finished in a first-place tie with international grandmaster Anthony Miles, scoring 6.5/8 points. During the event, it defeated grandmaster Bent Larsen and finished ahead of international grandmasters Samuel Reshevsky, Walter Browne, and former world champion Mikhail Tal. The victory over fifty-three-year-old Larson marked the first time a grandmaster had fallen to a computer in a regular tournament game. It was a fantastic performance. Not that computers hadn't defeated grandmasters before, but not in a regulation tournament game. Hitech two months earlier had defeated Arnold Denker in a four-game match by a 3.5–0.5 score, for example. However Larsen carried a 2580 FIDE (Fédération Internationale des Échecs) rating at the time, and Denker was effectively retired. Once a grandmaster, always a grandmaster, but Denker at seventy-three wasn't the player he had been when he won U.S. championships in 1944–46. Browne defeated Deep Thought 0.02 in the fourth round for the program's only loss.

November 25, 1988, Long Beach California
Round 3, Software Toolworks Chess Championship
White: Bent Larsen   Black: Deep Thought 0.02
Time Control: 40/2, 20/1 thereafter
English Opening

1 c4 e5 2 g3 Nf6 3 Bg2 c6 4 Nf3 e4 5 Nd4 d5 6 c×d5 Q×d5 7 Nc2 Qh5

With the intent of playing Bh3. Deep Thought 0.02 has active lines for its pieces.

8 h4 Bf5 9 Ne3 Bc5 10 Qb3 b6 11 Qa4 O-O 12 Nc3 b5 13 Qc2 B×e3 14 d×e3 Re8
15 a4 b4 16 Nb1 Nbd7 17 Nd2 Re6 18 b3 Rd8 19 Bb2 Bg6 20 Nc4 Nd5 21 O-O-O N7f6
22 Bh3 Bf5 23 B×f5 Q×f5 24 f3 h5 25 Bd4 Rd7 26 Kb2 Rc7

This threatens 27 . . . c5. Larsen, after the game was over, said he was in a
very strong position and made only this one bad move, getting the king in
the way of a good square for the bishop.

27 g4

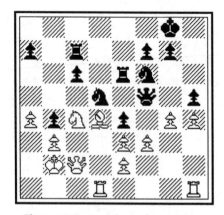

Figure 8.8. Position after 27 g4.

Black's strong knight and two advanced pawns are thorns in White's side;
White will be in trouble soon trying to cover all its weaknesses in this
highly complex tactical game.

27 . . . h×g4 28 Rhg1 c5 29 f×g4 N×g4 30 B×g7 Rg6

Black sees a forced win at this point.

31 Qd2 Rd7 32 R×g4 R×g4 33 Ne5 N×e3 34 Q×d7 N×d1+ 35 Q×d1 Rg3
36 Qd6 K×g7 37 Nd7 Re3 38 Qh2 Kh7 39 Nf8+ Kh8 40 h5 Qd5 41 Ng6+ f×g6
42 h×g6+ Kg7 43 Qh7+ Kf6 White resigns.

Several weeks later, when Larsen was participating in the Hasting International Tournament, David Levy interviewed the "Great Dane" and asked
him what he thought about the computer's performance during their game.
Larsen said that he "was not impressed at all. I thought it was rather ridicu-
lous. For instance there is a point where it protects the pawn on c6. It has a
weak pawn on c6 and it plays a clumsy rook move, 17 . . . Re6 I think it is,
to protect the pawn. But it is a pawn I cannot take, so I don't understand

why it protects it." [David Levy, "Computer Beats Grandmaster," *ICCA Journal* (December 1988): 168–170.] Levy also asked him when was the first time he thought it was possible that he might lose to a computer, and Larsen responded that he still didn't "think that is possible! What happened to me in Long Beach was that I got very angry when I had to play the machine. And then I get even more angry when I was told that I could have signed a note saying that I did not want to be paired against it. I did not know that."

♚

November 25, 1988, Long Beach, California
Round 4, Software Toolworks Chess Championship
White: DEEP THOUGHT 0.02   Black: Walter Browne
Time Control: 40/2, 20/1 thereafter
Sicilian Defense

———————

1 e4 c5 2 c3 Nf6 3 e5 Nd5 4 d4 c×d4 5 Nf3 Nc6 6 Bc4 Nb6 7 Bb3 d5 8 e×d6 Q×d6 9 O-O e6 10 c×d4 Be7 11 Nc3 O-O 12 Re1 Nd5

Browne said that he wanted to take DEEP THOUGHT 0.02 out of book and see how it would respond. He expected 13 B×d5 e×d5 14 Qb3 Be6 15 Q×b7 Rfb8 16 Qa6 N×d4!, not the computer's next move.

13 g3 Qd8 14 a3 N×c3 15 b×c3 b6 16 Qd3 Bb7 17 Bc2 g6 18 Bf4 Rc8 19 Bh6 Re8 20 Bd2

The three moves by White's bishop have improved the position of Black's rooks and left White's pieces on their original squares.

20 . . . Na5 21 Ba4

Figure 8.9. Position after 21 Ba4.

21 . . . Qd5

Browne observed that 21 . . . Bc6 was much stronger.

22 B×e8 R×e8 23 Kg2 Nc4 24 Bc1 g5 25 h3 h5 26 g4 e5 27 Qd1 f5

Browne has lost all his inhibitions and is on a roll!

28 g×h5 g4 29 h×g4 f×g4 30 Kg1 Q×f3 31 Q×f3 B×f3 32 Bh6 Kh7 33 Bd2

Yes, this is the move played.

33 . . . Rf8 34 R×e5 N×e5 35 Re1 Nc6 White resigns.

November 1988–March 1989: on the "Net"

Having served as the tournament director at a slew of computer chess tournaments beginning in the early 1980s, Mike Valvo was particularly tuned in to the style of computer play. Following the success of DEEP THOUGHT 0.02 at the Software Toolworks tournament, he took on the computer in a two-game correspondence match in which moves were made at a rate of one every three days, a rate that, in theory, gives the human better chances than a faster one, and this match would be a good test of that principle. Valvo had a USCF rating of 2488 while DEEP THOUGHT 0.02 weighed in at 2551. Valvo would post his analysis of the game as it went along on the net newsgroup rec.games.chess, where hundreds of chess aficionados would follow the games and his comments. Valvo won both games.

November 1988–March 1989 on the "Net"
Game 1, DEEP THOUGHT 0.02—Valvo match
White: Mike Valvo   Black: DEEP THOUGHT 0.02
Time Control: One move every three days
Alekhine's Defense

---

1 e4 Nf6 2 e5 Nd5 3 d4 d6 4 c4 Nb6 5 f4 d×e5 6 f×e5 Nc6 7 Be3 Bf5 8 Nc3 e6
9 Nf3 Bg4 10 Be2 B×f3 11 g×f3 Qh4+ 12 Bf2 Qf4 13 c5

In a game earlier in the year when playing Lev Alburt, Valvo played 13 Qc1 Q×c1+ 14 R×c1 O-O-O 15 Rd1 g6 16 a3 Bh6 17 b4 Rd7 18 Ne4 Rhd8 19 c5 Nd5 20 b5 Nce7 21 c6 b×c6 22 b×c6 N×c6 23 Bb5 Nde7 24 Ba6+ and won. Valvo was on familiar territory thus far.

13 . . . Nd7 14 Qc1 Qf5 15 Qb1

Valvo is determined to rid the game of queens.

Q×b1+ 16 R×b1 O-O-O 17 f4 Be7

DEEP THOUGHT 0.02, with this move, was out of book.

18 Rd1 g5 19 f×g5 B×g5

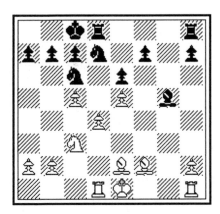

Figure 8.10. Position after 19 . . . B×g5.

20 Bf3

Valvo threatens to double Black's c-pawns, and DEEP THOUGHT 0.02, a bit out of ideas, will now advance its f-pawn, gaining some space but losing control of d6 and f6. After Black's next move, White will be in a position to force play for the remainder of the game.

20 . . . f5 21 O-O Nb4 22 Rfe1 Rhg8 23 Kh1 c6 24 a3 Na6 25 b4 Nc7 26 a4 a6
27 Re2 Be7 28 Rb2 Nd5 29 N×d5 c×d5 30 b5 a×b5 31 a×b5 Rg7 32 Ra1 Nb8
33 Rba2 Rdg8 34 Ra8 Bg5 35 b6 Bd8 36 Bh5 Rf8 37 Be2 Rfg8 38 Be3 h5

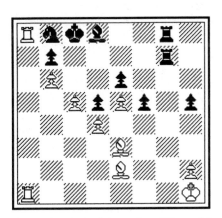

Figure 8.11. Position after 38 . . . h5.

39 Rb1

Valvo avoids the offering and prepares to push the c-pawn with his b-pawn now secure.

Be7 40 Bb5 Bd8 41 Ba4 f4

Black has only bad moves here and chooses the lesser of the evils.

42 B×f4 Rf7 43 Bh6 h4 44 Bb5 Be7 45 c6 b×c6 46 B×c6 Rf3 47 Rba1 Ba3 48 Bd2
Black resigns.

December 1988–March 1989 on the "Net"
Game 2, DEEP THOUGHT 0.02—Valvo match
White: DEEP THOUGHT 0.02   Black: Mike Valvo
Time Control: One move every three days
King's Gambit Declined (Falkbeer Counter Gambit)

---

1 e4 e5 2 f4 d5 3 e×d5 c6 4 Nc3 e×f4 5 Nf3 Bd6 6 d4 Ne7 7 d×c6 Nb×c6 8 d5 Nb4
9 Bc4 O-O 10 a3 b5 11 Bb3 Na6 12 N×b5 Qa5+ 13 Nc3 Nc5 14 Ba2 Ba6

Figure 8.12. Position after 14 . . . Ba6.

According to Valvo, the DEEP THOUGHT 0.02 team was in a "near panic after reception of Black's fourteenth. I believe . . . DEEP THOUGHT searched thirty-five plies (seventeen moves!) and could not find a refutation." Valvo will now sacrifice a knight only to recover it nine moves later.

15 b4 Qc7 16 b×c5 Rfe8 17 Ne2 Q×c5 18 c4 N×d5 19 Qd4 Q×d4 20 N×d4 Bc5
21 Kd2 Ne3 22 Kc3 Rac8 23 Bb2 N×g2

Valvo indicated that DEEP THOUGHT 0.02 considered Black's last move to be a mistake and that 23 ... Bb6 would have led to a large advantage for Black. "The human part in me, however, cried for some tangible compensation for the piece it gave up some nine moves earlier. I did not give enough weight to the 23 ... Bb6 and 24 ... Ba5+ idea. I just saw that 23 ... N×g2 would maintain an edge in initiative and recoups some material."

24 Raf1 Rcd8 25 Rhg1 Re3+ 26 Kd2 f3 27 R×f3 R×f3 28 R×g2 Rh3 29 Kc1 g6
30 a4 Bb7 31 Rf2 Ba8 32 Bb1 Rb8 33 Ba2 Rd3 34 Rf4 Rd2 35 K×d2 R×b2+
36 Nc2 R×a2 37 Nc3 Rb2 38 Rf6 Kg7

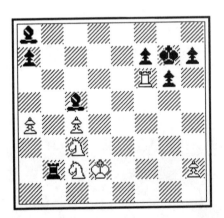

Figure 8.13. Position after 38 ... Kg7.

39 Rf1

Valvo thought White might have tried 39 Ra6, and if 39 ... Bb6 threatening to trap the rook, White plays 40 a5. The remaining knights and bishops will now be traded off, and Valvo will be left with a two pawn advantage and his second victory.

39 ... f5 40 Nd5 B×d5 41 c×d5 Rb3 42 h4 Kf6 43 Re1 Rh3 44 Re6+ Kf7 45 a5 R×h4
46 Rc6 Bb4+ 47 N×b4 R×b4 48 Rc7+ Kf6 White resigns.

April 9, 1989: Hilversum, the Netherlands

CHIPTEST-M participated in a match with eleven other computers against the top players from the Netherlands in a one-day match. The team of computers was outranked by their human opponents by approximately 150–200 rating points, but nevertheless managed to finish with 3.5/12. CHIPTEST-M, playing on top board against international grandmaster John van der Wiel (2560), put in a good performance but lost. DEEP THOUGHT 0.02 was undergoing major modifications at the time and was replaced by its older sibling.

May 28–31, 1989: Edmonton, Alberta

The sixth World Computer Chess Championship was held in Edmonton, Alberta, and saw a field of twenty-four entries compete. CRAY BLITZ returned as the reigning champion, but it didn't figure to repeat a third time; of course, going into the last world championship, it wasn't expected to repeat either but it did. The last time, however, there wasn't another entry that was clearly stronger. This time there was. DEEP THOUGHT 0.02 had finished ahead of CRAY BLITZ at the last two ACM championships and had reached new levels of excellence against humans in the last year. For this event, DEEP THOUGHT 0.02 was renamed simply DEEP THOUGHT by Hsu, Anantharaman, and Campbell. It trounced the field, winning the championship with a perfect 5-0 score. In the final round it met HITECH.

Feng-hsiung Hsu and Andreas Nowatzyk
in Edmonton, 1989, with DEEP THOUGHT.

Jaap van den Herik and his wife, Letty Raaphorst,
in Edmonton at the 1989 World Championship.

May 31, 1989, Edmonton
Round 5, sixth World Computer Chess Championship
White: HITECH   Black: DEEP THOUGHT
Time Control: 40/2, 20/1 thereafter
Queen's Pawn Opening

Ray Keene analyzed this game in the December 1989 *ICCA Journal*.

1 d4 d5 2 Nf3 Nf6 3 Bf4

Berliner takes DEEP THOUGHT out of book on this move.

3 . . . e6 4 e3 Nc6

This makes it difficult for Black to push the c-pawn, a natural move in this position.

5 Nbd2 Be7 6 h3 O-O 7 Be2 Nh5 8 Bh2 g6 9 O-O f5 10 Be5

Keene panned this move. He said it gave up a good bishop that was putting pressure on the pawn on c7 for a poorly placed knight. Moreover, in trading the knight for the bishop, White assists Black in preparing to push its c-pawn.

10 . . . N×e5 11 N×e5 Nf6 12 c4 c5 13 Ndf3 Bd6 14 a3 Qc7

Black eliminates White's d×c5 since the knight on e5 would be lost.

15 Rc1 a5 16 Qb3 b6 17 Qa4 Bb7

Figure 8.14. Position after 17 . . . Bb7.

HITECH's queen's moves give Black the best position in the game thus far, according to Keene.

18 Rc2 Kh8 19 c×d5 B×d5 20 Rd1 Rad8 21 Bb5 Ne4 22 Nd7

A classic computer move. HITECH must now be careful to keep the knight defended or able to flee safely.

22 . . . Rg8 23 Nfe5 Rg7 24 Rd3 Be7 25 Rd1 h5 26 Rdc1 Bg5 27 Re1 Bh4 28 Rf1 Be7 29 Rfc1

HITECH has been unable to develop any plan on how to proceed.

29 . . . g5 30 f3 Nf6 31 Kf1 g4 32 h×g4 h×g4 33 f4

DEEP THOUGHT puts on a tremendous attack now.

33 . . . Be4 34 Rd2 Nd5 35 Re2 Rh7 36 Ree1 N×e3+ 37 Kg1 Nd5 38 Ng6+ Kg7 39 N×e7 Q×f4 40 N×f5+ e×f5 41 R×e4 Q×c1+ 42 Bf1 f×e4 43 Qb3 Rh1+ 44 K×h1 Q×f1+ 45 Kh2 Rh8+ 46 Qh3 g3+ 47 K×g3 Qf4#.

In addition to participating in the world championship, DEEP THOUGHT played a two-game exhibition with Canada's top player, international grandmaster Kevin Spraggett. The first game was played at a speed of all moves in thirty minutes; the second was played at all in ten minutes.

May 1989, Edmonton
Game 1, Exhibition match
with international grandmaster Kevin Spraggett
White: DEEP THOUGHT   Black: Kevin Spraggett
Time Control: All/thirty minutes
Queen's Pawn Opening, Richter-Varesov Attack

1 d4 Nf6 2 Nc3 d5 3 Bg5 c6 4 e3 Bf5 5 Bd3 Bg6 6 Nf3 e6 7 O-O Be7 8 B×g6 h×g6
9 Re1 Nbd7 10 Qd3 Qc7 11 Bf4 Bd6 12 B×d6 Q×d6 13 e4 d×e4 14 N×e4 N×e4
15 R×e4 O-O-O 16 Rae1 Kb8 17 R4e2 Qf4 18 b4 Qf5 19 Qe3 Nb6 20 Qe5 Q×e5
21 N×e5 Rhf8 22 c3 Kc7 23 h4 Nd5 24 Rc2 Nf6 25 g3 Nd7 26 Nc4 Nb6 27 N×b6 a×b6

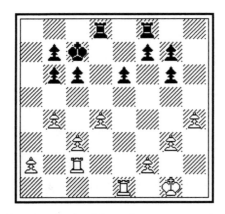

Figure 8.15. Position after 27 . . . a×b6.

The remainder of this game is a good lesson in rook and pawn endgames.
Another twenty-one moves follow without a capture. Only five of the
forty-two moves are pawn advances.

28 f4 b5 29 Kf2 Ra8 30 Ke3 Kd6 31 Kd3 Ra3 32 Rb1 Rfa8 33 Rbb2 Kd5 34 Re2 f6
35 Rh2 Rh8 36 Rbe2 Kd6 37 Re3 Raa8 38 Re1 Rae8 39 Re4 Re7 40 Rd2 Ra8
41 Ree2 b6 42 Re4 Rea7 43 Rde2 Re7 44 R4e3 Rh8 45 Kc2 Kd5 46 a3 Ra8
47 Kb1 Rae8 48 Kb2 Kd6 Drawn by agreement.

May 1989, Edmonton
Game 2, Exhibition match
with international grandmaster Kevin Spraggett
White: Kevin Spraggett   Black: Deep Thought
Time Control: All/ten minutes
King's Fianchetto Opening

1 g3 d5 2 Bg2 c6 3 d3 Nf6 4 Nc3 e5 5 Bg5 Be6 6 Nf3 Nbd7 7 O-O h6 8 B×f6 Q×f6
9 e4 d4 10 Ne2 Bd6 11 Nd2 g5 12 c3 d×c3 13 b×c3 O-O-O 14 d4 Qg6 15 Qa4 Kb8
16 Rab1 Nb6 17 Qa5 Bc7 18 Qb4 B×a2 19 Rb2 Be6 20 Ra1 Qh5 21 Nb3 Bc4 22 Nc5

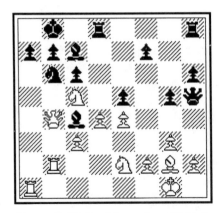

Figure 8.16. Position after 22 Nc5.

22 . . . Bb5

If Black plays 22 . . . B×e2, White can counter with 23 Qa5, forcing 23 . . .
a6 24 R×b6 and leaving Black in serious difficulties, although 22 . . . Bb5
is no better. Black's queen-side is too vulnerable to attack, and its rooks
and queen are of little help. In eight moves it will be forced to give up its
queen to avoid mate.

23 Bf1 e×d4 24 c×d4 Rhe8 25 Nc3 B×f1 26 R×f1 Qg4 27 Ra1 Qf3 28 Qa5 a6
29 R×b6 Kc8 30 R×c6 Qf4 31 g×f4 Rd7 32 Nd5 Re6 33 R×c7+ Kb8 34 N×d7+ Ka8
35 Qc5 Rc6 36 Qf8+ Ka7 37 Qb8#.

August 23, 1989 and September 2, 1989: Carnegie Mellon University

Robert Byrne, international grandmaster and *New York Times*'s chess columnist, played DEEP THOUGHT five games—three five-minute games and two at tournament speeds. He lost one five-minute game and drew two. The two tournament games were split. His loss occurred on August 23, 1989, and was the subject of his *New York Times* column on September 26, 1989. In a return game played on September 2, 1989, Byrne was victorious. In his younger days, Byrne was ranked among the top several players in the United States; his rating when he played DEEP THOUGHT was 2548.

August 23, 1989, Carnegie Mellon University
Game 1, Exhibition match with international grandmaster Robert Byrne
White: DEEP THOUGHT   Black: Robert Byrne
Time Control: 40/2, then all/thirty minutes
Sicilian Defense

---

1 e4 c5 2 c3 b6 3 d4 Bb7 4 Bd3 e6 5 Be3 Nf6 6 Nd2 Nc6 7 a3 d6 8 Qf3 g6 9 Ne2 Bg7 10 O-O O-O 11 b4 c×d4 12 c×d4 Qd7 13 Rac1 Rac8

Byrne notes that his 13 … Rac8 "was not accurate; 13 … Rfc8 would have kept the rooks united. Thus, quite soon, after 16 … Ne8, the black rook was out of action. DEEP THOUGHT's 17 Bb5 cost Black more time in retreat."

14 h3 Ne7 15 Bg5 R×c1 16 R×c1 Ne8 17 Bb5 Qd8 18 Qg3 h6 19 Be3 d5 20 f3 Nd6 21 Bd3 b5 22 Rc5

This seizes "on its one chance to keep the initiative," Byrne observed. "Of course, it ran the danger, after 22 … a6 23 Bf4 Nc4 24 B×c4 d×c4, of having the rook trapped, but I could not figure out how to bring that off."

22 … a6 23 Bf4 Nc4 24 B×c4 d×c4 25 Bd6 Re8 26 Rc7 Ba8 27 Rc5 Nc8 28 Be5 B×e5 29 Q×e5 Nd6 30 a4 Qd7 31 Qf4 Kg7 32 h4 Bc6 33 d5 Ba8 34 d×e6 R×e6 35 a×b5 a×b5 36 Nf1

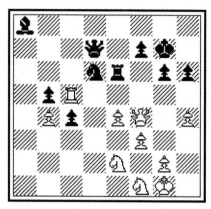

Figure 8.17. Position after 36 Nf1.

36 ... N×e4 37 f×e4 R×e4 38 Qf2 c3 39 N×c3 R×b4 40 Ne3 Bc6 41 Ned5 B×d5
42 N×d5 Rb1+ 43 Kh2 Qd6+ 44 g3 Qe5 45 Nc3 Qe1 46 Qd4+ Kg8 47 N×b1 Qe2+
48 Kg1 Black resigns.

Byrne said that he began to have serious problems when "DEEP THOUGHT
put the queen-side under pressure with 30 a4! and then broke open the
center with 33 d5! After 36 Nf1, I could find no antidote to the coming
Ne3 followed by N×c3 and Nd5." He then gambled that DEEP THOUGHT
could be "shaken up or flustered or bluffed," but he failed with 36 ...
N×e4 37 f×e4 R×e4 38 Qf2 c3, which he hoped would "get enough
pawns off the board to draw various possible endings that might arise."

September 2, 1989, Carnegie Mellon University
Game 2, Exhibition match with international grandmaster Robert Byrne
White: Robert Byrne   Black: DEEP THOUGHT
Time Control: 40/2, then all/thirty minutes
Queen's Gambit Accepted

---

1 d4 d5 2 c4 d×c4 3 Nf3 Nf6 4 Qa4+ c6 5 Q×c4 Bf5 6 Nc3 Nbd7 7 g3 Nb6 8 Qb3 Be6
9 Qd1 Nbd5 10 Bg2 N×c3 11 b×c3 Qa5 12 Qc2 Ne4 13 Bb2 Qf5 14 Qa4 a6 15 O-O Qh5
16 Rfe1 Qf5 17 c4 f6 18 Qb4 O-O-O 19 Rac1 Bf7 20 Qb6 g5 21 d5 c5 22 Bc3 e5
23 d×e6 B×e6 24 Rb1 Rd7 25 Nd2 N×c3 26 B×b7+ R×b7 27 Qc6+ Kd8 28 R×b7 Bd7
29 R×d7+ Q×d7 30 Q×f6+ Ke8 31 Q×c3 Bg7 32 Qe3+ Qe7 33 Ne4 Bd4 34 Qd3 Rf8
35 e3 Be5 36 Qd5 Rf7 37 N×c5 Qd6 38 Qa8+ Ke7 39 Ne4 Qd3 40 N×g5 Rf5 41 Qg8
Black resigns.

The DEEP THOUGHT team was awarded the $10,000 Fredkin Intermediate Prize for being the first to develop a chess program that played at the grandmaster level. It had established a USCF rating of 2551 based on its play in 1988. It was six years earlier that Ken Thompson was awarded $5000 for his success in bringing BELLE to the master level.

October 22, 1989: New York

For many years, researchers at IBM have dabbled with game-playing programs. In the late 1950s, Arthur Samuel explored learning by game-playing programs in the context of checkers, and Alex Bernstein developed one of the earliest chess programs. These were small but successful projects. Occasionally, IBM would provide support to the ACM for its annual competitions. But over the years the computing giant had taken a very cautious attitude toward making a major commitment to this activity. There had been many disappointments by those involved over the years, and in spite of the steady visible progress, the goal of catching the world human champion has been very elusive. Now IBM finally believed that Hsu, Campbell, and Anantharaman could, in fact, achieve this goal with the proper support. Randy Moulic, who would serve as their supervisor, brought the group to IBM, one at a time, beginning in the autumn of 1989; Campbell in September, Hsu the next month, and Anantharaman in February of 1990.

In October of 1989 and under the IBM banner for the first time, DEEP THOUGHT took on Garry Kasparov in a two-game match in New York and was routinely defeated. All of mankind's supporters would point to those games for several years as evidence of the distance computers had to go to reach the human champion. They generally would fail to mention that DEEP THOUGHT had some serious bugs in its king-safety algorithm in those two games, and that while the computer did have a long way to go, it was perhaps not as far as they imagined. The program actually avoided castling in both games because of a bug in its parallel search algorithm! In the first game it eventually castled after playing several strange moves; in the second game, it never castled. When playing this match, DEEP THOUGHT was running on a six-processor system that searched two million chess positions a second.

Until 1989, there was absolutely no question whether the human world champion, now Kasparov or before him Karpov, would find the best computer program any kind of a match. But the successes of DEEP THOUGHT

in games against grandmasters had raised the question of just how good computers were and whether they were ready to challenge the human world champion. Kasparov would not let the world down by avoiding his important role of shedding light on these intriguing questions.

Strong chess players have frequently avoided opportunities to play computers for a variety of reasons, but not Kasparov. With his intense love of the game and his fiercely competitive spirit, Kasparov was more than willing to pit his talent against the world's best chess machine. Kasparov probably would be first to line up for a match with some weird extraterrestrial creature who happened to land on earth claiming to be a chess champion. And so when New York chess promoter Shelby Lyman approached Kasparov with an offer of $10,000 to play DEEP THOUGHT, the champion accepted. Lyman had hosted the PBS show in 1972 covering the Bobby Fischer–Boris Spassky world championship in Iceland. On October 22, 1989, four hundred chess enthusiasts and one hundred people from the media gathered at the New York Academy of Art to see the human world champion sit down to a two-game match with DEEP THOUGHT.

The games were played with each side having ninety minutes of clock time and thus lasting at most three hours. This rate of play, faster than in major tournaments, was to the advantage of the computer; traditionally they have performed relatively better at fast rates of play than at slower rates, a phenomenon that became apparent in the mid-seventies when CHESS 4.9 started to beat masters in five-minute games but had less success in longer games.

Hsu and his colleagues didn't expect their computer to defeat Kasparov. They were hoping a miracle might lead to an even score but they were prepared for the worst. They wanted to play the match, but they would have preferred to wait until their new creation, which was expected to be about ten times as fast, was ready. Furthermore, Hsu and Campbell had only recently joined IBM, and their chess machine was still at CMU, giving them two additional reasons for preferring to wait. According to Campbell's wife, Gina, Hsu was the ultimate workaholic and had spent his first month at IBM too busy with DEEP THOUGHT to find time to acquire a bed for his apartment. Rumor has it that he spent that month sleeping on the floor! But Kasparov's schedule was filled with commitments all over the world, and the DEEP THOUGHT team realized it could not pass up this historic opportunity.

At a press conference one hour before the start of the match, Kasparov answered a multitude of questions while Hsu and Campbell sat alongside, listening and occasionally typing on a terminal connected to their computer at CMU. With the opportunity of asking the articulate champion all the questions they had always wanted to, and with Kasparov so obliging in his answers, Hsu and Campbell were completely neglected by the media. Nobody thought of asking them a single question!

The DEEP THOUGHT computer was actually a SUN computer housing three of Hsu's specially-designed dual-processor VLSI chess circuits. The dual-processor circuits shared the search of branches at positions deep in the tree, while the SUN divided up the search as dictated by the conventional principal variation splitting algorithm. Each dual-processor searched approximately 720,000 chess positions per second; the overall system searched 3 times 720,000 chess positions per second—somewhere between 200 million and 500 million positions per move!

At the press conference, Kasparov revealed that had done his homework. He said that he had studied about fifty of DEEP THOUGHT's games and felt confident he understood its style. When questioned on the program's strength, he credited it with a 2480–2500 FIDE rating, considerably less than his own 2800 rating, and he estimated that he would garner eight or nine points in a ten-game match. He said its style was aggressive, leading to active games. Kasparov granted that some day a computer might outplay him, but he believed the day was not just over the horizon. "I don't know how we can exist knowing that there exists something mentally stronger than us," he said. He contended that the best humans will improve when the day comes that a computer really challenges them.

The games were played in a room filled with paintings and pieces of sculpture, a more intimate and aesthetic setting than the sterile hotel meeting rooms where chess tournaments are usually held; a kibitzing room was set up on the second floor, where most of the audience gathered. Lyman acted as moderator with international grandmaster Edmar Mednis leading the analysis. A communication line connected the terminal at the game board with one in the kibitzing room upstairs. Photographs were taken of the participants during the first eight minutes of each game. After that, the game room became silent.

Garry Kasparov talking with Feng-hsiung Hsu and Murray Campbell just prior to the beginning of their 1989 two-game match in New York.

Feng-hsiung Hsu just prior to DEEP THOUGHT's 1989 match with Garry Kasparov in New York.

October 23, 1989, New York
Game 1, DEEP THOUGHT versus Garry Kasparov match
White: DEEP THOUGHT   Black: Garry Kasparov
Time Control: All/90 minutes
Sicilian Defense

---

1 e4 c5 2 c3

This variation of the Sicilian was used with great success by BELLE in the early 1980s at a time when computers were beginning to score victories over masters. It will be seen again in the first game of the ACM Chess Challenge, where Kasparov replied 2 . . . d5.

2 . . . e6 3 d4 d5 4 e×d5 e×d5 5 Nf3 Bd6 6 Be3

The bishop never moves again.

6 . . . c4

Black gains space on the queen-side with this move; it already has a space advantage on the king-side, with two strong bishops controlling many important squares.

7 b3 c×b3 8 a×b3

This is DEEP THOUGHT's first move out of book.

8 . . . Ne7 9 Na3 Nc6 10 Nb5

DEEP THOUGHT goes on a fishing expedition. Wasting a tempo against someone of Kasparov's strength can only lead to trouble.

10 . . . Bb8 11 Bd3 Bf5 12 c4

Computers handle passed pawns terribly, especially when there are many pieces on the board to distract them. White's 12 c4 invites a passed a-pawn, and in addition, weakens the b4 square. But the real problem here for DEEP THOUGHT is a bug that causes the computer not to castle. From here until move 17, DEEP THOUGHT has several chances to castle, but other moves received priority. The bug caused DEEP THOUGHT to want to castle, but only at the end of the principal continuation. It remained in the program until after the first round of the twentieth ACM North American

Computer Chess Championship in Reno three weeks later, when DEEP THOUGHT, after finding itself in a lost position midway through its game with SUN PHOENIX, backed into a victory. The bug was related to a problem in the parallel code. When DEEP THOUGHT ran on a single computer, the problem did not appear; but when it was running on more than one computer the bug materialized. A second bug in the parallel code also surfaced in this match: the program did not always choose the best move found by the processors. Which moves were adversely affected, however, is not clear.

12 ... O-O 13 Ra4

This is a strange way to protect b4, but computers have strange minds. Hsu and Campbell attributed this move to the castling bug. Kasparov, meanwhile, continues with his systematic development.

13 ... Qd7 14 Nc3

DEEP THOUGHT thinks Black has a small edge at this point.

14 ... Bc7 15 B×f5 Q×f5 16 Nh4

This is in the spirit of the earlier rook move. Campbell's immediate reaction was that this was also caused by a bug.

16 ... Qd7

Black's pieces are now all on active squares. White has yet to castle, has placed one rook on an unbelievably bad square, one knight on a square almost as bad, and has traded off its good bishop.

17 O-O

The audience applauded!

17 ... Rad8 18 Re1

DEEP THOUGHT imagines White has a small advantage now. In an interview after the game, Kasparov indicated that the game was wrapped up after the next two moves.

18 ... Rfe8 19 c5

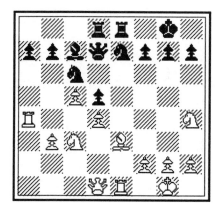

Figure 8.18. Position after 19 c5.

19 . . . Ba5

According to Kasparov, this was a particularly good move.

20 Qd3 a6 21 h3 B×c3 22 Q×c3 Nf5 23 N×f5 Q×f5

Black has a good knight and two well-placed rooks while White has a weak bishop and rooks that are poorly placed.

24 Ra2 Re6 25 Rae2 Rde8 26 Qd2 f6 27 Qc3 h5

Kasparov is gradually pulling the noose tighter.

28 b4 R8e7 29 Kh1

DEEP THOUGHT cannot find a move to improve its position and decides to mark time in a characteristically computer fashion. Kasparov continues with his theme:

29 . . . g5 30 Kg1 g4 31 h4 Re4 32 Qb2 Na7 33 Qd2 R4e6 34 Qc1 Nb5 35 Qd2

DEEP THOUGHT, the eternal optimist, thinks the game is about even.

35 . . . Na3 36 Qd1 Kf7 37 Qb3 Nc4 38 Kh2 Re4 39 g3

Turning pessimistic, DEEP THOUGHT now concludes that White is down about half a pawn.

39 . . . Qf3 40 b5 a5

Kasparov has finally created a passed a-pawn that eventually will be pushed and thereby lead to DEEP THOUGHT's demise. At this point, DEEP THOUGHT had about thirty-four minutes left and Kasparov had about twenty.

41 c6 f5 42 c×b7 R×b7 43 Kg1 f4 44 g×f4 g3 45 Qd1 Rbe7 46 b6 g×f2+
47 R×f2 Q×d1 48 R×d1 R×e3

A resignation is appropriate here, but DEEP THOUGHT is programmed to play on until it is behind seven points, the equivalent of a rook and two pawns.

49 Rg2 N×b6 50 Rg5 a4 51 R×h5 a3 52 Rd2 Re2 White resigns.

Kasparov finished with about ten minutes showing on his clock. DEEP THOUGHT had about twenty.

At Jonathan Schaeffer's suggestion Hsu and Campbell reprogrammed DEEP THOUGHT between games to take slightly more time on early moves in the game. Kasparov's style in the first game was conservative and methodical. He never exposed himself, took no chances, and one step at a time, nailed DEEP THOUGHT into a coffin. The game lacked the dramatic, but Kasparov was devastating in his simplicity and clarity. The game left Kasparov knowing that DEEP THOUGHT was no threat. In Kasparov's words, "after such a loss, no human would come back for more." But DEEP THOUGHT did come back for the second game after its programmers had had an early dinner.

October 23, 1989, New York
Game 2, DEEP THOUGHT versus Garry Kasparov match
White: Garry Kasparov   Black: DEEP THOUGHT
Time Control: All/90 minutes
Queen's Gambit Accepted

1 d4

Kasparov had been using this move as his primary weapon against the world's leading players, and by playing it here, he implicitly announced that he was all business.

1 . . . d5 2 c4 d×c4

Not a bad line for the computer, following the line played against Byrne (see pages 171–173). Since computers are naturally greedy, it makes good sense to use book lines consistent with this behavior. But DEEP THOUGHT's book is small, and the program's desire to hold the pawn quickly leads to trouble.

3 e4

This is a sharp line that Kasparov knows well; 3 e4 is more aggressive than Byrne's 3 Nf3.

3 . . . Nc6 4 Nf3 Bg4 5 d5 Ne5

This is DEEP THOUGHT's first move out of book. It carried out an eleven-ply search, concluding that White was down about a tenth of a pawn.

6 Nc3 c6

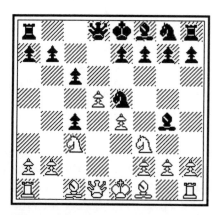

Figure 8.19. Position after 6 . . . c6.

The audience groaned when this move was made. One move out of book and the castling bug reappeared to haunt DEEP THOUGHT. Against someone at Kasparov's level, this move was sufficient to lose the game. DEEP THOUGHT met HITECH three weeks later at the twentieth ACM North American Computer Chess Championship in Reno with the bug corrected. Hans Berliner, having witnessed DEEP THOUGHT's 6 . . . c6 fiasco, had made extensive additions to HITECH's book anticipating that the two programs might meet and that HITECH might then waltz DEEP THOUGHT down the same or a similar garden path. This time DEEP THOUGHT played 6 . . . Nf6 and HITECH was booked to the hilt on this alternative. The game continued: 7 Bf4 Nfd7 8 Qa4 N×f3+ 9 g×f3 B×f3 10 Rg1 a6 11 Q×c4 Rc8

12 Rg3 Bh5 13 Bh3 f6 14 Qb4 (White's first move out of book, and it wastes valuable time moving its queen. Instead 14 Be6 leaves Black in a very cramped position.) 14 ... g5 15 Be3 b5 16 Qd4 (Once again HITECH passes up 16 Be6, although Black can gain some freedom with 16 ... Ne5 threatening 17 ... Nd3+.) 16 ... c5 17 d×c6 R×c6 18 R×g5 f×g5 19 Q×h8 Nf6 (HITECH's advantage, gained by its book, dissolves in six moves. White's queen is out of play, while Black's queen, rook, and bishop are well placed. DEEP THOUGHT is threatening 20 ... Qd3, 21 ... R×c3 followed by 22 ... Qe2#.) 20 Bf1 Qa5 21 Bd4 Qb4! 22 B×f6 R×f6 23 Rd1 B×d1 24 a3 Q×b2 25 N×d1 Q×a3 26 Q×h7 Qa5+ 27 Ke2 Rd6 28 Qh5+ Kd8 29 Q×g5 Bh6 30 Qg8+ Kc7 White resigns.

7 Bf4 Ng6 8 Be3 c×d5

DEEP THOUGHT's scoring function returns a value of −0.29 pawns for this position. Kasparov thought for much longer than usual on 8 Be3, but replies almost instantaneously to DEEP THOUGHT's 8 ... c×d5.

9 e×d5 Ne5

Black falls further behind in development while trying to hang on to its c-pawn.

10 Qd4

The first hard punch has been thrown. Black must reply 10 ... N×f3+ 11 g×f3 B×f3 attacking the rook, but this leaves White with an even larger lead in development. Black cannot make up for the sins of past moves at this point, and decides to go deeper into the hole.

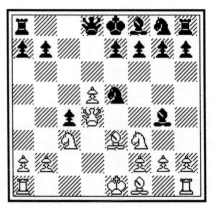

Figure 8.20. Position after 10 Qd4.

10 . . . N×f3+ 11 g×f3 B×f3

11 . . . Bd7 would be more circumspect.

12 B×c4

Kasparov is threatening 13 Bb5+, leaving DEEP THOUGHT in deep trouble.

12 . . . Qd6

DEEP THOUGHT naively thinks White is down a quarter of a pawn, while Kasparov prepares, and the audience eagerly awaits, the knockout blow. The alternative, 12 . . . a6, is met by 13 Rg1 with an overwhelming advantage for White. For example, 13 . . . Nf6 14 Bb3! b5 15 a4!, or 13 . . . e6 14 d×e6 f×e6 15 Qf4 Bd5 (15 . . . Bh5 16 B×e6) 16 B×d5 e×d5 17 O-O-O.

13 Nb5 Qf6

Computers are good at encouraging exchanges when they find themselves in trouble. Note that 13 . . . Qd7 is refuted by 14 N×a7, threatening 15 Bb5.

14 Qc5

The audience continues to expect mate shortly as Kasparov hammers away.

14 . . . Qb6

If 14 . . . B×h1 15 Nc7+ Kd8 16 N×a8 Qd6 17 Q×a7! with a killing attack.

15 Qa3 e6

DEEP THOUGHT now calculates that it is down the equivalent of two pawns. After only fifteen moves the knockout seems imminent. Kasparov has two choices here: 16 Qa4 Qd8 or the line he followed.

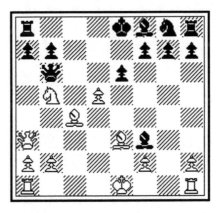

Figure 8.21. Position after 15 . . . e6.

16 Nc7+ Q×c7

Or 16 . . . Kd8 17 Q×f8+ K×c7 18 B×b6+.

17 Bb5+ Qc6 18 B×c6+ b×c6 19 Bc5 B×c5

If 19 . . . B×h1 20 B×f8, threatening 21 B×g7.

20 Q×f3 Bb4+

DEEP THOUGHT finally manages one harmless poke at the champion's chin. This is the only time Kasparov was placed in check in the two games.

21 Ke2 c×d5

Kasparov is ahead a queen for a knight, bishop, and two pawns, but Black's pieces have yet to develop. To DEEP THOUGHT's credit, it managed to escape mate here. Kasparov would have liked to have capped his performance with such a finale.

22 Qg4 Be7 23 Rhc1 Kf8 24 Rc7 Bd6 25 Rb7 Nf6 26 Qa4 a5 27 Rc1 h6 28 Rc6 Ne8 29 b4 B×h2 30 b×a5 Kg8 31 Qb4 Bd6 32 R×d6 N×d6 33 Rb8+ R×b8 34 Q×b8+ Kh7 35 Q×d6 Rc8 36 a4 Rc4 37 Qd7 Black resigns.

Kasparov received a standing ovation for a job well done; the human race would remain supreme. What conclusions could be drawn from the match? Certainly, Kasparov was the better player, but DEEP THOUGHT was better than these games show. In itself, the castling bug was sufficient to cost DEEP THOUGHT both games, and the bug that caused suboptimal moves to be selected didn't help either. Furthermore, Hsu and company hadn't taken adequate time to prepare an opening book for Kasparov, something absolutely necessary against someone of Kasparov's ability.

October 29, 1989: Harvard University

Chris Chabris and international master Dan Edelman have hosted the Harvard Cup since 1989. At their first event, Kasparov was their guest; he played a simultaneous exhibition against eight opponents, seven humans and SARGON IV, winning all games. The event itself featured four computers—DEEP THOUGHT, CHIPTEST-M, HITECH, and MEPHISTO PORTOROSE—and four humans—international grandmasters Lev Alburt, Maxim Dlugy, Boris Gulko, and Michael Rohde. The format of the match had each computer play each human, but no members of the same species would play against each other. Games lasted at most one hour with each side allotted 30 minutes to complete all moves, an increasingly popular speed. The humans outclassed the computers, winning the match with a score of 14.5/16. DEEP THOUGHT won one game against Dlugy, and MEPHISTO PORTOROSE draw one game with Alburt, and that was it. In 1990, the event was not held, but in 1991, the second Harvard Cup saw the computers do somewhat better, scoring 4/16; the following year in 1992 the computers did better yet, scoring 7/18.

October 29, 1989, Harvard University
Round 2, the Harvard Cup
White: DEEP THOUGHT   Black: Maxim Dlugy
Time Control: All/30 minutes
Sicilian Defense

---

1 e4 c5 2 d4 c×d4 3 c3 d×c3 4 N×c3 d6 5 Nf3 e6 6 Bc4 Be7 7 Bf4 Nc6 8 Rc1 Nf6 9 O-O O-O 10 Qd2 N×e4 11 N×e4 d5 12 Bd3 d×e4 13 B×e4 Q×d2 14 B×d2 Bd7 15 Rfe1 Rac8 16 Bf4 Bf6 17 Rcd1 Rfd8 18 b3 Be8 19 a4 h6 20 h3 g5 21 Be3 b6 22 R×d8 B×d8 23 Rc1 f5 24 Bd3 f4 25 Bd4 Bd7 26 Bb2 Na5 27 Rd1 Bc6 28 b4

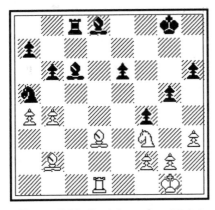

Figure 8.22. Position after 28 b4.

28 . . . Nb7

Black would have done better with 28 . . . B×f3 29 g×f3 Nc6. DEEP
THOUGHT now wins a bishop for a pawn.

29 Ba6 Be7 30 Rc1 B×b4 31 Ne5 Bc5 32 N×c6 R×c6 33 B×b7 Rd6 34 Bc3 Kf7 35 Bf3
Kg6 36 Re1 Kf7 37 Bg4 Rc6 38 Bh5+ Ke7

Black's active pieces keep White at bay a bit longer with a number of fruitless tries, all of which fall short.

39 Bg7 Bb4 40 Re4 Rc1+ 41 Kh2 Bd6 42 Bg4 f3+ 43 g3 Rf1 44 Bd4 Bc5 45 B×e6 Kd6
46 Bc4 Rc1 47 Bb3 Rf1 48 g4 B×d4 49 R×d4+ Kc5 50 Rc4+ Kd6 51 Kg3 Rb1
52 Rc3 Ke5 53 Re3+ Kd4 54 K×f3 a6 55 Bf7 b5 56 Re6 b×a4 57 R×a6 Rb4
58 R×h6 Kc3 59 Ke3 a3 60 Ra6 Kb2 61 Bd5 Rb5 62 Bc4 Rb8 63 Ra5 Rc8 64 Rb5+ Ka1
65 Kd3 Rf8 66 Rf5 Rh8 67 Re5 R×h3+ 68 Kc2 Rh1 69 Ra5 Rh3 70 Bd5 Rd3
71 K×d3 Kb2 72 Rb5+ Ka1 73 Kc2 Black resigns.

November 12–15, 1989: Reno, Nevada

Even though DEEP THOUGHT had lost to Kasparov just prior to the twentieth ACM championship, it was still the world computer champion, and it
came to this event as the clear favorite. It won its first three games but was
upset by MEPHISTO in the final round and settled for a tie for first place
with HITECH. DEEP THOUGHT's castling bug surfaced in its first-round game
with SUN PHOENIX and almost cost it that game, but the problem was finally driven home to the programmers. Watch how DEEP THOUGHT avoids
castling in that game. HITECH's only loss came at the hands of DEEP
THOUGHT (that game appears on pages 181–182). MEPHISTO almost defeated DEEP THOUGHT 0.02 at the previous ACM championship, but this
time it succeeded.

♚

November 12, 1989, Reno Nevada
Round 1, twentieth ACM North American
Computer Chess Championship
White: SUN PHOENIX   Black: DEEP THOUGHT
Time Control: 40/2, 20/1 thereafter
English Opening

---

1 c4 e5 2 Nc3 d6 3 Nf3 f5 4 d4 e4 5 Bg5 Be7 6 B×e7 N×e7 7 Nd2

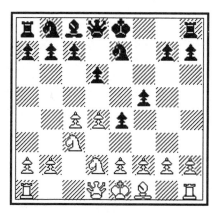

Figure 8.23. Position after 7 Nd2.

Note that Black can castle now, and until White checks on move 20, but it never does.

7 . . . c5 8 Nb3 Qb6 9 e3 Be6 10 Be2 Nd7 11 d5 Bf7 12 f3 e×f3 13 g×f3 Nf6 14 O-O a5 15 Qc2 Nd7 16 Bd3 Bg6 17 Nc1 Ra6

This move should be compared with DEEP THOUGHT's thirteenth move in its first game with Kasparov; it played 13 Ra4 there, which was matched in mentality by this one.

18 N1e2 Ne5 19 Nf4 N×d3 20 Qa4+ Kf8 21 N×d3 Be8 22 Qc2 Qd8 23 Nf4 Bd7 24 Kh1 Kg8 25 Rg1 g6 26 Nb5 Qf8 27 Nc7 Ra7 28 Nce6 Qf7 29 Qc3 B×e6 30 N×e6 b5 31 Rg2 b×c4 32 Q×c4 Ra8 33 Rag1 Qf6 34 Qd3 Kf7 35 e4 Rhb8 36 Qe3 Rb4 37 a3 Rb6 38 Qh6 Rh8 39 Re1 Kg8 40 Qd2 Rb5 41 Nc7 Rb7 42 Ne8 Qd4

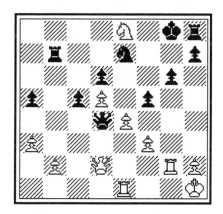

Figure 8.24. Position after 42 . . . Qd4.

43 Q×d4

White should first play 43 N×d6 avoiding the passed pawn that will lead to its undoing.

43 . . . c×d4 44 N×d6 Rb3 45 e×f5 Re3 46 R×e3 d×e3 47 f×g6 h×g6 48 Nc4 N×d5 49 R×g6+ Kh7 50 Rg1 e2 51 Re1 Nf4 52 b3 Re8 53 Nb2 Rc8 54 Nc4 a4 55 h4 a×b3 56 Nb2 Rc2 White resigns.

After this game, the castling bug was eliminated.

Richard Lang of MEPHISTO *in Reno, 1989.*

November 14, 1989, Reno, Nevada
Round 5, twentieth ACM North American
Computer Chess Championship
White: MEPHISTO   *Black:* DEEP THOUGHT
Time Control: 40/2, 20/1 thereafter
Queen's Gambit Accepted

---

1 d4 d5 2 c4 d×c4 3 Nf3 Nf6 4 e3 Bg4 5 B×c4 e6 6 h3 Bh5 7 Nc3 Nbd7 8 g4 Bg6 9 Nh4 Be4 10 N×e4 N×e4 11 Nf3 Nd6 12 Bb3 Qe7 13 Bd2 h5 14 Rg1 h×g4 15 h×g4 O-O-O 16 Ba5 b6 17 Bb4 a5 18 B×d6 Q×d6 19 Qc2 Be7 20 O-O-O Rh3

21 Nd2 c6 22 Rh1 Rdh8 23 R×h3 R×h3 24 Ne4 Qc7 25 Kb1 g5 26 Rc1 Kb7 27 Ba4 Nb8
28 Nd2 Qd7 29 Bb3 Na6 30 Qe4 Nb4 31 a3 Nd5 32 Qg2 Rh8 33 Ne4 f6 34 Qg3 Rg8
35 Rh1 f5 36 g×f5 e×f5 37 Qh3 Rf8 38 Nd2 Bf6 39 Qh7 Rf7 40 Qh6 Qe6 41 Qg6 Rg7
42 Rh7 R×h7 43 Q×h7+ Be7 44 Kc1 Kc7 45 Nf3 Kd8 46 Ne5 g4 47 Qh8+ Kc7
48 Kd2 Kb7 49 N×c6 Q×c6

White, down a knight for a pawn, will now win back a minor piece.

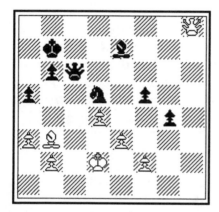

Figure 8.25. Position after 49 . . . Q×c6.

50 Qe5 Nc7 51 Q×e7 Qg2 52 Qh4 f4 53 e×f4 Qe4 54 Q×g4 Q×d4+ 55 Kc1 Q×f2
56 Qf5 Qf3 57 Kc2 Kc6 58 Qe5 Nd5 59 Qe6+ Kc5 60 B×d5 Q×d5 61 Q×d5+ K×d5
62 Kd3 a4 63 Kc3 Kc5 64 f5 Black resigns.

December 1989: London

For twenty-one years, David Levy had taunted the chess-playing computers of this world. In 1968, he wagered several leading British computer scientists that no computer would defeat him in the next ten years, winning
the wager in 1978 when CHESS 4.5 could take only 1.5 points in a five-
game match held in Toronto. *Omni* magazine then put up $4,000, and
Levy added another $1,000 and the bet was extended indefinitely. Levy
easily defeated CRAY BLITZ in 1984; CRAY BLITZ was world champion at
that time, having won the title the year before, but was plagued by bugs
during this match.

But this time, December of 1989, DEEP THOUGHT took Levy to the
cleaners in London. Levy, in all fairness, was not playing at the level he

used to play, mainly as a result of a lack of formal competition. In the weeks leading up to the match, he trained seriously with Danny Kopec, improving his playing strength, in his words, by about two hundred rating points. That wasn't enough. Levy felt that his understanding of computers might give him a 100–150 point advantage over someone who played at his strength but knew nothing about how computers were programmed to play chess, but he admitted that that still left him far from giving the computer a battle.

December 1989, London
Game 1, Exhibition match with international master David Levy
White: David Levy   Black: DEEP THOUGHT
Time Control: 40/2, 20/1 thereafter
Dutch Defense

1 d4 f5 2 Bg5 h6 3 Bh4 g5 4 e3

A dummy playing Black might overlook 4 ... g×h4 5 Qh5#, but Levy must be just teasing here.

4 ... Nf6 5 Bg3 d6 6 c3 Bg7 7 Nd2 O-O 8 f3

Levy regretted not playing 8 h4, forcing 8 ... g4 9 Ne2 followed by Ne4, putting long-term pressure on Black's king-side.

8 ... Nc6 9 Bc4+ d5 10 Bd3 Nh5 11 Bf2 e5 12 Qb3 f4 13 e4 e×d4 14 c×d4 B×d4
15 e×d5 Na5

Figure 8.26. Position after 15 ... Na5.

16 Qc2 B×f2+ 17 K×f2 Q×d5 18 Ne2 Bf5 19 Ne4 Qc6 20 N2c3 Qb6+ 21 Kf1 Rad8
22 Rd1 Rfe8 23 Be2 R×d1+ 24 Q×d1 B×e4 25 N×e4 Nf6 26 Qa4 Re5 27 Qd1 Nd5
28 Qa4 Q×b2 29 Qd7 Qc1+ 30 Kf2 Q×h1 31 Qd8+ Kg7 32 Qd7+ Ne7 33 Q×c7 Nac6
34 Nd6 R×e2+ 35 K×e2 Q×g2+ 36 Ke1 Qh1+ White resigns.

December 1989, London
Game 2, Exhibition match with international master David Levy
White: DEEP THOUGHT   Black: *David Levy*
Time Control: 40/2, 20/1 thereafter
English Opening

---

1 c4 d6 2 Nc3 g6 3 d4 Bg7 4 e4 a6 5 Be3 Nf6 6 Be2 O-O 7 f4 c6

Levy resorts to the classic style that leading players have found best when playing strong computers: play as dull a game as possible!

8 e5 Ne8 9 Nf3 d5 10 O-O Nc7 11 Rc1 e6 12 Qe1 b5 13 c×d5 c×d5 14 Nd1 Ra7
15 Nf2 Nd7 16 Qa5 Na8 17 Qa3 Qb6 18 Bd2 a5 19 Qd6 b4 20 Rc6 Qd8 21 Rfc1 Bb7
22 R6c2 Ndb6 23 Q×d8 R×d8 24 Be3 Rc8 25 Rc5 Bf8 26 Bd3 Rd8 27 R5c2 Rc8
28 R×c8 B×c8 29 Ng4 Be7 30 Nf6+

The beginning of the end for Black. Watch this!

30 . . . B×f6 31 e×f6 Rc7 32 Ne5 R×c1+ 33 B×c1 Bb7 34 a3 Nc7 35 a×b4 a×b4
36 Bd2 Na4 37 B×b4 N×b2 38 Ng4

The computer whispered mate in twelve to anyone who was around to hear except Levy! He played on for a few more moves.

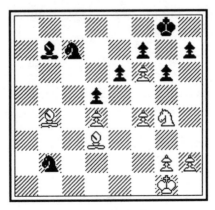

Figure 8.27. Position after 38 Ng4.

38 . . . e5 39 Nh6+ Kh8 40 N×f7+ Kg8 41 Nh6+ Kh8 42 f5 Black resigns.

December 1989, London
Game 3, Exhibition match with international master David Levy
White: David Levy   Black: DEEP THOUGHT
Time Control: 40/2, 20/1 thereafter
Dutch Defense

Now Levy must win the last two games in order not to lose the match. He was defeated in twenty-two moves in this game!

1 d4 f5 2 Bg5 c6 3 c3 h6 4 Bf4 Nf6 5 Nd2 d6 6 e4 g5 7 e5 Nh7 8 Nc4 g×f4
9 Qh5+ Kd7 10 Q×f5+ Kc7 11 Q×f4 Be6 12 Nf3 Rg8 13 Ne3 Ng5 14 e×d6 e×d6
15 d5 B×d5 16 N×d5+ c×d5 17 Nd4 Qe7+ 18 Be2 Nc6 19 Nb5+ Kb8 20 h4 Ne6
21 Qf3 Ne5 22 Q×d5 Nf4 White resigns.

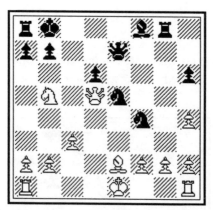

Figure 8.28. Position after 22 . . . Nf4 White resigns.

In the final game, Levy goes down like a lamb.

December 1989, London
Game 4, Exhibition match with international master Dav..
White: DEEP THOUGHT   Black: David Levy
Time Control: 40/2, 20/1 thereafter
English Opening

---

1 c4 d6 2 Nc3 Nd7 3 d4 g6 4 Nf3 Bg7 5 e4 c5 6 Be2 c×d4 7 N×d4 Ngf6 8 Be3 O-O
9 O-O a6 10 f3 Re8 11 Qd2 Ne5 12 f4 Nc6 13 h3 Bd7 14 Nf3 Qa5 15 a3 Rad8
16 b4 Qc7 17 Rac1 b6 18 Bd3 Qb7 19 Qf2 Rb8 20 e5 Nh5 21 b5 a×b5 22 c×b5 Nd8
23 g4 Bh8 24 g×h5 B×h3 25 h×g6 h×g6 26 Rfd1 Qd7 27 Ng5 Bg4 28 Qh4 Bg7
29 Rd2 Bh5 30 Nd5 Qa7 31 Rc7 Rb7 32 e×d6 e×d6 33 Rc8 Q×a3 34 Ne4 Black resigns.

Thus, at the dawn of the last decade of the twentieth century, there is no question that DEEP THOUGHT was well beyond Levy's level. After the match, Levy said he had no excuse—the room was not too hot, there was no noise, the lighting was fine, and the computer operator, Peter Jansen, was not smoking. Jansen assisted the DEEP THOUGHT team while completing his doctoral studies at CMU. In Levy's words, he lost "because an international master who has not played serious chess for eleven years is no match for the enormous power of DEEP THOUGHT." He left the door open a bit on whether an international master who had practiced over the last eleven years would be a match!

February 2, 1990: Harvard University

Three months after DEEP THOUGHT was routinely defeated by Kasparov, it became the turn of the second, super-grandmaster of the present era, Anatoly Karpov, to take on the machine. Karpov reigned as world champion from 1975 to 1985, having assumed the title in 1975 when Bobby Fischer yielded without a contest. In 1985 Karpov lost the title to Kasparov after battling in Moscow for seventy-two games over a 229 day period. Since then, Karpov has remained the world's second-strongest player, with a FIDE rating over 2700.

Karpov took on DEEP THOUGHT in a one-game match at Harvard University on February 2, 1990. He had arrived in the United States the evening before, not having slept for the previous twenty-four hours. To

.pensate for his state of fatigue Karpov insisted on playing White. The
.te of play agreed upon was all moves in one hour by each player.

February 2, 1990, Harvard University
Exhibition match with international grandmaster
and former world champion Anatoly Karpov
White: Anatoly Karpov   Black: DEEP THOUGHT
Time Control: All/1
Caro-Kann Defense

1 e4 c6 2 d4 d5 3 Nd2 g6 4 c3 Bg7 5 e5 f6

At the cost of creating a slight weakening in its king-side pawn structure
DEEP THOUGHT immediately attacks the head of White's central pawn
chain.

6 f4 Nh6 7 Ngf3

This move was criticized by the spectators and by DEEP THOUGHT, all of
whom considered 7 Ndf3 to be best, followed by Bd3 and Ne2. After the
move played, Karpov's knight does not have a great future.

7 . . . O-O 8 Be2 f×e5 9 f×e5 c5 10 Nb3

If 10 d×c5, then 10 . . . Ng4 gives Black an active game.

10 . . . c×d4 11 c×d4 Nc6 12 O-O Qb6 13 Kh1 a5 14 a4 Bf5 15 Bg5 Be4 16 Nc5

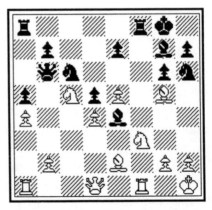

Figure 8.29. Position after 16 Nc5.

16 . . . Q×b2

DEEP THOUGHT could not restrain itself from snitching a pawn.

17 N×e4 d×e4 18 Rb1 Qa3

If 18 . . . Qc3, then 19 Rb3, traps the queen. Also bad is 18 . . . Qa2 because 19 Nd2 eventually wins the pawn on e4.

19 Bc1 Qc3 20 Bd2 Qa3 21 Bc1 Qc3

Karpov repeated moves to gain time on the clock.

22 Rb3 Qa1 23 Bc4+ Kh8 24 B×h6 Q×d1 25 B×g7+ K×g7 26 R×d1 e×f3 27 g×f3

Karpov could have tried for more with 27 R×b7, putting the rook on the seventh rank. The computer's next move prevented that idea.

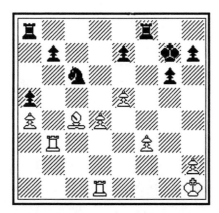

Figure 8.30. Position after 27 g×f3.

27 . . . Ra7

Although the spectators criticized this move, Karpov said after the game that it was the program's only chance.

28 Bd5 Rd8 29 Rb5 Ra6 30 Bc4 Ra7 31 Bd5 Ra6 32 Rc5

Karpov avoided a draw by repetition.

32 . . . Rd7 33 Kg2 Rb6 34 B×c6 b×c6 35 Kf2

If 35 R×a5, Black can equalize with 35 . . . Rb4.

35 ... Rd5 36 R×d5 c×d5 37 Rc1 Rb4 38 Ke3 R×a4

38 ... Rb3+ 39 Ke2 Rb4 forces White to accept a draw. Otherwise he must give up his pawn on e4, which he cannot afford to do.

39 Rc5 e6 40 Rc7+ Kg8 41 Re7 Ra3+ 42 Kf4 Rd3 43 R×e6 R×d4+ 44 Kg5 Kf7 45 Ra6

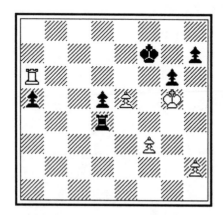

Figure 8.31. Position after 45 Ra6.

45 ... a4

DEEP THOUGHT could have forced a draw by 45 ... h6+ 46 K×h6 Rh4+ 47 Kg5 Rh5+ 48 Kf4 Rf5+ followed by 49 ... R×e5, but the program thought that having the distant passed a-pawn as well as an extra pawn gave it an advantage, and so 45 ... a4 was a winning try!

46 f4 h6+ 47 Kg4 Rc4

Again, DEEP THOUGHT could have drawn with 47 ... g5, because it forces the exchange of pawns. Karpov was now able to mobilize his king-side pawns.

48 h4 Rd4 49 Rf6+ Kg7 50 Ra6 Kf7 51 h5

Karpov passed on a draw with this move, showing he felt he had winning possibilities and could take the draw later if necessary.

51 ... g×h5

A better drawing try was 51 ... g5, though Karpov believed that he would still have winning chances.

52 Kf5 Kg7 53 Ra7+ Kf8

White has forced Black's king to the side of the board and placed his own in the middle of the board. His rook has just enough time to catch Black's passed pawns.

54 e6 Re4 55 Rd7 Rc4 56 R×d5 h4 57 Rd3 Ke7 58 Rd7+ Kf8 59 Rh7 h5 60 Ke5 h3 61 f5 Kg8 62 R×h5 a3 63 R×h3 a2

63 ... Ra4 would not save the game: 64 e7 Kf7 65 Rh7+ and 66 f6 etc.

64 Ra3 Rc5+ 65 Kf6 Black resigns.

The most impressive game by a computer to date. DEEP THOUGHT outplayed Karpov in the opening and early middle game, and had many opportunities to force a draw in the endgame.

February 1990: Germany

DEEP THOUGHT played a two-game match with German international grandmaster Helmut Pfleger drawing both games. The first game is presented here.

February 1990, Germany
Game 1, Exhibition match
with international grandmaster Helmut Pfleger
White: Helmut Pfleger   Black: DEEP THOUGHT
Time Control: 40/2, 20/1 thereafter
English Opening

1 c4 e5 2 Nc3 d6 3 g3 g6 4 Bg2 Bg7 5 Nf3 f5 6 d3 Nf6 7 O-O O-O 8 Rb1 a5 9 a3 Nh5
10 Bg5 Nf6 11 Qd2 Nc6 12 b4 a×b4 13 a×b4 Be6 14 b5 Ne7 15 Ra1 Qc8
16 R×a8 Q×a8 17 Ne1 c6 18 Nc2 Qe8 19 Rb1 Qd7 20 Na4 Qc7 21 b×c6 b×c6
22 Qb4 h6 23 Bd2 Nd7 24 Qb7 Rc8 25 Q×c7 R×c7 26 f4 Ra7 27 Nc3 e×f4
28 g×f4 Rc7 29 Nd1 d5 30 c×d5 c×d5 31 Nb4 d4 32 Kf2 Bf6 33 Rc1 R×c1
34 B×c1 Nb6 35 Nb2 Bh4+ 36 Kf1 Kg7 37 Bd2 Bf6 38 Na6 Ned5 39 Nc5 Bf7
40 Nca4 N×a4 41 N×a4 Ne3+ 42 B×e3 d×e3 43 Nb6 Bd4 44 Nc4 B×c4 45 d×c4 Bc5
46 Bd5 Bd6 47 c5 B×c5 48 Kg2 g5 49 f×g5 h×g5 50 h3 Drawn by agreement.

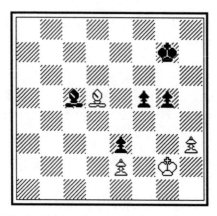

Figure 8.32. Position after 50 h3 Drawn by agreement.

November 11–14, 1990: New York

At the twenty-first ACM North American Computer Chess Championship in New York, the IBM team returned to an earlier version, DEEP THOUGHT/88—the version used at the ACM tournament in 1988—for this event. Anantharaman had left the team to accept a position with an investment firm in Connecticut, and was effectively replaced by Joe Hoane. Hoane was primarily concerned with the parallel search algorithm. The team had also enjoined Jerry Brody to provide technical support. They were hard at work on the new version and not particularly interested in this competition. DEEP THOUGHT/88 was weaker than the program that was used against the K's (Kasparov and Karpov, that is) approximately a year ago, and it could only tie for first place with MEPHISTO, losing to HITECH in the final round.

November 14, 1990, New York
Round 4, twenty-first North America Computer Chess Championship
White: HITECH   *Black:* DEEP THOUGHT/88
Time Control: All/2
Sicilian Defense

1 e4 c5 2 Nf3 Nc6 3 Bb5 g6 4 O-O Bg7 5 c3 Nf6 6 Re1 O-O 7 d4 c×d4 8 c×d4 d5
9 e5 Ne4 10 Nc3 N×c3 11 b×c3 Bg4 12 h3 Bf5 13 B×c6 b×c6 14 Ba3 Rb8 15 Bc5 Qc7

16 Qc1 Rb7 17 Nh4 Be4 18 Qe3 Rfb8 19 f3 Bc2 20 Rec1 Ba4 21 f4 Bb5
22 f5 Kh8 23 e6 Bf6 24 e×f7 Kg7 25 Nf3 g×f5 26 Re1 K×f7 27 Qh6 Qg3
28 Q×h7+ Ke8 29 Q×f5 Qg7 30 Re6 Bc4 31 R×c6 Kd8 32 Bd6 Bb5 33 Ne5 B×e5
34 B×e5 Q×e5 35 Q×e5 B×c6 36 Qe6 Rb1+ 37 R×b1 R×b1+ 38 Kh2 Rb6
39 g4 Bb7 40 Qg8+ Kc7 41 Qf7 Bc6 42 Q×e7+ Bd7 43 Qc5+ Rc6 44 Q×d5 Re6
45 Kg3 Re1 46 c4 Re2 47 Qa5+ Kb7 48 Qb4+ Kc8 49 Qa3 Kb8 50 d5 Re4 51 c5 B×g4
Black resigns.

May 1991: Hanover, Germany

The new DEEP THOUGHT II appeared at the CeBIT computer fair in Hanover for the first time. The new version used twenty-two custom chess processors, according to Frederic Friedel, who was involved in the organization of the event. IBM Germany put on the tournament featuring seven grandmasters and DEEP THOUGHT II. This was the strongest tournament that ever had a computer participant, with the average rating of DEEP THOUGHT II's seven opponents exceeding 2500. DEEP THOUGHT II's best performance was against international grandmaster Uwe Bonsch in round 4.

May 1991, Hanover, Germany
Round 4, Hanover grandmaster event
White: DEEP THOUGHT II   Black: Uwe Bonsch
Time Control: 40/2, 20/1 thereafter
Queen's Gambit Declined

---

1 d4 Nf6 2 c4 e6 3 Nc3 d5 4 Bg5 Be7 5 Nf3 h6 6 B×f6 B×f6 7 e3 O-O
8 Qd2 a6 9 Be2 Nc6 10 O-O d×c4 11 B×c4 e5 12 d5 Ne7 13 Ne4 Nf5
14 Qc3 Re8 15 Bb3 Nd6 16 N×f6+ Q×f6 17 Q×c7 Bg4 18 Nd2 Rac8 19 Qb6 e4
20 Rab1 Qg6 21 Kh1 Be2 22 Rfe1 Bd3 23 Rbd1 Re5 24 f4 Rh5 25 Kg1 Rh4
26 Nb1 B×b1 27 R×b1 Rg4 28 Re2 Qf6 29 Bd1 Rg6 30 Rc2 R×c2 31 B×c2 Qf5
32 Qd4 Qg4 33 g3 h5 34 B×e4 f5 35 Bd3 h4 36 Kg2 Ne4 37 Qc4

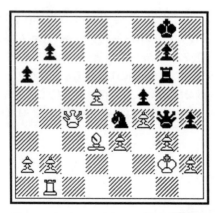

Figure 8.33. Position after 37 Qc4.

37 ... N×g3

Black can win with 37 ... h3+. If 38 Kf1, then 38 ... Nd2+ winning a queen for a knight. Otherwise if 38 Kg1, then Black mates in four with 38 ... Qf3 39 Bf1 R×g3+ 40 h×g3 Qf2+ 41 Kh1 N×g3#.

38 h3 Qh5 39 Kf2 Kh7 40 Qb4 a5 41 Qe7 Qh6 42 Q3b7 Rd6 43 Qb5 Qg6 44 Qc5 Rb6
45 b3 Nh11 46 Ke1 Rf6 47 Q3a5 Qg2 48 Qc5 Ng3 49 d6 Ne4 50 B3e4 Q3e4
51 Rc1 Rg6 52 Kd2 Rg21 53 Kc3 Re2 54 d7 R3e31 55 Kb2 Rd3 56 Qf2 Qe7
57 Rc7 R3h3 58 Qd2 Qf61 59 Kb1 Rh11 60 Kc2 Qa1 61 d8Q Q3a21 62 Kc3 Qa51 63
Kc4 Qa61 64 Kc5 Qa31 65 b4 Rc11 66 Kb5 Black resigns.

Kasparov came to the event and put on a simultaneous exhibition on the final day. In addition, Friedel had prepared a test for the champion. Friedel had not permitted Kasparov to see any of the twenty games that were played during the tournament. Then he gave Kasparov the games from each round— one round at a time—and asked him to identify DEEP THOUGHT II. Kasparov correctly identified the computer in two of its five games, and actually picked Bonsch as the computer in the fourth round game presented above. Kasparov was given thirty minutes for the test, or ninety seconds per game.

August 28, 1991: Sydney

The twelfth International Joint Conference on Artificial Intelligence (IJCAI) was held in Sydney, Australia, on August 24–30, 1991. It brought together many of the leaders in the world of AI, and as a special event, DEEP THOUGHT II took on Australia's number-two-ranked player, international master Darryl Johansen, in a two-game match. Each game was played at a speed of all moves in one hour for each side. Johansen had defeated Deep Thought eighteen months earlier. This time, Deep Thought II was running on an IBM RS/6000 with twenty-four custom chess processors, searching six to seven million positions per second.

August 28, 1991, Sydney
Game 1, IJCAI exhibition match
with international grandmaster Darryl Johansen
White: Deep Thought II   Black: Darryl Johansen
Time Control: All/1
Franco-Benoni Defense

1 d4 e6 2 Nf3 c5 3 e3 b6 4 d5

Johansen wanted to take Deep Thought II out of book with 3 . . . b6. He was surprised with 4 d5 because it forces the computer to prematurely get its queen into the fray.

4 . . . e×d5 5 Q×d5 Nc6 6 Bc4 Qe7

The correct move here is 6 . . . Qf6, giving support to the knight on c6.

7 Ne5 Q×e5 8 Q×f7+ Kd8 9 Q×f8+ Kc7 10 Nc3 Nce7 11 Qf3 Kb8 12 e4

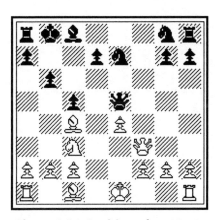

Figure 8.34. Position after 12 e4.

White has a commanding lead at this point as a result of Black's weak sixth move.

12 . . . Ng6 13 h4 h5 14 Bg5 N8e7 15 Rd1 a6 16 Qe3 Rf8 17 Be2 Nf4 18 Bf3 Nc6
19 g3 Ne6 20 B×h5 Ncd4 21 Kd2 N×g5 22 h×g5 Bb7 23 f4 Qe6 24 Rh4

At first this looks quite strange, but it will give White the option of doubling rooks on the h-file; it will also make Bg4 playable.

24 . . . Ka7 25 Bg4 Qf7 26 Rdh1 d6 27 Rh7 b5

Black tries storming White with a pawn attack on the king, but it is not enough.

28 Kc1 b4 29 Nd5 B×d5 30 e×d5 Rae8 31 Qd3 Q×d5 32 c3 b×c3 33 b×c3 Nb3+
34 Kc2 Qg2+ 35 Kb1 Qe4 36 R×g7+ Kb6 37 Rd1 Q×d3+ 38 R×d3 Re1+ 39 Kc2 Na5
40 R×d6+ Kb5 41 a4+ K×a4 42 Bd7+ Ka3 43 R×a6 Re2+ 44 Kd3 Black resigns.

August 28, 1991, Sydney
Game 2, IJCAI exhibition match
with international master Darryl Johansen
White: Darryl Johansen   Black: DEEP THOUGHT II
Time Control: All/1
English Opening

———————

1 e3 e5 2 c4 Nf6 3 Nc3 Bb4 4 Nge2 O-O 5 a3 Be7 6 d4 d6 7 d5 c6 8 Ng3 Bg4 9 f3

White's 9 f3 shows that Black's previous move 8 . . . Bg4 was an error, wasting a tempo while simultaneously allowing White to strengthen its center pawns.

9 . . . Bd7 10 Be2 c×d5 11 c×d5 Be8 12 O-O Nbd7 13 Kh1 Rc8 14 e4 a6 15 Be3 Kh8

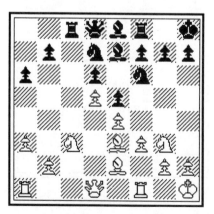

Figure 8.35. Position after 15 . . . Kh8.

Black is hopelessly cramped, and matters get only worse.

16 Rc1 h6 17 Nf5 Nc5 18 b4 Ncd7 19 a4 Ng8 20 a5 Ngf6 21 Qd2 Rg8 22 Na4 Bf8
23 Nb6 N×b6 24 B×b6 Qd7 25 R×c8 Q×c8 26 Rc1 Qa8 27 Bc7 Nh5 28 N×d6 B×d6
29 B×d6 f6 30 Qe3 Ba4 31 g3 Rc8 32 Bc7 Be8 33 Qb6 Bf7 34 b5 a×b5 35 B×b5 Be8
36 d6 B×b5 37 Q×b5 Black resigns

November 17–20, 1991: Albuquerque

DEEP THOUGHT II came to the twenty-second ACM International Computer
Chess Championship running on the same system it did in Australia. It won
all five games, including victories over ZARKOV, HITECH, CRAY BLITZ,
MCHESS, and CHESS MACHINE/SCHRODER. At last year's ACM championship, HITECH had defeated DEEP THOUGHT/88 after having lost the three
previous encounters. Of course, last year it was DEEP THOUGHT/88 that participated, while this year it was a new, stronger DEEP THOUGHT II that was
entered. This year's contest figured to be an exciting battle, but it turned out
that apparently an error in HITECH's opening book led to its downfall.

November 18, 1991
Round 3, twenty-second ACM International
Computer Chess Championship
White: DEEP THOUGHT II   Black: HITECH
Time Control: 40/2, 20/1 thereafter
French Defense

---

1 e4 e6 2 d4 d5 3 Nd2 c5 4 e×d5 e×d5 5 Ngf3 Nf6 6 Bb5+ Bd7 7 B×d7+ Nb×d7
8 O-O Be7 9 d×c5 N×c5 10 Nb3 O-O 11 N×c5 B×c5 12 Bg5

Figure 8.36. Position after 12 Bg5.

12 ... d4 13 Qd3 h6 14 Bh4 Rc8 15 Rfd1 Re8 16 Qf5 Qb6 17 B×f6 Q×f6
18 Q×f6 g×f6

Black's pawns are a real liability and will ultimately spell defeat.

19 Kf1 f5 20 Rac1 Rcd8 21 Rd3 Rd6 22 a3 a5 23 Rb3 b6 24 Ne1 Rc6 25 Rb5 Kg7
26 Nf3 Rd8 27 Ne5 Rc7 28 Nd3 a4 29 Re1 Bf8 30 Re2 Bc5 31 g3 Rdc8 32 Re5 Kf6
33 Rd5 Re7 34 c3

Black cannot take the pawn offering without getting into more difficulties.

34 ... Re4 35 c×d4 R×d4 36 R×d4 B×d4 37 Rb4 Rd8 38 R×a4 Ke6 39 Rb4 Kd5
40 a4 Ra8 41 b3 Ra5 42 Ke2 b5 43 R×b5+ R×b5 44 a×b5 Bb6

The remainder of the game is nicely played by White.

45 h4 Bc7 46 h5 Ba5 47 f4 f6 48 Nb2 Bb4 49 Nc4 Bc5 50 Kf3 Bf8 51 Ne3+ Kc5
52 N×f5 K×b5 53 Ke4 Kc5 54 Ne3 Kb4 55 Kf5 Black resigns.

In the spring of 1992, Chung-Jen Tan took over the supervision of the
chess project from Randy Moulic. The composition of the team has remained the same since then. Later that year, the seventh World Computer
Chess Championship was held in Madrid, Spain, and the IBM team passed
it up. Again, they were hard at work on their new version and had nothing
new to offer and little to gain by winning. They had only one concern and
that was to complete their new system. In February of 1993, the ACM
hosted the twenty-third ACM International Computer Chess Championship in Indianapolis, and again there was no entry from IBM.

February 24–28, 1993: Copenhagen

Bent Larsen and the Danish national team challenged the IBM computer to
two separate matches that took place during the same few days. In one
match Larsen would take on the computer, and in the other the Danish national team would take it on. Each match was four games, but the fourth
Larsen game would count in both matches, so actually only seven games
were played. The IBM computer was called NORDIC DEEP BLUE for the
match, essentially what was subsequently called DEEP BLUE PROTOTYPE. It
was a DEEP BLUE simulation running on the DEEP THOUGHT II hardware, an
RS/6000 550 workstation connected to fourteen VLSI chess processors.
The system searched, according to Hsu, four to five million chess positions
per second. Larsen won his match with a score of 2.5–1.5, and the other

match went to NORDIC DEEP BLUE 2.5-1.5. The fourth Larsen versus NORDIC DEEP BLUE game was drawn, and that game was included in both matches.

This was the first event in which the name DEEP BLUE was attached to the IBM effort. It was determined by an in-house naming contest.

February 24, 1993, Copenhagen
Game 1, Larsen match
White: Bent Larsen   Black: NORDIC BLUE PROTOTYPE
Time Control: 40/2, 20/1 thereafter
Four Knights Opening

---

1 e4 e5 2 Nf3 Nc6 3 Nc3 Nf6 4 Bb5 Bb4 5 O-O O-O 6 B×c6 d×c6 7 d3 Qe7 8 Ne2 Bg4
9 Ng3 Nh5 10 h3 N×g3 11 f×g3 Bc5+ 12 Kh2 Bc8 13 g4 Be6 14 Qe2 f6 15 Be3 B×e3
16 Q×e3 h6 17 a4 Qb4 18 b3 b6 19 Rf2 c5 20 Kg3 Qa5 21 h4 Qc3 22 Raf1 Rad8 23 g5

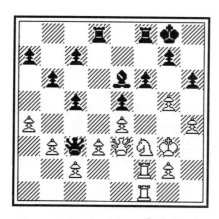

Figure 8.37. Position after 23 g5.

Black, trying to find some counterplay, proposes a sacrifice that comes up short.

23 . . . B×b3 24 c×b3 R×d3 25 Qe2 h×g5 26 h×g5 f×g5 27 Rd1 Re3 28 Qb2 Q×b3
29 Q×b3+ R×b3 30 Rd5 Ra3 31 R×e5 g4 32 K×g4 c4 33 Rd2 R×a4 34 Rd7 Rc8
35 Ng5 Ra2 36 R×c7 Ra8 37 g3 Rf2 38 Ree7 Kh8 39 R×g7 Rh2 40 e5 Rd8
41 Rh7+ R×h7 42 N×h7 Rg8+ 43 Ng5 Black resigns.

February 28, 1993, Copenhagen
Game 4, Larsen match and match with Danish national team
White: NORDIC BLUE PROTOTYPE   Black: Bent Larsen
Time Control: 40/2, 20/1 thereafter
Sicilian Defense

1 e4 c5 2 Nf3 d6 3 d4 c×d4 4 N×d4 Nf6 5 Nc3 a6 6 a4 g6 7 Be2 Bg7 8 O-O O-O
9 f4 Nc6 10 Be3 Bd7 11 Nb3 Be6 12 Ra3 Rc8 13 Kh1 Re8 14 f5 B×b3 15 R×b3 Qd7
16 f×g6 h×g6 17 Nd5 N×d5 18 e×d5 Ne5 19 a5 Bf6 20 c3 Kg7 21 Rb4 Rh8
22 Qb3 Rc7 23 Bb6 Rcc8 24 Kg1 Rh4 25 Bd4 Rc7 26 B×e5 d×e5 27 R×h4 B×h4
28 R×f7+ K×f7 29 d6+ Kg7 30 d×c7 Q×c7 31 Qb4 Bg5 32 Bf3 b5 33 a×b6 Be3+
34 Kh1 B×b6 35 Qe4 Qc5 36 Qb1 a5 37 Be4 g5 38 Bh7 Kf8 39 Bf5 Qf2 40 Bg6 Kg7
41 Bh7 Kh8 42 Bf5 Kg7 43 Bd3 Be3 44 Bh7 Kh8 45 b3 Bd2 46 c4 Be3 47 Bg6 Bd4
48 Bf5 Bc5 49 Be4 Be3 50 Qd1 Kg7 51 Qa1 Bd4 52 Qc1 Drawn by agreement.

April 20, 1993: New York University, New York

The New York University Chess Club hosted a one-game match between
the new DEEP BLUE PROTOTYPE and international grandmaster Michael
Rohde. DEEP BLUE PROTOTYPE ran on a sixteen-processor system.

April 20, 1993, New York University
The DEEP BLUE Challenge
White: DEEP BLUE PROTOTYPE   Black: Michael Rohde
Time Control: 40/2, 20/1 thereafter
Sicilian Defense, Taimanov Variation

1 e4 c5 2 Nf3 Nc6 3 d4 c×d4 4 N×d4 Qc7

Characterizing the Taimanov Variation.

5 Nc3 e6 6 Be2 a6 7 O-O Nf6 8 Be3 Bb4 9 Na4 O-O 10 N×c6 b×c6 11 Nb6 Rb8
12 N×c8 Rf×c8 13 B×a6 Rf8 14 Bd3 Bd6 15 f4 e5

To here, Mark Ginsburg, an international master and one of the commentators of the match, notes that the game followed standard lines.

16 b3 e×f4 17 Bd4 Be5 18 B×e5 Q×e5 19 Qf3 d5 20 e×d5 N×d5 21 Qe4 Qh5
22 Rae1 g6 23 Bc4 Rbc8 24 a4 g5 25 B×d5 c×d5 26 Q×d5 R×c2 27 R×f4 Qg6

28 Rd4 Rfc8 29 a5 R8c5 30 Qd8+ Kg7 31 b4 Rf5 32 Rd2 Qc6 33 Qd4+ Kg6 34 Rb1 f6
35 R×c2 Q×c2 36 Qb2 Qd3 37 Ra1 Qe3+ 38 Kh1 Rf2 39 Qb1+ Kh6 40 Qg1 Qd2
41 a6 Qb2 42 a7 R×g2 43 a8Q R×g1+ 44 R×g1 Q×b4 45 Rf1 Kg7 46 Qd5 h6 47 Qd7+

The computer announced mate in eight.

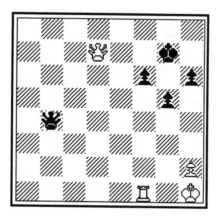

Figure 8.38. Position after 47 Qd7+.

47 ... Kg8 48 Qe6+ Kh7 49 Qf7+ Black resigns.

August 20, 1993: Yorktown Heights, New York

The following two games were played at IBM's T. J. Watson Research Center in Yorktown Heights, New York, on August 20, 1993. They were played at a speed of all moves in thirty minutes per player per game. IBM had invited international grandmaster Judit Polgar, rated 2630 by FIDE, to their world-famous research center for the encounter. Judit arrived in a Rolls Royce with her mother, Klara, and the Hungarian consul general and his wife.

♚

August 20, 1993, T. J. Watson Research Center, IBM
Game 1, Exhibition match with international grandmaster Judit Polgar
White: Deep Blue Prototype   Black: Judit Polgar
Time Control: All/30 minutes
Sicilian Defense

1 e4 c5 2 Nf3 e6 3 d4 c×d4 4 N×d4 Nc6 5 Nc3 Qc7 6 Be2 a6 7 O-O Bb4 8 N×c6 b×c6
9 Qd4 Bd6 10 Q×g7 B×h2+ 11 Kh1 Be5 12 Bf4 B×g7 13 B×c7 d5 14 Rad1 Ne7

15 Na4 Ra7 16 Bb6 Ra8 17 c3 Ng6 18 Bc7 Ra7 19 Bb8 Rb7 20 Bg3 O-O 21 e×d5 c×d5
22 Rfe1 f5 23 Bd6 Rd8 24 Ba3 Rc7 25 Bb4 Rc6 26 Ba5 Rf8 27 Bb6 Rf7 28 Kg1 Bf8
29 b3 Bb7 30 Bh5 Re7 31 Kf1 Kf7 32 c4 Rc8 33 Ba5 d×c4 34 Nb6 Rb8

Figure 8.39. Position after 34 . . . Rb8.

35 Nd7 Rc8 36 Bb4 c×b3 37 N×f8 R×f8 38 a×b3 Rb8 39 B×e7 K×e7 40 Rd4 a5
41 Ra4 Bc6 42 R×a5 R×b3 43 Ra7+ Kf6 44 R×h7 Nf4 45 g3 Bb5+ 46 Kg1 Nh3+
47 Kg2 Ng5 48 Rh6+ Ke7 49 Re5 Bc6+ 50 Kf1 Rb1+ 51 Re1 Rb2 52 Be2 Ne4
53 Rd1 Bd5 54 Rc1 Nd2+ 55 Ke1 Ne4 56 Ra1 Nc3 57 Bd3 Na2 58 Kf1 Nb4

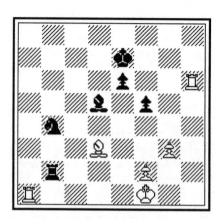

Figure 8.40. Position after 58 . . . Nb4.

Hsu, in his write-up of this match in the *ICCA Journal,* asks the readers: "What is White's shot here?"

59 B×f5 Nc6 60 Rd1 Bc4+ 61 Bd3 Bb3 62 Rb1 R×b1 63 B×b1 Bd5 64 Rh7+ Kf6
65 Rh4 Ne5 66 Ke2 Bf3+ 67 Ke3 Bc6 68 f4 Nf7 69 g4 e5 70 g5+ Kg7 71 Rh7+ Kg8
72 g6 e×f4 73 K×f4 Black resigns

August 20, 1993, T. J. Watson Research Center, IBM
Game 2, Exhibition match with international grandmaster Judit Polgar
White: Judit Polgar   Black: DEEP BLUE PROTOTYPE
Time Control: All/30 minutes
Reti Opening

1 Nf3 Nf6 2 g3 d5 3 d3 Nbd7 4 Nbd2 e5 5 Bg2 c6 6 O-O Bd6 7 Nh4 O-O 8 e4 Nc5
9 Re1 Bg4 10 f3 Be6 11 Nf1 Qb6 12 Kh1 d×e4 13 d×e4 Rfd8 14 Qe2 Na4 15 g4 Bc5
16 Ne3 Bd4

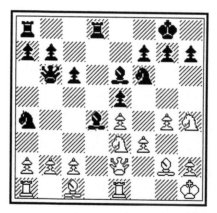

Figure 8.41. Position after 16 . . . Bd4.

17 c3 N×c3 18 b×c3 B×c3 19 Nc2 Qa5 20 Bg5 h6 21 Be3 b6 22 Nf5 Qa4 23 g5 h×g5
24 B×g5 B×e1 25 R×e1 B×f5 26 e×f5 Rd6 27 Ne3 Re8 28 Rg1 Nh7 29 Bf1 N×g5
30 R×g5 Qf4 31 Rg4 Qh6 32 Rg1 Kf8 33 Qe1 Rd4 34 Bg2 Qf4 35 Ng4 Q×f5
36 Qh4 Qg6 37 Qh8+ Ke7 38 Qh4+ Kd6 39 Qf2 c5 40 Ne3 Kc7 41 f4 e×f4
42 Nd5+ Kd8 43 Nc3 Qd3 44 Qb2 Re3 45 Nb5 Rb4 46 Q×g7 Q×b5 47 Qf6+ Kc7
48 Q×f7+ Qd7 49 Qf8

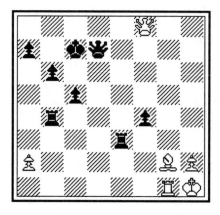

Figure 8.42. Position after 49 Qf8.

49 ... Ra4 50 Qa8 R×a2 51 Qb7+ Kd8 52 Qb8+ Ke7 53 Q×f4 Qd4 54 Qc7+ Kf6
55 Rf1+ Kg5 56 Qf7 Ra1 57 Qf5+ Kh6 58 Qf8+ Kh5 59 Qf5+ Kh4 60 Qh7+ Kg5
61 Qf5+ Drawn by agreement

Hsu observed that "17 c3 might be questionable, although White does
have some compensation for the material deficit. At move 49, the machine
had a completely winning position, but 49 ... Ra4? gave Judit some
counter-chances and 50 ... R×a2?? surrendered the win. It needed ten seconds of thinking time, which it did not have, to avoid the draw."

May 1994: Munich, Germany

The following game was played in the Intel World Chess Express Challenge tournament in Munich in May 1994. At this event FRITZ 3 was allowed five minutes per game for all of its moves; the seventeen grandmasters each had six minutes. But the grandmasters had to play the program
from a computer screen, using a mouse to make their moves. The result of
the round-robin tournament was a phenomenon! FRITZ 3 shared first
place with Garry Kasparov with a score of 12.5/17, ahead of sixteen top-
class grandmasters. In the playoff that followed Kasparov scored a con-
vincing victory. Kasparov's loss to FRITZ 3 follows. The world champion
erred on 35 ... e4 but nevertheless had the advantage when he lost on
time.

May 1994, Munich
Intel World Chess Express Challenge
White: FRITZ 3   Black: Garry Kasparov
Time Control: All/5 minutes for FRITZ 3
All/6 minutes for the human
Irregular Opening

1 e3 d5 2 c4 d×c4 3 B×c4 e5 4 d4 e×d4 5 e×d4 Bb4+ 6 Nc3 Nf6 7 Nf3 O-O 8 O-O Bg4
9 h3 Bh5 10 g4 Bg6 11 Ne5 Nc6 12 Be3 N×e5 13 d×e5 Nd7 14 f4 Nb6 15 Bb3 Bd3

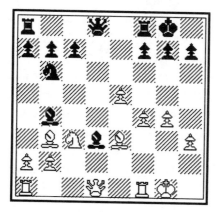

Figure 8.43. Position after 15 . . . Bd3.

16 Qf3 B×f1 17 R×f1 c6 18 f5 Qe7 19 f6 Q×e5 20 f×g7 K×g7 21 Ne4 Nd5
22 B×d5 c×d5 23 Ng3 Kg8 24 Nf5 Rac8 25 Qf2 Rc4 26 Nh6+ Kh8 27 B×a7 f6
28 Nf5 Re8 29 a3 Be1

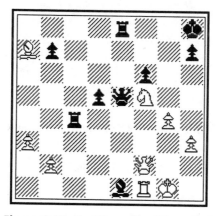

Figure 8.44. Position after 29 . . . Be1.

30 Qg2 Re4 31 Nh6 Re7 32 Rf5 Re2 33 R×e5 R×g2+ 34 K×g2 f×e5 35 Bb8 e4
36 Be5+ R×e5 37 Nf7+ Kg7 38 N×e5 Bd2 39 Kf1 Bc1 40 b3 B×a3 41 g5 d4
42 Ke2 d3+ 43 Kd2 Bd6 44 Nc4 Bf4+ 45 Kc3 b5 White wins on time.

June 25–27 1994: Cape May, New Jersey

DEEP BLUE PROTOTYPE participated in the twenty-fourth ACM International Computer Chess Championship at Cape May, New Jersey, June 25–27, 1994. It won its first-round game against John Stanback's ZARKOV, but a summer thunderstorm in Yorktown Heights caused the program to default its second-round game. In the third round, it defeated David Kittinger's WCHESS and then played the crucial game of the tournament in the next round against STAR SOCRATES. STAR SOCRATES played 8 O-O-O and found itself on the defensive shortly thereafter. On move 40, STAR SOCRATES went down an exchange, and with DEEP BLUE PROTOTYPE keeping up the pressure, resigned twenty-one moves later. At the end of four rounds, DEEP BLUE PROTOTYPE and STAR SOCRATES each had three points. In the final round DEEP BLUE PROTOTYPE defeated Marty Hirsch's MCHESS, while STAR SOCRATES was defeated by ZARKOV. Thus, despite forfeiting its second-round game, DEEP BLUE PROTOTYPE won the five-round event with a 4-1 score. The DEEP BLUE PROTOTYPE team was delighted to have won the event outright.

June 26, 1994, Cape May
Round 4, twenty-fourth ACM International
Computer Chess Championship
White: STAR SOCRATES   Black: DEEP BLUE PROTOTYPE
Time Control: 40/2, 20/1 thereafter
Sicilian Defense

1 e4 c5 2 Nc3 Nc6 3 Nge2 Nf6 4 d4 c×d4 5 N×d4 d6 6 Bg5 e6 7 Qd2 a6
8 O-O-O h6 9 Bf4 Bd7 10 N×c6 B×c6 11 f3 d5 12 Qe1 Bb4 13 a3 Ba5
14 Bd2 O-O 15 e×d5 e×d5 16 Bd3 Re8 17 Qh4 d4 18 Na2 B×d2+ 19 R×d2 a5
20 Bc4

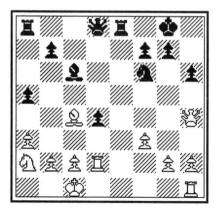

Figure 8.45. Position after 20 Bc4.

20 . . . b5 21 R×d4

Playing 21 Bb3 keeps White in the game. If 21 . . . a4, then 22 Nb4 gives White better chances than the line played.

21 . . . Qe7 22 Bf1 Qe3+ 23 Rd2 b4 24 Qd4 b×a3 25 Q×e3 a×b2+ 26 K×b2 R×e3 27 Rd6 Rb8+ 28 Kc1 Ra3 29 R×c6 R×a2 30 g3 Ra1+ 31 Kd2 a4 32 Bg2 Rd8+ 33 Ke2 R×h1 34 B×h1 Ra8 35 Rb6

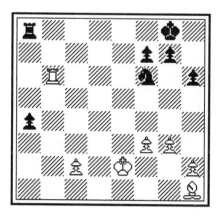

Figure 8.46. Position after 35 Rb6.

Black plays perfectly from here to the end. Its passed a-pawn is pushed until White gives up its rook for it and the knight. Black then forces a passed h-pawn and repeats a similar scenario on the king-side.

213

35 ... Nd5 36 Rd6 Nc3+ 37 Kd3 a3 38 K×c3 a2 39 Rd1 a1Q+ 40 R×a1 R×a1
41 Bg2 Rg1 42 Bh3 Rh1 43 Bc8 R×h2 44 g4 Rf2 45 Bb7 g6 46 Kd3 h5 47 g×h5 g×h5
48 Be4 h4 49 Ke3 Rg2 50 Bf5 Rg5 51 Bh3 Rg3 52 Bf1 h3 53 Kf2 h2 54 Bg2 Rg7 55 f4 f5
56 Kf3 Kf7 57 Kf2 Rg4 58 Kf3 Ke7 59 Kf2 Rg8 60 Kf1 Kd6 61 Kf2 White resigns.

August 31, 1994: London

On August 31, 1994, chess history was written when Richard Lang's PEN-
TIUM CHESS GENIUS defeated Garry Kasparov in the Intel Rapid Chess Tournament in London. The games were played at a speed of all moves in twenty-
five minutes per player per game. This event was a knockout tournament
involving many of the world's top grandmasters. Lang's program was paired
against the world champion in the first round, and by winning the match 1.5-
0.5 the program knocked Kasparov out of the tournament. In the second
round, the program scored another dramatic victory, winning both games
against international grandmaster Predrag Nikolic, from Bosnia. It was only in
the semifinal round that the program was to meet its match—the cool Vish-
wananthan Anand of India, who strategically outplayed it for a 2-0 victory.

August 31, 1994, London
Game 1, Intel Speed Chess Grand Prix
White: Garry Kasparov   Black: PENTIUM CHESS GENIUS
Time Control: All/25 minutes
English Opening

1 c4 c6 2 d4 d5 3 Nf3 Nf6 4 Qc2 d×c4 5 Q×c4 Bf5 6 Nc3 Nbd7 7 g3 e6 8 Bg2 Be7
9 O-O O-O 10 e3 Ne4 11 Qe2 Qb6 12 Rd1 Rad8 13 Ne1 Ndf6 14 N×e4 N×e4

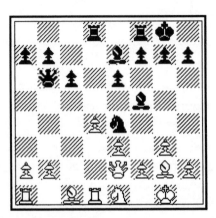

Figure 8.47. Position after 14 ... N×e4.

15 f3 Nd6 16 a4 Qb3 17 e4 Bg6 18 Rd3 Qb4 19 b3 Nc8 20 Nc2 Qb6 21 Bf4 c5
22 Be3 c×d4 23 N×d4 Bc5 24 Rad1 e5 25 Nc2 R×d3 26 Q×d3 Ne7 27 b4 B×e3+
28 Q×e3 Rd8 29 R×d8+ Q×d8 30 Bf1 b6 31 Qc3 f6 32 Bc4+ Bf7 33 Ne3 Qd4
34 B×f7+ K×f7

Figure 8.48. Position after 34 . . . K×f7.

35 Qb3+ Kf8 36 Kg2 Qd2+ 37 Kh3 Qe2 38 Ng2 h5 39 Qe3 Qc4 40 Qd2 Qe6+
41 g4 h×g4+ 42 f×g4 Qc4 43 Qe1 Qb3+ 44 Ne3 Qd3 45 Kg3 Q×e4 46 Qd2 Qf4+
47 Kg2 Qd4 48 Q×d4 e×d4 49 Nc4 Nc6 50 b5 Ne5 51 Nd6 d3 52 Kf2 N×g4+
53 Ke1 N×h2 54 Kd2 Nf3+ 55 K×d3 Ke7 56 Nf5+ Kf7 57 Ke4 Nd2+ 58 Kd5 g5
59 Nd6+ Kg6 60 Kd4 Nb3+ White resigns.

By move 20, Kasparov had acquired a strong position, but exchanges over
the coming moves reduced his advantage. Frederic Friedel, when writing
this match up in the September 1994 *ICCA Journal,* noted that "Instead of
35 Qd4 with an easy draw he played 35 Qb3+? for a win. The resulting
position was one in which computers revel, and GENIUS had found all the
tactical resources it required."

Friedel noted that "The second game saw Kasparov, playing Black, sacrifice a pawn and then go on to entrap White positionally and gain a winning advantage. But the computer defended stubbornly and the inevitable
moment of inattention came. 55 . . . Qd4?? allows 56 Qb1 and the double
threat 57 g4 and 57 Q×b5, so that Black has lost the extra pawn for nothing. A horrified Kasparov submitted to a draw."

August 31, 1994, London
Game 2, Intel Speed Chess Grand Prix
White: PENTIUM CHESS GENIUS   Black: Garry Kasparov
Time Control: All/25 minutes
Queen's Gambit Opening

1 d4 Nf6 2 c4 e6 3 Nf3 b6 4 a3 Bb7 5 Nc3 d5 6 Bg5 Be7 7 e3 O-O 8 Bd3 Nbd7
9 c×d5 e×d5 10 O-O c5 11 Rc1 Ne4 12 Bf4 a6 13 Qc2 Ndf6 14 d×c5 B×c5
15 Rfd1 Qe8 16 b4 Be7 17 Be2 Rc8 18 Qb2 b5 19 Nd4 Nd6 20 Bd3 Nc4 21 Qb3 Nh5
22 Bf5 Ra8 23 Nde2 Nf6 24 Bg5 Rd8 25 Nf4

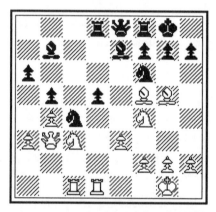

Figure 8.49. Position after 25 Nf4.

25 ... d4 26 e×d4 h6 27 B×f6 B×f6 28 Nce2 Be4 29 B×e4 Q×e4 30 Qg3 Rfe8
31 Qc3 Rd6 32 Re1 Red8 33 Rcd1 B×d4 34 N×d4 Q×f4 35 Ne2 Qe5
36 R×d6 R×d6 37 a4 Re6 38 Qc1 Qd6 39 a×b5 a×b5 40 Ng3 Q×b4
41 R×e6 f×e6 42 h3 Qc5 43 Nf1 Qd5 44 Qa1 Qe5 45 Qa7 Kh7 46 Qd7 Qd5
47 Qe7 Qd6 48 Qb7 Qd5 49 Qe7 Qe5 50 Qd7 Nd6 51 Ne3 Nf5 52 Qd3 Kg8
53 Qd8+ Kf7 54 Qd7+ Kg6 55 Qd3

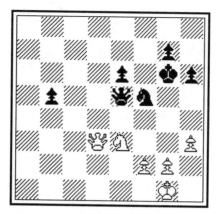

Figure 8.50. Position after 55 Qd3.

55 . . . Qd4 56 Qb1 Drawn by agreement.

The countdown to Philadelphia

In the weeks following Cape May, I had discussions with Chung-Jen Tan and the DEEP BLUE Team. They said that their new system was making good progress and would be ready soon. Plans for the next world championship were discussed, and IBM indicated it would be willing to sponsor the event if it were held in Hong Kong sometime in the spring of 1995. They hoped to introduce the new DEEP BLUE there. IBM was expanding its presence in the Far East, and in China in particular. They were planning to open a major research laboratory in Beijing in 1995. They thought the world championship in Hong Kong would draw some international attention to their efforts in that region. Omar Wing, dean of the faculty of engineering at the Chinese University of Hong Kong, had been a friend of Tan and mine for many years. He agreed to host the event at his university in one of the most beautiful settings in which a chess tournament was ever held.

In some sense, the countdown to Philadelphia actually began a long time ago. In 1967, I completed my graduate studies at the Ohio State University and accepted a position as an assistant professor at Columbia University in New York City. In my first week there I met Tan, who was then a doctoral student, and for the next several years we collaborated on research in the area of computer circuit design. We became good friends,

published a number of joint papers, ate many good Chinese meals, and discussed the raging bull-market run on the New York Stock Exchange. It was roaring then almost as it is now, and every graduate student was in close contact with his broker! Tan joined IBM shortly after receiving his Ph.D. in 1969 and has been one of their pioneers in the design of supercomputers ever since. In 1992 he was placed in charge of the DEEP BLUE computer chess project.

In my capacity as chairman of the ACM Computer Chess Committee, I discussed with Tan various possibilities for a match between DEEP BLUE and Kasparov. Such a match had been one of the goals of our committee for many years, and now it made some sense. DEEP BLUE looked as if it could turn in a respectable performance, and if their new version was ready and performed at design specifications, it could be a close match. We concluded it could be done in Philadelphia at the ACM Computing Week '96 if Kasparov would agree to come. As part of the festivities, the ACM was planning to celebrate the fiftieth birthday of the ENIAC computer, built at the University of Pennsylvania in 1946. Joe DeBlasi, executive director of the ACM and former IBMer, joined Tan and me in December of 1995, and we formed a three-man organizing committee. We approached David Levy as vice-president of the ICCA, feeling the event would benefit from being under the auspices of that organization. Further, Levy was on good terms with Kasparov's agent, Andrew Page, and thus the links connecting DEEP BLUE and the ACM and the ACM and Kasparov were established.

After several months of discussions and negotiations, the contract was signed in Hong Kong at the eighth World Computer Chess Championship in May of 1995 by IBM, the ACM, the ICCA, and Kasparov. There would be a prize fund of $500,000, $400,000 to the winner and $100,000 to the loser. Kasparov initially preferred "winner-take-all," since he viewed the prize as essentially a charitable contribution—to him! His memory of his match with DEEP THOUGHT in New York was still vivid in his mind. The match would be six games played over an eight-day period. All games would begin at 3:00 P.M. to fit Kasparov's schedule. They would be played at a rate of forty moves in the first two hours, twenty moves in the next hour, and the remaining moves in thirty minutes; a game would thus last at most seven hours.

A press conference was held, and the match was announced to the world on "CNN Worldwide" later that day and in *USA Today,* the *London Times,* and many other papers in the next day or so. IBM was working hard to finish their new machine in time for Hong Kong and then test it thoroughly in the months leading up to the match, but the chip was not yet ready to go into production. Progress was always a bit slower than expected, and they wound up playing in Hong Kong with DEEP BLUE PROTOTYPE. Even so, they were the best there in spite of finishing in third place. Going into the last round, they only needed a draw to win the event, but a glitch in their opening book, combined with a crash when their program left book, cost them the last-round game and the title.

May 1995: Cologne, Germany

Kasparov played PENTIUM CHESS GENIUS two games in Cologne, Germany, in May of 1995. Kasparov won the first and settled for a draw in the second.

May 1995, Cologne, Germany
Game 1, Intel World Chess WDR
White: Garry Kasparov   Black: PENTIUM CHESS GENIUS
Time Control: All/25 minutes
English Opening

1 c4 c6 2 d4 d5 3 Nf3 Nf6 4 Nc3 a6 5 c5 g6 6 Bf4 Bg7 7 h3 O-O 8 e3 Nbd7 9 Bd3 Ne8
10 Rc1 f6 11 e4 e5 12 d×e5 N×c5 13 e×d5 f×e5 14 Be3 N×d3+ 15 Q×d3 e4
16 Q×e4 Nf6 17 Qc4 N×d5 18 N×d5 Be6 19 O-O B×d5 20 Qg4 B×f3 21 g×f3 Qd5
22 Rcd1

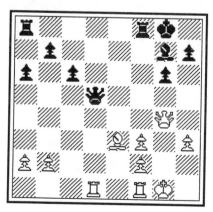

Figure 8.51. Position after 22 Rcd1.

Black has a good position here. It must decide now which pawn to capture. Capturing the a-pawn leaves White with an isolated pawn, while capturing the pawn on f3 eliminates a doubled pawn. The predictable mind of the computer says that capturing the pawn on a2 is therefore preferable to capturing the pawn on f3.

22 . . . Q×a2 23 Rd7 Rf7 24 Rfd1 Qb3

PENTIUM CHESS GENIUS wastes a move here. Perhaps better was 24 . . . Re8 or even 24 . . . b5. Black's position quickly deteriorates now.

25 R1d3 Q×b2 26 Qc4 Rf8 27 R×f7 R×f7 28 Rd8+ Bf8 29 Bh6 Qa3 30 Qe6 Qc5
31 h4 Qb4 32 f4 Qb1+ 33 Kh2 Qb4 34 Kg2 Qa3 35 h5 g×h5 36 f5 Qb4
37 R×f8+ Q×f8 38 B×f8 K×f8 39 f6 R×f6 Black resigns.

In the second game, Kasparov avoided taking any risks, content with a draw.

May 1995, Cologne, Germany
Game 2, Intel World Chess WDR
White: PENTIUM CHESS GENIUS   Black: Garry Kasparov
Time Control: All/25 minutes
Reti Opening

---

1 Nf3 c5 2 g3 g6 3 Bg2 Bg7 4 O-O Nc6 5 Nc3 d6 6 d3 Nf6 7 Bg5 O-O 8 Qd2 Rb8
9 Bh6 b5 10 B×g7 K×g7 11 a3 a5 12 Ng5 Bd7 13 Nce4 N×e4 14 N×e4 h6 15 e3 b4
16 a×b4 a×b4 17 Qe2 Qc8 18 Rfc1 Bg4 19 Qf1 Qc7 20 Ra6 Rb6 21 Rca1 R×a6
22 R×a6 Bc8 23 Ra1 Bb7 24 Qd1 Rc8 25 b3 Qb6 26 Ra2 d5 27 Qa1+ Kg8 28 Nd2 e6
29 Nf3 Qc7 30 h3 Qd6 31 Nh2 e5 32 Ng4 h5 33 Nh2 Qd8 34 Nf3 Ra8 35 R×a8 Q×a8
36 Q×a8+ B×a8 37 g4 h×g4 38 h×g4 f6 39 g5 Kf7 40 Nh2 Nb8 41 Ng4 Nd7
42 g×f6 Ke6 43 f4 e×f4 44 e×f4 N×f6 45 N×f6 K×f6 46 Kf2 Kf5 47 Kg3 g5
48 Bh3+ Kf6 49 f×g5+ K×g5 50 Bg2 Kf5 51 Kf2 Ke5 52 Ke2 Drawn by agreement.

May 25–30, 1995, Hong Kong

The Hong Kong Tournament looked from the beginning as though it would be a week-long ceremony that culminated in crowning DEEP BLUE PROTOTYPE as world champion. The DEEP BLUE PROTOTYPE ancestor, DEEP THOUGHT, had won the 1989 world championship, but it passed up defending its title in 1992. The 1992 champion, CHESS MACHINE/SCHRÖDER, decided not to defend its title this time. The competition included FRITZ 3,

Star Socrates, Pentium Chess Genius, Hitech, Wchess, and Zugzwang, each having a small chance to be an upset winner of the event. But the cumulative chances of one of them finishing ahead of Deep Blue Proto-type in a five-round event, as the championship was, were significant.

Deep Blue Prototype breezed through the first three rounds, defeating Star Socrates in the first round, Hitech in the second, and Ulf Lorenz's Cheiron in the third. Its victory over Hitech was the most lopsided of its six encounters. The IBM program lead the field of twenty-four competitors by a full point with two games to go. But in the fourth round, it had to settle for a draw with Wchess, narrowing their lead to a half point. In the fifth round, Deep Blue Prototype was paired with Fritz 3. Playing White, the program startled everyone when it castled on the thirteenth move only to find itself under a powerful Black attack, and then missing the only way to save the game on the sixteenth move.

May 26, 1995, Hong Kong
Round 2, eighth World Computer Chess Championship
White: Hitech   Black: Deep Blue Prototype
Time Control: 40/2, 40/1 thereafter
Sicilian Defense

---

1 e4 c5 2 c3 Nf6 3 d3 Nc6 4 Nf3 d6 5 Nbd2 e5 6 Qa4 Be7 7 d4 c×d4 8 c×d4 Bd7
9 Bb5 a6 10 B×c6 B×c6 11 Qc2 O-O 12 d5 Bd7 13 O-O Rc8 14 Qb3 Bb5 15 Re1 Nd7
16 Re3 Nc5 17 Qa3 f5 18 e×f5 R×f5 19 h3 a5 20 Rc3 Bf6 21 g4 Rf4 22 Rc2 Ra4
23 Qe3 Nd3 24 R×c8 Q×c8 25 b3

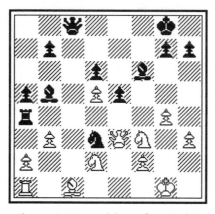

Figure 8.52. Position after 25 b3.

25 ... R×g4+

HITECH will not bite the Trojan horse, but either way, the game is lost! If 26 h×g4, Black wins with 27 Q×g4+, followed by 28 Nf4 threatening mate in one. But what transpires is not any better.

26 Kh1 Rf4 27 Kg2 R×f3 28 N×f3 Nf4+ 29 Q×f4 e×f4 30 Bb2 B×b2 31 Re1 Qf5 32 a4 Bd7 33 Ng1 f3+ 34 Kh2 Be5+ 35 Kh1 Qf4 36 R×e5 d×e5 37 b4 B×h3 38 N×h3 Qg4 39 Nf4 e×f4 40 b×a5 Qg2#.

David Kittinger, author of WCHESS, *enjoying an apple while his program was hard at work finding a move, 1988.*

♚

May 28, 1995, Hong Kong
Round 4, eighth World Computer Chess Championship
White: WCHESS   *Black:* DEEP BLUE PROTOTYPE
Time Control: 40/2, 40/1 thereafter
Sicilian Defense

---

1 e4 c5 2 c3 d5 3 e×d5 Q×d5 4 d4 Nf6 5 Nf3 e6 6 Be2 Nc6 7 O-O c×d4 8 c×d4 Be7 9 Nc3 Qd6 10 Nb5 Qd8 11 Bf4 Nd5 12 Bg3 a6 13 Nc3 O-O 14 Qb3 Nf6 15 Rfd1 b5

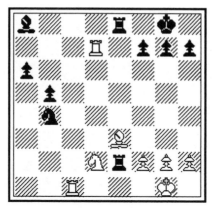

Figure 8.53. Position after 28 . . . N×b4.

16 a3 Bb7 17 Qa2 Na5 18 b4 Rc8 19 Rac1 Nc6 20 Bf4 Re8 21 d5 e×d5 22 N×d5 N×d5
23 Q×d5 Q×d5 24 R×d5 B×b4 25 a×b4 R×e2 26 Be3 Re8 27 Rd7 Ba8 28 Nd2 N×b4

While Black has two passed pawns on the queen-side, it is about to be forced to exchange a rook for a bishop. Its only chance for victory rests in pushing its passed pawns, but White's active pieces and Black's remote king make that impossible; after the rooks come off on move 39, any chance for victory evaporates.

29 Kf1 R2×e3 30 f×e3 Nd5 31 Kf2 h6 32 Nf1 Nb4 33 Nd2 Bd5 34 Rb1 Be6
35 Ra7 Nd3+ 36 Ke2 Nc5 37 Rb4 Bd5 38 g3 Ra8 39 R×a8+ B×a8 40 Rd4 Kh7
41 Rd8 Bb7 42 Rb8 Bh1 43 Rc8 Ne6 44 e4 Bg2 45 Ke3 Bh3 46 Rc6 f5 47 R×a6 Nc5
48 Rd6 N×e4 49 N×e4 f×e4 50 Kf2 Bg4 51 Rb6 Bf3 52 R×b5 g5 53 Ke3 Kg7
54 Rb7+ Kg6 55 Rb6+ Kg7 56 Re6 h5 57 Rd6 h4 58 g4 B×g4 59 K×e4 Bh3
60 Rd3 Bg4 Drawn by agreement.

May 29, 1995, Hong Kong
Round 5, eighth World Computer Chess Championship
White: DEEP BLUE PROTOTYPE   Black: FRITZ 3
Time Control: 40/2, 40/1 thereafter
Sicilian Defense

---

1 e4 c5 2 Nf3 Nc6 3 d4 c×d4 4 N×d4 Nf6 5 Nc3 e5 6 Ndb5 d6 7 Bg5 a6 8 Na3 b5
9 B×f6 g×f6 10 Nd5 f5 11 Bd3 Be6 12 Qh5 f4

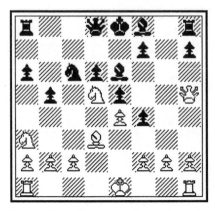

Figure 8.54. Position after 12 . . . f4.

13 O-O

Hsu said that the normal book line is to play Bg7 before f4. He indicated that their opening database did contain the transposition and it realized that O-O and O-O-O were not good moves, recommending c3 or g3 instead. But somehow, DEEP BLUE PROTOTYPE didn't use the book correctly, and in fact, was out of book. The prototype had to carry out a search for a move, and as is usually the case when leaving book, was taking an extra amount of time to calculate a reply. It actually saw the problem with castling, but then the communication line dropped! After the computer was reconnected, it had about half the time to search that it had before the line went down—not enough time to see the trap. Even if the program had played 13 g3, its position still would have been weak.

The other systems, especially the commercial ones, employ full-time people, usually grandmasters, just for opening book preparations and advising on chess strategies. This error pointed out to the DEEP BLUE team the importance of doing the same. They had not been sufficiently concerned with this aspect of their preparation.

13 . . . Rg8 14 Kh1 Rg6 15 Qd1 Rc8 16 c4

Here Hsu said that 16 g3 should hold against FRITZ 3, although he wasn't so sure it would do so against Kasparov.

16 ... Qh4 17 g3 Qh3 18 Qd2 f3 19 Rg1 Rh6 20 Q×h6 Q×h6 21 c×b5 B×d5
22 e×d5 Nb4 23 Bf5 Rc5 24 b×a6 N×a6 25 Nc2 Qd2 26 Ne1 R×d5
27 N×f3 Q×f2 28 Be4 Ra5 29 Rg2 Qe3 30 Re1 Qh6 31 Bc6+ Kd8 32 a3 f5
33 Rc2 Rc5 34 R×c5 N×c5 35 Rf1 Be7 36 a4 f4 37 g×f4 Q×f4 38 Rg1 N×a4
39 b4 Q×b4 White resigns.

After the championship ended, Hsu took the opportunity to visit his family in Taiwan for a week. It was perhaps his first time off in some time. Most of us in attendance used our free time to explore Hong Kong. Robert Byrne, who was with us as an honored guest, showed great energy in traversing the interesting old streets of Hong Kong under the dynamic leadership of Tan and Tony Marsland. Marsland was spending the year in Hong Kong, on sabbatical from the University of Alberta and attached to Hong Kong University. Some of the participants took advantage of a one-day trip to China and explored China's tiny south-east tip adjacent to Hong Kong.

Even though contracts had been signed in Hong Kong, there were many months between the signing and the match, and anything could happen. The biggest problem was getting the new DEEP BLUE up and running. Most plans for exhibitions involving DEEP BLUE were postponed or called off entirely when the group returned to Yorktown, although they did fulfill two commitments made prior to going to Hong Kong—a trip to Spain in July and another to China in October. While on the one hand there was concern that DEEP BLUE might not be ready, there was also some chance that Kasparov could lose the world champion title in his September-October match with Anand or that another program might challenge and defeat Kasparov in the meanwhile. Everyone was hoping for a healthy, ready-to-go, new DEEP BLUE and a similarly healthy, ready-to-go, world champion Garry Kasparov.

July, 1995: Barcelona

In July of 1995, DEEP BLUE PROTOTYPE traveled to Spain to take on the top-rated Spanish player, international grandmaster Miguel Illescas. Hsu and company had originally planned to take DEEP BLUE there, but DEEP BLUE PROTOTYPE went instead. DEEP BLUE was not ready, and the days were passing quickly. Illescas has a rating of approximately 2625. The match was played using the "Fischer Clock," whereby the time remaining for each side is adjusted after each move. In the first game, after Illescas played

31 ... N×c8, the game was quickly drawn. In the second game, DEEP BLUE PROTOTYPE lost on time while in a strong position.

July 1995, Barcelona
Game 1, Exhibition match with international grandmaster Miguel Illescas
White: DEEP BLUE PROTOTYPE   Black: *Miguel Illescas*
Time Control: 40/2, Fischer Clock
Queen's Gambit Declined

---

1 d4 d5 2 c4 c6 3 Nc3 Nf6 4 e3 e6 5 Qc2 Nbd7 6 Bd2 Be7 7 Nf3 O-O 8 Bd3 d×c4
9 B×c4 c5 10 d×c5 B×c5 11 O-O b6 12 Rfd1 Bb7 13 Be2 h6 14 Rac1 Qb8 15 Nb5 a6
16 Nc3 Rc8 17 Qa4 b5 18 Qh4 Bd6 19 a3 Ne5 20 N×e5 B×e5 21 f3 Bd5 22 f4 B×c3
23 B×c3 Ne4 24 Bd4 Qb7 25 Qg4 f5 26 Qg6 Qf7 27 Q×f7 K×f7 28 Bd3 Nd6
29 Be5 R×c1 30 R×c1 Rc8 31 R×c8 N×c8 32 a4 Bc6 33 b3 Ne7 34 a×b5 B×b5
35 Bb1 Nc6 36 Bd6 g6 37 Kf2 a5 38 Bc7 a4 39 b×a4 B×a4 40 e4 Bb3 41 h3 h5
42 g3 Ne7 43 Bd3 Ba2 44 Be5 Bb3 45 Bd4 Ba2 Drawn by agreement.

July 1995, Barcelona
Game 2, Exhibition match with international grandmaster Miguel Illescas
White: *Miguel Illescas*   Black: DEEP BLUE PROTOTYPE
Time Control: 40/2, Fischer Clock
English Opening

---

1 c4 e5 2 Nc3 Nc6 3 Nf3 Nf6 4 d3 g6 5 e3 Bb4 6 Bd2 d6 7 Be2 Be6
8 O-O h6 9 a3 B×c3 10 B×c3 O-O 11 d4 e4 12 d5 e×f3 13 B×f3 B×d5
14 c×d5 Ne5 15 Be2 Ne4 16 Ba5 Rc8 17 f3 Nf6 18 e4 Qe7 19 Bc3 c6
20 d×c6 b×c6 21 f4 Ned7 22 Bf3 Rfe8 23 Re1 d5 24 e5 Nh7 25 Bg4 Nhf8 26 Qd4
Black lost on time.

DEEP BLUE PROTOTYPE lost the game on time when a bug appeared in a newly programmed algorithm to handle the Fischer Clock. It must defend itself against White's threat of 27 e6.

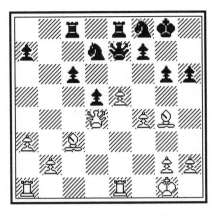

Figure 8.55. Position after 26 Qd4 Black lost on time.

In October of 1995, IBM was opening a new research center in China and wanted to use DEEP BLUE to kick off the opening day with a match against Jun Xie, one of the world's strongest female players. When the decision to go to China was initially made, it seemed a certainty that the new DEEP BLUE would be ready, but it turned out that the chip came back from fabrication in just the nick of time and went there totally untested. Some problems were discovered immediately, but it was too late to correct them by modifying the hardware. By changing the microcode that controlled the chip, Tan said that the circuit functioned satisfactorily, although the modifications reduced chip's functional capabilities by a factor of two. A factor of two could be lived with, but any sacrifice from the design specification was a step in the wrong direction—though not necessarily a big surprise. In computer chess, the norm is surprise. Nevertheless, it was ready, and that was a big relief for the DEEP BLUE team. If the circuit hadn't been ready for China, the match with Kasparov might have been postponed, as the senior staff at IBM was probably getting concerned about the delays in getting DEEP BLUE into the starting gate. The contract for the match was designed to permit either party to postpone the date without penalty if requested before November 1. DEEP BLUE played two games with Xie, winning one and losing one. Given that the system they used was a peanut of the system to be used against Kasparov, the DEEP BLUE team was satisfied with the results.

Our organizing committee held its breath when Kasparov drew game after game with Anand in New York at the world championship match in October and November. And when he lost the ninth game, we really became concerned. However, Kasparov straightened matters out immediately, winning the next game and coasting to an eventual easy victory, much to our relief. At least he would come to Philadelphia as the world champion. While DEEP BLUE might not be the world champion of computers, those in the know realized it was the best computer; I suppose even if Kasparov had lost to Anand, it could be argued that he was still the best of his species.

December 14, 1995: London

We all held our breath again when we found out that Kasparov was playing an Intel-sponsored match against FRITZ 4 in London in December. Anything could happen, although it was felt Kasparov had learned from his earlier experiences with the PC-based programs. Further, even if by some strange reason Kasparov lost, these games were being played at accelerated rates and could be taken only so seriously. Kasparov came though with flying colors—although his victory in the first game was made easy by an operator error on the seventh move!—defeating FRITZ 4 1.5-0.5. We were all quite relieved after that final potential disaster failed to materialize.

December 14, 1995, London
Game 1, Intel-sponsored match between Garry Kasparov and FRITZ 4
White: FRITZ 4   Black: Garry Kasparov
Time Control: All/25 minutes
Nimzo-Indian Defense

---

1 d4 Nf6 2 c4 e6 3 Nc3 Bb4 4 Qc2 O-O 5 a3 B×c3+ 6 Q×c3 b6 7 Bg5 Ba6

An error was made by FRITZ 4's operator, who entered 7 . . . Bb7 instead of the move played by Kasparov.

8 e3 d6 9 f3

This was probably a result of FRITZ 4 seeing the bishop on the wrong square.

9 . . . Nbd7 10 Bd3 h6 11 Bh4 c5 12 Rd1 Rc8 13 Ne2 c×d4 14 Q×d4 Ne5
15 b3 N×d3+ 16 Q×d3 d5

The error was finally found and the bishop placed on a6 in FRITZ 4's memory, but it's too late!

17 Qc3 Ne4 18 Q×g7+ K×g7 19 B×d8 Rf×d8 20 f×e4 d×c4 21 b×c4 R×d1+
22 K×d1 R×c4 23 Kd2 Ra4 24 Ra1 B×e2 25 K×e2 b5 26 Rb1 a6 27 Rb3 R×e4
28 Rc3 Ra4 29 h3 h5 30 g3 f5 31 Rb3 Kf6 32 Rc3 Ke5 33 Kf3 Kd5 34 Rd3+ Kc4
35 Rd6 Kb3 36 R×e6 K×a3 37 Ke2 a5 38 Re5 b4 39 Rb5 b3 40 Kd3 Kb2 41 h4 Ra1
42 R×f5 a4 43 R×h5 a3 44 Ra5 a2 45 h5 Rh1 46 Kc4 a1Q White resigns.

December 14, 1995, London
Game 2, Intel-sponsored match between Garry Kasparov and FRITZ 4
White: Garry Kasparov   Black: FRITZ 4
Time Control: All/25 minutes
Queen's Gambit Declined

---

1 d4 d5 2 c4 e6 3 Nf3 c5 4 c×d5 e×d5 5 g3 Nf6 6 Bg2 Nc6 7 O-O Be7 8 Nc3 O-O
9 Bg5 c×d4 10 N×d4 Qb6 11 Nb3 Be6 12 B×f6 B×f6 13 N×d5 B×d5 14 Q×d5 Rfd8
15 Qf5 B×b2 16 Rab1 Ba3 17 e3 Rac8 18 h4 Qc7 19 Rfd1 h6 20 h5 Ne7 21 Qe4 b5
22 Nd4 a6 23 Qb7 Rd6 24 Rb3 Q×b7 25 B×b7 Rc7 26 Be4 Bc5 27 Rbd3 Bb6
28 Nf5 R×d3 29 R×d3 Rc1+ 30 Kg2 N×f5 31 B×f5 a5 32 Rd7 b4 33 Be4 Kf8
34 Bd5 Rc7

Figure 8.56. Position after 34 . . . Rc7.

Kasparov, needing only a half-point to win the match, now trades off the rooks, leading to a drawn ending. Playing 35 Rd6 gives Black a few more problems but not enough to change the final result.

35 R×c7 B×c7 36 Bb3 Be5 37 f4 Bf6 38 Kf3 Bd8 39 e4 g6 40 h×g6 f×g6 41 g4 h5
42 g×h5 g×h5 43 e5 Bc7 44 Ba4 Kg7 45 Bc6 Kg6 46 Ke4 Bb6 47 f5+ Kg5 48 f6 Bc5
49 Kd5 Bf8 50 Be8 h4 51 Bd7 Kg6 52 Ke6 h3 53 Be8+ Kg5 54 Kf7 Bc5 55 e6 Bd4
56 e7 B×f6 57 Bd7 B×e7 58 B×h3 a4 59 Be6 Bd8 60 Ke8 Kf6 61 Bg8 Be7 62 Kd7 Bf8
Drawn by agreement.

With the Kasparov match nearing, Tan hired international grandmaster Joel Benjamin. Benjamin played the program many games and interacted with the team quite productively. In addition, he assisted in adding new book lines. From the time the team returned from China until the match with Kasparov, the DEEP BLUE team kept a low profile, working long hours to get their system together. There was no end to the work to be done.

References

The following publications are technical in nature and authored by one or more members of the DEEP BLUE team.

M. S. Campbell, "Algorithms for the Parallel Search of Game Trees" (M.Sc. thesis, Department of Computing Science, University of Alberta, Edmonton, 1981).

F.-h. Hsu, "A two-million moves/s CMOS single chip chess move generator," *IEEE Journal of Solid-State Circuits* 22, no. 5 (1987): 841–46.

M. Campbell, "Chunking as an Abstract Mechanism" (Ph.D. thesis, Report CMU-CS-88-116, Carnegie Mellon University, 1988).

T. S. Anantharaman, M. S. Campbell, and F.-h. Hsu, "Singular extensions: adding selectivity to brute force searching," *Proceedings of the AAAI Spring Symposium.* Also in the *ICCA Journal* 11, no. 4 (December 1988): 135–143, and *Artificial Intelligence* 43, no. 1 (1990): 99–109.

F.-h. Hsu, "Large Scale Parallelization of Alpha-Beta Search: An Algorithmic and Architectural Study with Computer Chess" (Ph.D. thesis, Carnegie Mellon University, Technical Report CMU-CS-90-108, Pittsburgh, 1990).

T. S. Anantharaman, "A Statistical Study of Selective Min-Max Search in Computer Chess" (Ph.D. thesis, Carnegie Mellon University, Technical Report CMU-CS-90-173, Pittsburgh, 1990).

G. Goetsch and M. S. Campbell, "Experiments with the null move heuristic," *Computers, Chess and Cognition,* eds. T. A. Marsland and J. Schaeffer, (New York: Springer-Verlag, 1990), 159–68.

F.-h. Hsu, T. S. Anantharaman, M. S. Campbell, and A. Nowatzyk, "DEEP THOUGHT," in *Computers, Chess and Cognition* eds. T. A. Marsland and Jonathan Schaeffer (New York: Springer-Verlag, 1990), 55–78.

F.-h. Hsu, T. Anantharaman, M. Campbell, and A. Nowatzyk, "A Grandmaster chess machine," *Scientific American* 263, no. 4 (October 1990): 44–50.

T. S. Anantharaman, "Confidently selecting a search heuristic," *ICCA Journal* 14, no. 1 (March 1991): 3–16. [An edited version of Chapter 3 of the author's doctoral thesis.]

T. S. Anantharaman, "Extension heuristics," *ICCA Journal* 14, no. 2 (June 1991): 47–65. [An edited version of Chapter 4 of the author's doctoral thesis.]

P. J. Jansen, "Using Knowledge About the Opponent in Game-Tree Search," (Ph.D. Thesis, Carnegie Mellon University, Pittsburgh, 1990).

The following articles primarily report on computer chess events in which DEEP BLUE or Garry Kasparov participated.

The editors, "Chess grandmasters versus chess computers," *ICCA Journal* 8, no. 1 (March 1986): 51–53.

D. Kopec and M. Newborn, "BELLE and MEPHISTO DALLAS capture computer chess titles at FJCC," *Communications of the ACM* 30, no. 7 (July 1987): 640–44.

M. Newborn and D. Kopec, "Results of ACM's Eighteenth Computer Chess Championship," *Communications of the ACM* 31, no. 8 (August 1988): 992–95.

M. Campbell, F.-h. Hsu, and G. Goetsch, "Report on the 1988 Fredkin Masters Open," *ICCA Journal* 11, no. 2/3 (June/September 1988): 105–10.

D. Maddox, "Flowers refuse to burn . . . Gurevich sizzles in Boston," *Chess Life* (December 1988): 26–30.

M. Newborn and D. Kopec, "Results of the Nineteenth ACM North American Computer Chess Championship," *Communications of the ACM* 32, no. 10 (October 1989): 1225–30.

D. Kopec and M. Valvo, "Report on the ACM Nineteenth North American Computer Chess Championship," *ICCA Journal* 11, no. 4 (December 1988): 181–84.

R. Keene, "MEPHISTO vs. DEEP THOUGHT analyzed," *ICCA Journal* 11, no. 4 (December 1988): 189–91.

E. Gufeld, "DEEP THOUGHT vs. HITECH analyzed," *ICCA Journal* 11, no. 4 (December 1988): 193–95.

J. Hanken, "DEEP THOUGHT has miles to go before it sleeps," *Chess Life* (March 1989): 22–28.

F.-h. Hsu, "The Software Toolworks Open Championship," *ICCA Journal* 11, no. 3 (December 1988): 199–200.

D. Levy, "Computer beats grandmaster," *ICCA Journal* 11, no. 3 (December 1988): 168–70.

M. Valvo, "The Valvo-DEEP THOUGHT UNIX Mail Match," *ICCA Journal* 12, no. 3 (September 1989): 183–90.

D. Levy, "The Netherlands versus the computer world," *ICCA Journal* 12, no. 2 (June 1989): 111–12.

G. E. Courtois, Jr., "The Sixth World Computer-Chess Championship," *ICCA Journal* 12, no. 2 (June 1989): 84–99.

R. Keene, "Deep Thoughts from Edmonton," *ICCA Journal* 12, no. 2 (June 1989): 108–110.

The editors, "DEEP THOUGHT vs. Spraggett exhibition games," *ICCA Journal* 12, no. 2 (June 1989): 99.

R. Byrne, *New York Times,* September 26, 1989.

The DT Team, "DEEP THOUGHT versus Byrne," *ICCA Journal* 12, no. 3 (September 1989): 191.

The editors, "Champ meets champ," *ICCA Journal* 12, no. 4 (December 1989): 230.

C. Chabris, "The Harvard Cup Man-Versus-Machine Chess Challenge," *ICCA Journal* 16, no. 1 (March 1993): 57–61.

M. Newborn and D. Kopec, "The Twentieth Annual ACM North American Computer Chess Championship," *Communications of the ACM* 33, no. 7 (July 1990): 94–103.

D. Levy, "The ACM 20th North American Computer Chess Championship," *ICCA Journal* 12, no. 4 (December 1989): 238–43.

L. Evans, "The key game," *ICCA Journal* 12, no. 4 (December 1989): 244–45.

B. Mittman, "Deep preparations," *ICCA Journal* 12, no. 4 (December 1989): 246–47.

D. Levy, "The end of an era," *ICCA Journal* 13, no. 1 (March 1990): 34–35.

M. Valvo, "Moral victory: Karpov versus DEEP THOUGHT at Harvard," *ICCA Journal* 13, no. 1 (March 1990): 37–40.

F. Friedel, "Pfleger versus DEEP THOUGHT," *ICCA Journal* 13, no. 1 (March 1990): 40.

M. Newborn and D. Kopec, "The Twenty-First ACM North American Computer Chess Championship," *Communications of the ACM* 34, no. 11 (November 1991): 85–92.

R. Levinson, "The ACM Twenty-First North American Computer-Chess Championship," *ICCA Journal* 13, no. 4 (December 1990): 208–14.

F. Friedel, "Not the mother of all machines," *ICCA Journal* 14, no. 2 (June 1991): 101–107.

R. Levinson, "Man and machine, theory and practice square off in Sydney," *ICCA Journal* 14, no. 3 (September 1991): 150–52.

ICCA Editorial Board, "Johansen vs. DEEP THOUGHT II: A correction," *ICCA Journal* 14, no. 4 (December 1991): 233.

D. Kopec, M. Newborn, and M. Valvo, "The 22nd ACM International Computer Chess Championship," *Communications of the ACM* 35, no. 11 (November 1992): 100–10.

D. Beal, "Report on the 22nd ACM International Computer Chess Championship," *ICCA Journal* 14, no. 4 (December 1991): 214–22.

F.-h. Hsu, "IBM DEEP BLUE in Copenhagen," *ICCA Journal* 16, no. 1 (March 1993): 53–56.

M. Ginsburg, "The DEEP BLUE Challenge," *ICCA Journal* 16, no. 2 (June 1993): 111–13.

F.-h. Hsu, "DEEP THOUGHT vs. Judit Polgar," *ICCA Journal* 16, no. 3 (September 1993): 150–51.

M. Newborn, "The 24th ACM International Computer-Chess Championship," *ICCA Journal* 17, no. 3 (September 1994): 159–64.

F. Friedel, "PENTIUM GENIUS Beats Kasparov," *ICCA Journal* 17, no. 3 (September 1994): 153–58.

H. K. Tsang and D. Beal, "The 8th World Computer-Chess Championship," *ICCA Journal* 18, no. 2 (June 1995): 93–111.

O. Weiner, "A vengeful return," *ICCA Journal* 18, no. 2 (June 1995): 125–26.

F. Friedel, private correspondence, March 1996. [Games from FRITZ 4 versus Kasparov, London 1995.]

http://www.chess.ibm.park.org

9 DEEP BLUE and Garry Kasparov in Philadelphia

Sunday, February 4, 1996

Garry Kasparov arrived in Philadelphia with his fiancée, Ioulia Vovk—Julia Wolk, when Anglicized—on a connecting flight from Miami around noon. As their host, I watched for them as the passengers left the airplane, but somehow they got by. A certain amount of panic briefly set in until they were found down by the luggage carousel. Kasparov was in good spirits and we discussed a number of things about chess, IBM, politics, Botvinnik, and his just-completed match in Brazil that he had no trouble winning. His fiancée was from Riga, Latvia, and a university student. She was bright, beautiful, and somewhat shy, understanding English quite well but hesitant to try it out. The drive from the airport to the Philadelphia Marriott Hotel, where they would stay, went quickly. They checked into their suite and were very happy with it. There were three rooms, with the middle room serving as a place for interviews, training sessions, and dining. The ACM had arranged a large fruit dish for them as well as flowers and a bottle of champagne. Lunch followed in the hotel coffee shop, and although Kasparov suggested going to an early movie, he later decided not to go, opting for dinner at nine o'clock with his fiancée, Terrie Phoenix, and me. Phoenix, the ACM director of public relations, arrived late in the afternoon. She took us to a hip Philadelphia steakhouse,

Julia Wolk, in good spirits on the final day of the ACM Chess Challenge.

where over dinner she informed Kasparov of the interviews lined up for Monday and Tuesday.

Monday, February 5, 1996

The interviews took place in Phoenix's suite and consumed the entire morning. Kasparov spoke with James Kim of *USA Today,* Bill Macklin of the *Philadelphia Inquirer,* and Bruce Weber of the *New York Times.* All three went on to report the match every day in their respective publications, but when the interviews were held, it wasn't clear that this was their intentions; even if it was, it wasn't clear whether their publications would give the match such prominent coverage. By the end of the match, front page coverage on countless newspapers around the world became the norm. Kasparov spent the remainder of the day relaxing.

Tuesday, February 6, 1996

Phoenix invited us to her suite for breakfast. Meetings with the press followed. Peter Coy from *Business Week* and Don Steinberg from *Gentlemen's Quarterly* occupied most of the time, although telephone calls were coming in from all over the world. By lunch, Kasparov was already becoming concerned that the press was taking too much of his time. He didn't anticipate the extent of the coverage that was to follow, although as the event grew in magnitude, he became more comfortable spending time with the press, realizing how good it was for him and for chess. Kasparov was becoming a national hero in the United States as the savior of the human race, and he was enjoying this aspect of the attention he was receiving.

There was never any doubt, however, that his involvement with the press always played second fiddle to his need to devote his energy to defeating DEEP BLUE. Nevertheless, for another day or so he was relaxing, an important part of his prematch preparation, as important as the chess training itself. In the afternoon, he visited the Philadelphia Aquarium, fascinated by a large pool of sharks that quietly roamed their limited space. His mother, Clara Kasparova arrived around dinner time with coach Yuri Dohokian. She moved into her son's suite, while Dohokian occupied a room across the corridor. In addition to his human entourage, Kasparov had brought a copy of FRITZ 3 for his PC and used it during the match for analysis. A Japanese sushi dinner that evening was Kasparov's last night on the town before the big match.

Over dinner, we discussed the match. When Kasparov mentioned that he had seen an article in *Popular Science* in which I had speculated that the computer might win, he fell silent for some time, I believe, in disbelief, after I confirmed that that was, in fact, what I had said. I will never know for sure what he was thinking, and maybe it was about another matter altogether; but I imagine that until then I had seemed to be a reasonable person, and no reasonable person that he had met thus far ever thought he might lose. Michael Antonoff, the author of the *Popular Science* article, had discussed the match earlier with David Levy, and Levy had indicated he was prepared to jump off a bridge if the computer even garnered a point. From all I knew, the computer had a reasonable chance to do well, although nobody outside IBM including me knew exactly how strong the new DEEP BLUE would be.

After that meal and until the match was over, Kasparov's mother would take control of her son's daily activities, especially such incidental matters as feeding the neurons of his unique cerebral cortex. Most meals were in their suite with food brought up by the hotel staff.

Wednesday, February 7, 1996

Clara Kasparov is a special person, a very strong but delightful woman, young in spirit, with a good grasp of English. She understands what has to

be done to keep her son at the top of the chess world, and she performs her job in a forceful yet charming way. That afternoon, she, Wolk, Dohokian, and I went to the Pennsylvania Convention Center, which was adjacent to the Marriott, to check things out. After raising a number of concerns, mainly related to noise and lighting in the game room, she expressed her approval of the arrangements.

My belief that DEEP BLUE had good chances against Kasparov was based on data that correlated the performance of chess programs with their search capabilities. In 1993 at the twenty-third ACM International Computer Chess Championship, a panel discussion was held, and it was generally concluded that a fourteen-ply search by DEEP THOUGHT or an equivalent program would be enough to defeat Kasparov. A thirteen-ply search might, in fact, be sufficient, while a twelve-ply search was probably not enough. In talks with Chung-Jen Tan today, he seemed to indicate that DEEP BLUE was not going to be searching as deeply as originally planned. There had not been enough time to put the entire system together as de-signed, and IBM was coming with a scaled-down version. The good news for the DEEP BLUE team, in this regard, is that it will be easy to make im-provements that will strengthen DEEP BLUE. The scaling down occurred in the number of processors that were to be used, 192 as opposed to 1,024, and in the speed of each processor. Next time DEEP BLUE will run on more processors and design changes to the move generator will be made that will speed up each processor. DEEP BLUE could gain as much as a factor of ten in strength from these changes.

Because the IBM team was working night and day to be ready for the match, they had avoided playing in any formal contests with DEEP BLUE in the months leading up to the event. In the contractual agreement for the match, signed in May of 1995, it was agreed that the two sides would ex-change all officially played games, but there were none by DEEP BLUE. In every contest that Kasparov had ever participated in, he had games played by his opponents to study. For this match, he had set aside several days for this purpose, but there were no games and Kasparov was frustrated.

Kasparov indicated that he was willing to go to Yorktown to play several speed chess games with DEEP BLUE, but the DEEP BLUE team said they couldn't sacrifice the development time during this crucial period. They were also concerned that Kasparov could use any information that he gathered very ef-fectively. For example, knowing who was working on their opening book would be very useful. Knowing how deeply it was searching would have also been very useful. A couple of games would have given Kasparov a feeling for the computer's positional play that would have been very valuable. Of course, the Deep Blue team could have turned off the opening book and played with a scaled-down version so that Kasparov wouldn't have seen his real Philadelphia opponent. But he still would have gained enough information to develop some feeling for what he was up against. There was quite a bit of mystery surrounding Deep Blue's strength outside of IBM.

We asked Kasparov what he wanted for a chess set for the match and found out that the Manhattan Chess Club had just what he wanted. They had provided the equipment for the Kasparov-Anand match in New York the previous year. We needed two chess sets in case one side promoted a pawn. The pieces were to be wooden, heavily weighted, not too glossy, no seams, and the king had to be 3.75 inches in height. They should be dark brown and cream-colored. The board, too, should be brown and cream-colored, not too glossy, with each square 2.25 inches. Total cost—just over $700.

Thursday, February 8, 1996

Kasparov was in training for the match and wasn't seen all day, evidently sequestered in his suite with his coach and family. It was understood that he was considering various opening lines. Chung-Jen Tan, Joe DeBlasi, and David Levy arrived in the afternoon and I joined them, along with DeBlasi's son, Pat DeBlasi, and Terrie Phoenix, for dinner in the Marriott's steakhouse. The match was discussed, and the usual speculation transpired. Tan seemed quite optimistic, and my reading of his conjecture that Deep Blue might win "one, two, or three" points was that he was playing it a bit conservative. As proud of his team's accomplishments as he was, he was always modest in his speculations. I interpreted his words as an indication that Deep Blue would put up a real struggle.

Friday, February 9, 1996

The troops were all gathering. A successful press conference took place at 11:30 A.M. Kasparov was in super spirits. He responded to my story about the birds, paraphrased in the first chapter of this book, pointing out that no bird has crashed into the sea as airplanes do. Tan represented the Deep

BLUE team at the conference and painted a picture of guarded optimism. That evening, the ACM hosted a prematch dinner with DeBlasi, Levy, Mike Valvo, Ken Thompson, Tony Marsland, Yasser Seirawan and his friend Yvette Nagel, and me at an outstanding Italian restaurant down by the waterfront. We invited Clara Kasparova to join us, but she declined, being occupied with activities in her suite.

Mike Valvo, the arbiter, had been looking forward to the match for some time. He had served as the arbiter at ACM computer chess events for fifteen years, and had earned the respect of the participants because of his impartiality and fairness, and his ability to make difficult decisions after appropriate consultation. Valvo is rated over 2400 and is one of the top blindfold players in the world. He also has considerable experience playing computers, including DEEP BLUE's predecessors. As detailed in the previous chapter, beginning in late 1988 and continuing for the next five months, Valvo played DEEP THOUGHT two e-mail games.

Thompson had agreed to serve as an assistant to Valvo if his expertise on computer-related matters was required. Kasparov had asked the organizers for this on the advise of Frederic Friedel. Friedel was Kasparov's consultant on such matters as well as a good friend of Thompson.

Tony Marsland, president of the ICCA, and Jonathan Schaeffer,
author of CHINOOK, *the world's best checker program.*

*Maurice Ashley, co-anchor commentator
at the ACM Chess Challenge.*

Tony Marsland attended in his capacity as the president of the ICCA. He had spent a lifetime working on chess programs, having participated in the ACM's 1970 championship in New York and many others subsequently. He had assisted in formulating the original rules for the ACM tournaments. His program AWIT had its greatest success at the fourth world championship in New York, where it finished in third place.

Yasser Seirawan, co-anchor commentator at the ACM Chess Challenge.

David Levy, vice-president of the ICCA.

While chess has never been a great spectator sport—some say watching chess is about as exciting as watching paint dry—nevertheless, events of this magnitude draw audiences ranging from several hundred to over a thousand. We had no idea what to expect, but we wanted to have the games discussed, brought to life as they were in progress, in our "commentary room." We had invited international grandmaster Yasser Seirawan, a former United States Open champion (three times) and international master Maurice Ashley to serve as anchor commentators. Ashley didn't arrive in time to join us for dinner, being busy at home helping his wife with their young daughter. The two had been the commentators at the Kasparov-Anand world championship match and were well known in the chess community for their dynamism. They would be assisted from time to time by several other leading players, including Hans Berliner, Danny Kopec, Dan Heisman, and David Levy. Unlike many sports, where the action occurs too quickly to speculate on strategy, chess is ideal for such second-guessing. There are approximately three minutes to analyze each move and predict the future. During the match, Seirawan and Ashley held the audience's attention with their creative analysis, entertaining many questions, bouncing them around and getting advice from FRITZ 4. FRITZ 4 sat on a table on stage carrying out its own analysis on a large screen for the audience to observe. During the course of the match, there was hardly a person that left before the end of a game, a tribute to the exciting chess that took place and the ability of the Seirawan-Ashley team to bring it to life.

Saturday, February 10, 1996

The day began early for those involved in the organization of the event. There were many last-minute details. Finding the proper chair for Kasparov was a big problem. It had to be soft but not too soft, with arms that were comfortable. The lighting for the stage was difficult to work out. IBM wanted to film the stage and that implied a lot of light, but Kasparov wanted much less. Eventually a compromise was reached by Kasparov's mother and the organizers. Kasparov was unhappy with the clock that Levy had brought from London. After the first game, he requested a new board and clock for the next game.

The Russian flag flew from Kasparov's side of the board, and a United States flag flew from the DEEP BLUE side. Before the match, there was

Ken Thompson, relaxing at the board
before the final game of the ACM Chess Challenge.

Yuri Dohokian, Kasparov's "second" at the ACM Chess Challenge.

considerable discussion about this, as the members of the DEEP BLUE team come from several countries and IBM is a multinational company. Perhaps no flags on the table would have been best. It was really not a match between Russia and the USA. But Kasparov wanted a Russian flag and so the option of no flags was ruled out. And the only flag appropriate to

Frederic Friedel, Kasparov's advisor on computer-related matters.

Chung-Jen Tan, head of the DEEP BLUE team at IBM.

fly opposite the Russian flag was an American one, so an American flag there was.

The usual media were there at the start. About twenty videocameras were filming Kasparov in the minutes leading up to the event. About three hundred people were in the commentary room, where Seirawan and Ashley were entertaining. There were three large twelve-foot by twelve-foot

Joe Hoane, member of the DEEP BLUE team.

screens; one had FRITZ 4's display showing and was used for analysis, the second had the actual board, and the third showed the participants.

Kasparov stayed in his hotel room until just before the match, coming down to the game room at about 2:50 P.M. He looked around the room, checked out his adjacent dressing room, and then sat down at the table. His mother, coach, and fiancée were there watching every move.

As 3:00 neared and then passed, and with the arbiter, Valvo, and Kasparov on the stage, DEEP BLUE was having some last-minute technical problems, and in fact, since it was playing White as had been decided at the press conference on the previous day, its clock was started while its handlers were working out the details. DEEP BLUE's supporters were holding their breaths waiting for the computer to go on the air! The many "experts" present were all concerned that last-minute preparations would plague DEEP BLUE during the match, and their fears seemed to be materializing even before the match began. However, after a minute or so, the program was ready, and the first move, 1 e4, was played, followed by nine more moves in relatively fast order until 10 . . . Bb4 took DEEP BLUE out of its book.

DEEP BLUE was running on a thirty-two-node IBM RS/6000 SP high-performance computer located at the IBM Thomas J. Watson Research Center in Yorktown Heights, New York. Each node of the SP employed a single multichannel card containing six dedicated VLSI chess processors, for a total of 192 processors working in tandem. DEEP BLUE's programming code was developed in C and ran under the AIX operating system. The highly parallel system was capable of searching one hundred billion chess positions when making a move.

Each node of the SP could have handled eight chess processors, rather than the six that were used, but it was necessary to remove some of the processors and use them in the "backup" system that IBM had brought to Philadelphia. If they were unable to use the Yorktown system for some reason or other, they would use the smaller system in Philadelphia. They never did.

Seirawan provided his account of the match in the March 1996 issue of the *ICCA Journal,* and we quote his observations in the material that follows. He brings the match to life with his vivid, perceptive comments, reflecting his own extensive knowledge of the game.

Feng-hsiung Hsu and Murray Campbell making final preparations before beginning the final round of the ACM Chess Challenge.

Joel Benjamin, chess advisor to the Deep Blue team.

February 10, 1996, Philadelphia
Game 1, ACM Chess Challenge
White: DEEP BLUE   Black: Garry Kasparov
Time Control: 40/2, 20/1, All/30 minutes
Sicilian Opening

---

1 e4 c5 2 c3

This line of play was popularized for computer play by Thompson's BELLE. It gives White's pieces good freedom of movement.

2 ... d5 3 e×d5 Q×d5 4 d4 Nf6 5 Nf3 Bg4 6 Be2 e6 7 h3 Bh5 8 O-O Nc6 9 Be3 c×d4
10 c×d4 Bb4

DEEP BLUE was now out of book. Its pawns were not as well organized as Kasparov's for the endgame, although that seemed a long way off at this point. Kasparov's last move encouraged White to chase the bishop, further weakening its queen-side pawns.

11 a3 Ba5 12 Nc3 Qd6

The third time Kasparov retreated a piece. DEEP BLUE didn't make any of Black's pieces feel very much at home on the far side of the board. Seirawan felt Kasparov was simply testing the computer, trying to understand its strengths and weaknesses. He thought that Kasparov would probe the program for the first two games.

13 Nb5

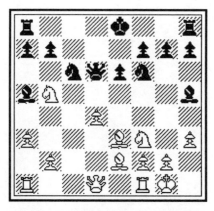

Figure 9.1. Position after 13 Nb5.

13 ... Qe7

It might have been better for Black to have played 13 ... Qb8. Observers felt 13 ... Qe7 was a bit too passive.

14 Ne5 B×e2 15 Q×e2 O-O 16 Rac1 Rac8 17 Bg5 Bb6

Kasparov was not happy here, leading Bob Rice, commissioner of the Professional Chess Association, to observe that "now we know Kasparov does not deliberately pull those faces to disturb his opponents."

18 B×f6 g×f6

Kasparov probably felt that he might eventually use the g-file for attacking White with his rooks. Moreover recapturing with the queen would have given White 19 Nd7 forking the queen and the rook on f8.

19 Nc4 Rfd8

Kasparov could not play 19 ... N×d4 because of 20 N×d4 B×d4 Qg4+ winning Black's bishop.

20 N×b6 a×b6 21 Rfd1 f5 22 Qe3 Qf6 23 d5

DEEP BLUE proposed a dangerous pawn trade with this move, and then went on to play very strongly.

23 ... R×d5 24 R×d5 e×d5 25 b3

The position was judged equal here. It was understood that White would soon recover the pawn. But Black had a potentially dangerous d-pawn now. Kasparov thought for a long time before making his next move.

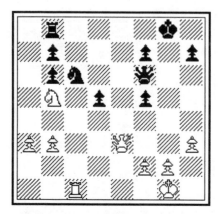

Figure 9.2. Position after 25 b3.

25 . . . Kh8

This move was judged an error. Seirawan felt attacking on the g-file with no real advantage on the kingside was a mistake. It would have been better to play 25 . . . Rd8, preparing to push the d-pawn.

26 Q×b6 Rg8 27 Qc5

Of course, 27 Q×b7 is refuted by 27 . . . Qg4 threatening mate and the rook.

27 . . . d4

Kasparov began harassing his opponent, but he was always one move late.

28 Nd6 f4

More hassling, but he underestimated the inhuman move:

29 N×b7

This dramatic move was unexpected by the audience; 29 Qd5 was suggested by Seirawan and Ashley because it seemed less risky and yet maintained the slight advantage that White had. It seemed that Black was closing in on White's king and that placing the knight on the periphery of the battle was to White's disadvantage. No human would have shown such disregard for a Kasparov attack!

29 . . . Ne5 30 Qd5

It was downhill quickly from here on for Kasparov.

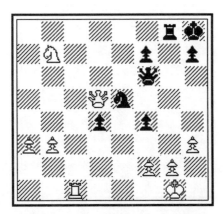

Figure 9.3. Position after 30 Qd5.

30 . . . f3

Kasparov still had some resources to attack and they might have worked against lesser players. But if he could not win material through attacking White's king, he was lost eventually to White's queen-side pawns. So he fought on in the only way possible.

31 g3 Nd3 32 Rc7

Both sides were now on the edge of disaster, though White was one step the better and Black could not turn the tables.

**32 . . . Re8 33 Nd6 Re1+ 34 Kh2 N×f2 35 N×f7+ Kg7 36 Ng5+ Kh6
37 R×h7+ Black resigns.**

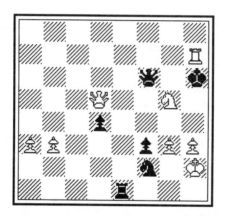

Figure 9.4. Position after 37 R×h7+ Black resigns.

The game could be described as one in which standard lines were followed until Kasparov played 10 . . . Bb4. Then for the next several moves, both sides carried out some minor skirmishes, trying to place their pieces on good squares, while avoiding any major conflict. Kasparov made some minor attacking moves but they were all refuted by DEEP BLUE. DEEP BLUE slowly built up small advantages, clinching the game with the dramatic 29 N×b7. In the final position, Black must play 37 . . . Kg6 and faces devastation after 38 Qg8+ Kf5 39 N×f3.

Kasparov was in some time-trouble throughout the game, and when it ended only five minutes remained on his clock, while DEEP BLUE had about one hour. That seemed to be an ominous sign for the future five games. Kasparov had to play more quickly, but if he did he could not play any weaker, and that was his dilemma. It appears as though DEEP BLUE had been programmed not to use all its time, in case unforeseen problems caused it to lose time.

Kasparov quickly shook hands with Hsu, who was on the other side of the table at the time. They examined the final few moves for a minute or so, and then Kasparov left the room. The IBM team was ecstatic; they had been bracing for anything to happen for a long time.

Over dinner with Seirawan, Ashley, Levy, and Berliner, we observed that the match would not be decided before game five if Kasparov were to win and game four if DEEP BLUE were to win. Those at the table still felt, except for me, that Kasparov would win the match. We also were well aware that Kasparov would learn from this first game and do better with each successive game. (After game two, I spoke with Tan, and he observed that Kasparov might learn some incorrect things as well. We'd see!) Most now felt Kasparov would win the match, but it would be closer than originally anticipated.

Kasparov requested that the board on which the game was played be replaced. Upon close inspection, it was clear that there was some warping, so at seven o'clock on Saturday evening, DeBlasi, Valvo, Thompson, and I met to see how to find a suitable board. We arranged to have a new one there on Sunday.

The event was reported on ABC's National News and was reported on page thirty of the *New York Times* and the front page of both the *Philadelphia Inquirer* and *USA Today*. In addition, the game was broadcast over the Internet and was accepting hits at a rate of 1,200 a minute, about two million for the day, making this one of the largest events in Internet history. Day two saw a hit rate of six million, when IBM increased the number of servers from one to ten.

Kasparov said at a press conference the next day he had trouble sleeping that evening, digesting the implications of his loss and how to proceed.

Sunday, February 11, 1996

After losing the first game, the second game became crucial for Kasparov to win. He appeared in the game room about five minutes to three and sat down promptly while photographers went to work. Some of the concerns about DEEP BLUE's bugs surfaced in game two as early as the second move, when DEEP BLUE fell out of book. After 1 Nf3 d5 2 d4, DEEP BLUE began to calculate a reply, much to the surprise of its programmers and everyone around. Evidently, the computer was not initialized quite correctly! This cost the computer time that could have been saved for later moves. On move nine, Hsu entered the wrong move and after a few seconds, Campbell came running into the room in horror to tell Hsu that he had made a made a mistake. It was quickly corrected and the game went on. Later in the game the telephone line went dead, costing Deep Blue some more time. Glitches like these give one little faith in such things as antiballistic systems that depend on computers working correctly the first time.

♛

February 11, 1996, Philadelphia
Game 2, ACM Chess Challenge
White: *Garry Kasparov*   Black: Deep Blue
Time Control: 40/2, 20/1, All/30 minutes
Catalan Opening

---

1 Nf3 d5 2 d4

As said before, an immediate reply was expected, but instead, the computer took several minutes to respond, indicating that it was out of book. It wasn't supposed to be out of book, but an initialization error evidently had been made. This left the program out of book after only one move. Deep Blue played the following moves satisfactorily, but lost valuable time that could have been used later.

2 . . . e6 3 g3

The next few moves by Kasparov characterize a rather quiet opening and may reflect his concern about getting into a brawl before fully developing his pieces.

3 . . . c5 4 Bg2 Nc6 5 O-O Nf6 6 c4 d×c4

Hsu mistakenly input 6 . . . c×d4 and Campbell, who was watching in the IBM operations room, realized the error immediately and rushed to the game room to tell Hsu and Valvo. The move was undone and play resumed. Kasparov seemed to take the problem in stride.

7 Ne5 Bd7 8 Na3 c×d4 9 Na×c4

Kasparov got up here to take a walk, a sign that so far so good.

9 . . . Bc5 10 Qb3 O-O 11 Q×b7 N×e5 12 N×e5 Rb8 13 Qf3 Bd6

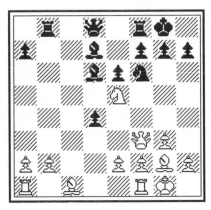

Figure 9.5. Position after 13 . . . Bd6.

14 Nc6

Kasparov thought for twenty minutes before making this last move.

14 . . . B×c6 15 Q×c6 e5 16 Rb1 Rb6 17 Qa4 Qb8 18 Bg5 Be7 19 b4

Kasparov dared DEEP BLUE to take a pawn.

19 . . . B×b4

And the computer bit!

20 B×f6 g×f6 21 Qd7 Qc8 22 Q×a7 Rb8

Seirawan felt that Black could hang on for a draw if it had forced the trade of queens with 22 . . . Ra6 23 Qb7 Q×b7 24 B×b7. Now Seirawan says "the win is easy. White will just shift his focus and occupy the light squares on the king-side for a decisive attack. The extra a2-pawn is a big plus, too."

23 Qa4 Bc3

Kasparov observed after the game that 23 . . . Bd6 was better and that 23 . . . Bc3 left White with a decisive advantage.

24 R×b8 Q×b8 25 Be4 Qc7 26 Qa6 Kg7 27 Qd3 Rb8

DEEP BLUE signaled that it would trade its h-pawn for White's a-pawn. The fewer pawns at this point, the better for Black, who found itself on the defense. In addition, DEEP BLUE's scoring function viewed the exchange favorably as the distant a-pawn would have been judged more valuable than its own h-pawn. Kasparov willingly went along.

28 B×h7 Rb2 29 Be4 R×a2

Figure 9.6. Position after 29 . . . R×a2.

One of Black's long-term problems has been eliminated, but its exposed king and ineffective bishop remain as major handicaps.

30 h4 Qc8 31 Qf3 Ra1 32 R×a1 B×a1 33 Qh5 Qh8 34 Qg4+ Kf8 35 Qc8+ Kg7
36 Qg4+

Kasparov repeated the position to make completing his fortieth move before time control less of a hassle.

36 . . . Kf8 37 Bd5

We see that Kasparov really didn't want a draw.

37 . . . Ke7

Black's king should be used to hold off the h-pawn.

38 Bc6 Kf8 39 Bd5 Ke7 40 Qf3

Again Kasparov backed off from a draw.

40 . . . Bc3 41 Bc4 Qc8 42 Qd5 Qe6 43 Qb5 Qd7 44 Qc5+ Qd6 45 Qa7+ Qd7
46 Qa8 Qc7 47 Qa3+ Qd6 48 Qa2 f5

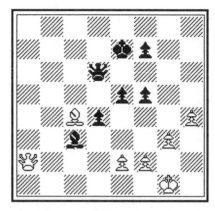

Figure 9.7. Position after 48 . . . f5.

Kasparov's maneuver won a pawn. From here until the game ended, DEEP BLUE was in deep goo, although it squirmed and squirmed.

49 B×f7 e4 50 Bh5 Qf6 51 Qa3+ Kd7 52 Qa7+ Kd8 53 Qb8+ Kd7 54 Be8+ Ke7 55 Bb5 Bd2 56 Qc7+ Kf8 57 Bc4

Kasparov said after the game, "I was pretty sure I was winning when I put my bishop on c4."

57 . . . Bc3 58 Kg2 Be1 59 Kf1 Bc3 60 f4 e×f3 61 e×f3 Bd2 62 f4 Ke8 63 Qc8+ Ke7 64 Qc5+ Kd8 65 Bd3 Be3 66 Q×f5 Qc6 67 Qf8+ Kc7 68 Qe7+ Kc8 69 Bf5+ Kb8 70 Qd8+ Kb7 71 Qd7+ Q×d7 72 B×d7 Kc7 73 Bb5 Black resigns.

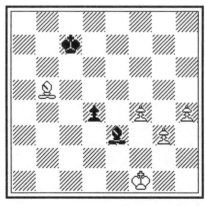

Figure 9.8. Position after 73 Bb5 Black resigns.

Kasparov came into the commentary room with a grin from ear to ear, clearly relieved that he had tackled the monster, or better, had been able to catch the slippery eel, and spoke to the audience for over thirty minutes. He praised the computer and discussed his concerns. The computer should not be allowed to think on his time, he said, and he should be able to bring books to the table. He indicated that if aided appropriately by a strong program, he was capable of playing much stronger chess. He said he had played many computers in the past and had no real problems defeating them. It was like playing little children; but this time instead of a kid, he said, big daddy appeared and a real battle took place. His mother, standing at the rear of the room, tried to signal to him to stop, perhaps concerned that he might give away too much information to his opponents, but he enthusiastically carried on. The audience gave Kasparov a standing ovation when he left the room.

With the match now tied at 1-1, the remaining four games figured to be particularly exciting. It seemed that Kasparov had learned from the first game. At least he played the second game more confidently, and the question now was whether he would push the computer around in the coming games. We had the next day off, and with today's game going the distance, a day's rest was very useful for Kasparov.

According to Seirawan, Kasparov would make a poor poker player. Seirawan said Kasparov removes his watch when he feels a bit of pressure, and then his jacket if things get even worse. He puts them back on when his position improves, indicating that he's collecting his things, getting ready to go to dinner. In the second game he only went as far as to remove his watch, and when late in the game Seirawan pointed out that he had put it back on the audience roared in laughter. In the first game he had lost both his watch and jacket by the end!

Kasparov also would sit for long stretches with his hands on his forehead, almost as though he was receiving energy from them; sometimes he closed his hands over his mouth, and almost always sat with an intense look of concentration on his face. He would get up for a break every ten moves or so. His physical demeanor was a direct reflection of his mental state, said Seirawan!

On the other side of the board, Hsu sat stonefaced, emotionless for the entire first game, even though his imagination was going wild with visions of victory and fears of the unpredictability of his computing system. Near the end, it seemed that he was looking off into space. In spite of the fact that DEEP BLUE had no technical problem, Hsu, who might have given up his seat

to Campbell, was too absorbed with his protégé to leave the board. In the second game, Campbell took over as operator midway through the game.

The game room, itself was usually empty except for Kasparov's entourage and one or two people from the media, who would sit there for a few minutes and then leave. Kasparov's mother and his fiancée and his coach spent most of their time in the game room.

February 12, 1996

A day off and a welcomed rest for the world champion. Terrie Phoenix took Clara Kasparov shopping at the King of Prussia shopping center with Frederic Friedel. That evening I had dinner with Tan and some of his group, and in spite of their loss the day before, they were very happy with DEEP BLUE's performance so far. Campbell, Hoane, and Benjamin stayed behind to work! The IBM team worked every minute they could between rounds. Kasparov, too, wasted little time. CNN ran a brief report on the match once an hour that evening.

February 13, 1996

Kasparov and the DEEP BLUE team were becoming national heroes, with CNN featuring them on hourly spots. *USA Today* ran an editorial on the subject. Today's game promised to be the most dramatic yet. Not that the second one hadn't been dramatic. Had the champion figured out how to play the computer? Was Kasparov back in control of the match, as he had been after he defeated Anand in New York just one game after Anand had defeated him in their ninth game? It took a win by Anand to bring out the fire in Kasparov's game. It was felt that if he won today, he would coast to an easy overall win. As usual, the game started at 3:00 P.M. sharp.

♚

February 13, 1996, Philadelphia
Game 3, ACM Chess Challenge
White: DEEP BLUE   Black: Garry Kasparov
Time Control: 40/2, 20/1, All/30 minutes
Catalan Opening

---

1 e4 c5 2 c3 d5 3 e×d5 Q×d5 4 d4 Nf6 5 Nf3

A glitch somewhere in the DEEP BLUE system required its operators to reboot the system here.

5 . . . Bg4 6 Be2 e6 7 O-O

This game followed the first game through Black's last move. Deep Blue decided to castle here rather than to play 7 h3, maybe gaining a small tempo. This may have been Benjamin's idea.

7 . . . Nc6 8 Be3 c×d4 9 c×d4

As in game one, White's pawns had potential long-term weaknesses after only nine moves.

9 . . . Bb4 10 a3 Ba5 11 Nc3 Qd6 12 Ne5

Deep Blue was still in book, with this move being Benjamin's innovation. It turned out that the computer was not prepared for the consequences. The line was booked following the first game. Perhaps Benjamin felt this move gave White some tactical possibilities.

Garry Kasparov on stage following his victory in the ACM Chess Challenge.

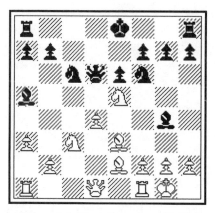

Figure 9.9. Position after 12 Ne5.

12 ... B×e2 13 Q×e2

To be sure that White cannot cause problems by playing its queen to b5 and weaken White's pawns further, Kasparov decided to simplify the position with

13 ... B×c3 14 b×c3

This left White's pawns in more of a mess than before.

14 ... N×e5 15 Bf4

This was better than 15 d×e5, leaving an isolated pawn on the c-file.

15 ... Nf3+ 16 Q×f3 Qd5

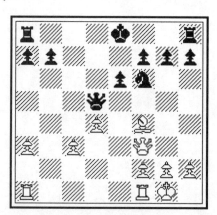

Figure 9.10. Position after 16 . . . Qd5.

Kasparov seemed to have a decisive advantage here. Black has a strong knight while White has a weak bishop, Black's pawns are organized better than White's, and the backward pawn is vulnerable to attack.

17 Qd3

White could hardly afford to let Black capture its queen and further weaken its pawns.

17 . . . Rc8

This prevented White from advancing the c-pawn, thereby eliminating the weakness of a backward pawn.

18 Rfc1

Seirawan felt "Benjamin could only moan after he saw this move. His idea had been the forced 18 Be5, seeking advantageously to swap bishop for knight."

18 . . . Qc4

For the second time, Kasparov offered an exchange of queens and was ready to enter the endgame, with the objective of continuing to build pressure on the c-pawn. He was threatening to play Nd5 and tie up all of White's pieces defending the c-pawn.

19 Q×c4 R×c4 20 Rcb1

A big surprise and a key move for White. This turned out to be much better than 20 Rab1. It was the beginning of a slow comeback by DEEP BLUE.

20 . . . b6 21 Bb8

A second surprise move, and typical of the twisted mind of a computer!

21 . . . Ra4 22 Rb4 Ra5 23 Rc4

This was also entirely unexpected and completed the rehabilitation of DEEP BLUE. Leave it to a computer to figure out a way to hold on to a weak backward pawn: simply move a rook *in front of* the pawn!

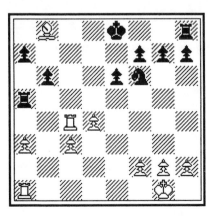

Figure 9.11. Position after 23 Rc4.

23 ... O-O

Kasparov finally castled, adding a second rook to the fray just as DEEP BLUE was gaining its equilibrium.

24 Bd6 Ra8 25 Rc6 b5 26 Kf1

DEEP BLUE's scoring function went to work here, and with no other crisis on the board, encouraged the computer to centralize its king.

26 ... Ra4 27 Rb1 a6 28 Ke2 h5

Both sides now have eliminated back-rank mate threats.

29 Kd3 Rd8 30 Be7 Rd7 31 B×f6 g×f6

DEEP BLUE has managed to get rid of its weak bishop for the strong knight and leave Kasparov with nothing more than a draw.

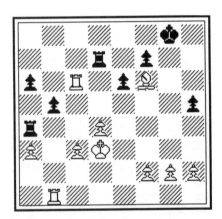

Figure 9.12. Position after 31 ... g×f6.

32 Rb3 Kg7 33 Ke3 e5 34 g3 e×d4+ 35 c×d4 Re7+ 36 Kf3 Rd7 37 Rd3 Ra×d4
38 R×d4 R×d4

Kasparov informed Campbell, who was sitting across the table, that the game was a draw, but they played on for another move.

39 R×a6 b4 Drawn by agreement.

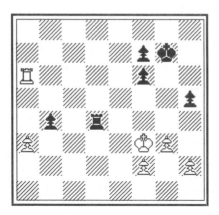

Figure 9.13. Position after 39 . . . b4 Drawn by agreement.

Kasparov had some chances to win this game, but the computer squirmed its way out of an almost airtight cage. Thus after three games, the score stood even at a point and a half apiece. With Kasparov having White in two of the three remaining games, he had the advantage now. But the match figured to be very close and it was quite possible that a blunder by Kasparov or a bug in the program would be enough to decide the match. That would have been a shame but that didn't happen.

Yasser Seirawan, Hans Berliner, and Maurice Ashley
discussing one of the games at the ACM Chess Challenge.

February 14, 1996

This day came quickly. DEEP BLUE had played three terrific games and had surpassed the expectations of most of the experts. The following game, the fourth, was perhaps the best.

♚

February 14, 1996, Philadelphia
Game 4, ACM Chess Challenge
White: Garry Kasparov   Black: DEEP BLUE
Time Control: 40/2, 20/1, All/30 minutes
Slav Defense

The game began sharply at 3:00 P.M. with increasing media interest. An audience of about two hundred attended, up a bit from the third game, but down from the first two, which were played on the weekend.

1 Nf3 d5 2 d4 c6

DEEP BLUE, in book for this move, veered from the line played in the second game when its book wasn't used.

3 c4 e6

The characteristic first three moves of the Slav Defense. Kasparov has played well against this defense according to Seirawan. But he was afraid to march the computer too far along standard lines and decided to try a quiet move next. He probably would have preferred a more dynamic move against even the strongest of human opponents. But after playing even with the machine for three games, he had developed a certain respect for it and wanted to avoid riling it up at this point.

4 Nbd2 Nf6 5 e3

Kasparov might have continued his quiet development with g3 and then Bg2, but he may not have wanted to give up his c-pawn to the machine only to have to fight to get it back.

5 . . . Nbd7 6 Bd3 Bd6 7 e4

Kasparov found it hard not to throw the first jab.

7 . . . d×e4 8 N×e4

Kasparov got up from the table and took his first break, evidently feeling that he was in good shape.

8 . . . N×e4 9 B×e4 O-O 10 O-O h6

White's pieces are more active than Black's, enough so that Kasparov was looking for ways to begin an attack against Black's king, but 10 . . . h6 very effectively kept White at bay.

Figure 9.14. Position after 10 . . . h6.

11 Bc2 e5

This was DEEP BLUE's first move that recovered some space for itself.

12 Re1 e×d4

This seemed to help Black, but White's pieces still had considerable scope on Black's kingside and Kasparov seemed to be weighing sacrificial possibilities.

13 Q×d4 Bc5 14 Qc3 a5

Black prevented White from chasing the bishop with his b-pawn while threatening to pin the queen to the rook on e1. This move was considered by some to be one of DEEP BLUE's best moves of the entire match.

15 a3 Nf6 16 Be3

Kasparov developed his last minor piece and seemed to have a clear advantage at this point.

16 . . . B×e3 17 R×e3 Bg4 18 Ne5 Re8 19 Rae1

Kasparov took twenty minutes before playing the last move, possibly concerned about tactical shots. All his pieces were active and it seemed to be only a matter of a few moves before he would find a way to cause serious damage to DEEP BLUE.

19 . . . Be6 20 f4

Kasparov decided to expand on the king-side, plotting to play f5 and g4, g5.

20 . . . Qc8

DEEP BLUE had few moves to improve its position, but the move played prepared for one possibility: advancing its b-pawn.

21 h3 b5

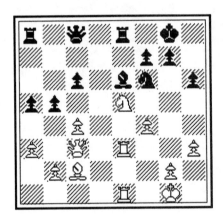

Figure 9.15. Position after 21 . . . b5.

22 f5

White continued to expand on the king-side. Black's bishop had to move and it could capture either the c-pawn or the f-pawn. It chose the c-pawn, somewhat to the surprise of the audience. After the game, Kasparov said that that was the better choice. Before choosing it, however, the computer went down briefly and had to be resuscitated.

22 . . . B×c4 23 N×c4 b×c4 24 R×e8+ N×e8 25 Re4 Nf6

DEEP BLUE seemed a bit better off here than previously, although Kasparov still seemed to hold a clear lead.

Bruce Weber, of the New York Times.

26 R×c4 Nd5 27 Qe5 Qd7 28 Rg4 f6

DEEP BLUE drew even here, and except for a potentially weak square on g6, ended pressure on its king for the remainder of the game.

29 Qd4 Kh7 30 Re4 Rd8 31 Kh1

Kasparov was beginning to feel time pressure, having to make nine moves in twenty-one minutes. After the game he said that this move was a bad mistake.

31 . . . Qc7 32 Qf2 Qb8

Here White was attempting to maneuver its queen to g6, while Black was pressuring White's b-pawn.

33 Ba4 c5 34 Bc6 c4 35 R×c4 Nb4

A poisonous knight! Kasparov had less than five minutes to make the remaining five moves to the first time control. DEEP BLUE had about half an hour, and its last move threatened White in several ways.

36 Bf3 Nd3 37 Qh4 Q×b2

DEEP BLUE evidently understood that White could not cause problems on the king-side, but Seirawan felt 37 . . . N×b2 38 Rd4 Nd3 was better. Now White's queen can get back into the game.

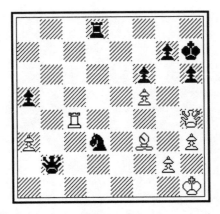

Figure 9.16. Position after 37 . . . Q×b2.

38 Qg3 Q3a3 39 Rc7 Qf8 40 Ra7 Ne5 41 R3a5

It looked like a draw from here on, although Black's pieces were a bit stronger.

41 . . . Qf7 42 R×e5

Kasparov indicated his willingness to draw the game with this move.

42 . . . f×e5 43 Q×e5 Re8 44 Qf4 Qf6 45 Bh5

Kasparov was so tired and concerned about his position at this point that his hand visibly shook when he made this move.

45 . . . Rf8 46 Bg6+ Kh8 47 Qc7 Qd4 48 Kh2 Ra8 49 Bh5 Qf6 50 Bg6 Rg8 Drawn by agreement.

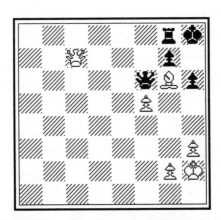

Figure 9.17. Position after 50 . . . Rg8 Drawn by agreement.

Thus after four games, the match stood at two points apiece. After the game, Kasparov returned to his room looking very tired and happy to have escaped the tentacles of DEEP BLUE. He later went to Philadelphia's top French restaurant, Le Bec Fin, with his friends. Thursday was a day off and you can be sure he was plotting for Friday's fifth game.

The results of the last two games have shown that while Kasparov was learning how to play against DEEP BLUE, he has not yet become master of the house.

February 15, 1996

This was a day off from over-the-board battle, but a busy one for both Kasparov and the DEEP BLUE team. Kasparov was busy digesting what he had learned in the four games thus far, while the DEEP BLUE team worked on opening lines.

The publicity surrounding the match continued at a high level. Today Tan and Seirawan were guests of "The News Hour with Jim Lehrer" on PBS, and CNN regularly ran occasional spots on the match.

February 16, 1996

The excitement surrounding the match continued to build with CNN back to its extensive coverage of the event after a one-day hiatus. As usual, Kasparov came down to the game room several minutes before 3:00 P.M., and Game five started on schedule.

February 16, 1996, Philadelphia
Game 5, ACM Chess Challenge
White: DEEP BLUE   Black: Garry Kasparov
Time Control: 40/2, 20/1, All/30 minutes
Four Knights Opening

---

1 e4 e5

Kasparov avoided his favorite Sicilian Defense.

2 Nf3 Nf6

Now he suggested the Petroff Opening, but DEEP BLUE preferred another line altogether.

3 Nc3 Nc6

This transformed the game into the Four Knights Opening.

4 d4 e×d4 5 N×d4 Bb4 6 N×c6 b×c6 7 Bd3 d5 8 e×d5 c×d5 9 O-O O-O 10 Bg5 c6
11 Qf3 Be7 12 Rae1

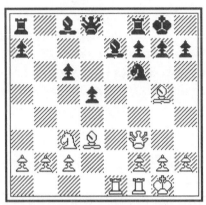

Figure 9.18. Position after 12 Rae1.

White's nicely developed pieces are balanced by Black's strong pawns on c6 and d5. White has no tactical possibilities here and will drift for the next several moves. On move seventeen, the audience felt Black was better.

Danny Kopec and Maurice Ashley analyzing the position after Kasparov's nineteenth move in Game Five. DEEP BLUE *played 20 R×e8+.*

Mike Valvo, arbiter at the ACM Chess Challenge.

12 ... Re8 13 Ne2 h6 14 Bf4 Bd6

Kasparov thought for twenty-six minutes in deciding upon this move.

15 Nd4 Bg4 16 Qg3 B×f4 17 Q×f4 Qb6 18 c4 Bd7 19 c×d5 c×d5 20 R×e8+ R×e8
21 Qd2 Ne4 22 B×e4 d×e4 23 b3 Rd8

At this point, Kasparov offered a draw. The DEEP BLUE team gathered and called upon their strongest chess expert Joel Benjamin to decide; in spite of the fact that DEEP BLUE thought its score was slightly negative, a decision was made to play on. The decision was made a bit murky; the DEEP BLUE team took so long to decide that DEEP BLUE came back with its twenty-fourth move while the discussion was going on. The rules normally require a player to accept or reject a draw before making a move. In this case, the computer had made the move but the operator had not made it on the board. For future matches this point should be clarified. Kasparov evidently felt that the only way to improve Black's position was to push the f-pawn, but was concerned that if that failed to crack White, he could be left in a lost position. Benjamin underestimated Kasparov's position and overestimated the difficulties Kasparov faced in making time control. Kasparov had been playing a bit slowly, but that was the pattern of the match. With the position relatively simple, this factor should not have been an issue in the decision. Had DEEP BLUE accepted the draw, the match would have gone into the final round with the possibility of either side winning or even a drawn match. Kasparov played on with a heightened resolve to teach his annoying, tenacious, though unperturbable opponent a lesson.

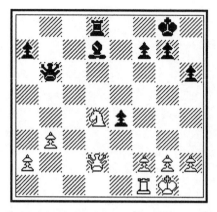

Figure 9.19. Position after 23 . . . Rd8.

24 Qc3 f5 25 Rd1 Be6 26 Qe3 Bf7 27 Qc3 f4

Here Kasparov could force a draw himself with 27 . . . Be6, but he avoided repeating the position, playing 27 . . . f4 and quickly getting the better of DEEP BLUE.

28 Rd2 Qf6 29 g3 Rd5 30 a3 Kh7 31 Kg2 Qe5 32 f3 e3

The commentators felt that 32 . . . f×g3 would have made the victory even easier.

33 Rd3 e2 34 g×f4 e1Q 35 f×e5 Q×c3 36 R×c3 R×d4 37 b4

Kasparov was up a piece and DEEP BLUE could give up at any time.

37 . . . Bc4 38 Kf2 g5 39 Re3 Be6 40 Rc3 Bc4 41 Re3 Rd2+ 42 Ke1 Rd3 43 Kf2 Kg6
44 R×d3 B×d3 45 Ke3 Bc2 46 Kd4 Kf5 47 Kd5 h5 White resigns.

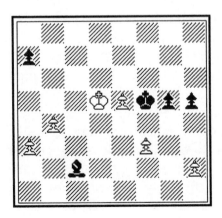

Figure 9.20. Position after 47 . . . h5 White resigns.

Black could now force one of its king-side pawns to the eighth rank. DEEP BLUE understood this and resigned.

Kasparov again meets with the audience and media following the game with lots of smiles. He said he "was very hesitant before the game, because I felt that it was time to change my opening. You know, I normally stick with my favorite opening, and I do not betray my opening, but I felt that I had to find something, and my choice was the Petroff Defense, and normally you play that with Black when you want to have a safe game, a draw, but I came to the conclusion that the positions in the middlegame are quite complicated." He went on to say that he was "very surprised that they played this opening. I think I played it twice in my life. One was against Karpov in the world championship match, and I tried to see what he could play with White, because I had difficulty with the white pieces against Karpov, and I wanted to turn the tables on him. And another one, I think, when I played against Kramnik in New York, when I had to make a draw."

When Kasparov offered the draw, he implied he was prepared to go into the last game of the match needing a victory to win the match. Now he can finish with a draw. He noted that "here, for the first time, we are seeing something intelligent." Other lesser players had seen the light several years earlier.

Philadelphia Inquirer's *William Macklin talking with IBM's Chung-Jen Tan in the press room. At the rear is IBM's Marcie Holle.*

February 17, 1996

While Kasparov only needed a draw to win the match, he had to be very careful to ensure that the game was played his way. Over the course of the five games, Kasparov had learned how to play the computer while the computer had learned nothing about playing him—although the programmers had worked hard between rounds to prepare the computer for its next game. His one-point lead, though, included a game that could well have been a draw (Game five) and a game in which the program had failed to use its opening book (Game two). Winning or drawing this final game was worth $150,000 to Kasparov, giving him $400,000; a loss would mean he would have to settle for $250,000.

♚

February 17, 1996, Philadelphia
Game 6, ACM Chess Challenge
White: Garry Kasparov   Black: DEEP BLUE
Time Control: 40/2, 20/1, All/30 minutes
Slav Defense

---

1 Nf3 d5 2 d4 c6 3 c4 e6 4 Nbd2 Nf6 5 e3 c5 6 b3 Nc6 7 Bb2 c×d4 8 e×d4 Be7
9 Rc1 O-O 10 Bd3 Bd7 11 O-O Nh5

"You know what I thought of this," said Seirawan. "My peals of laughter could be heard throughout the lobby. Why, these guys have cheek! As an earlier teacher of mine once said, 'Black is cruising for a bruising.'"

Figure 9.21. Position after 11 . . . Nh5.

12 Re1 Nf4 13 Bb1 Bd6 14 g3 Ng6 15 Ne5 Rc8 16 N×d7 Q×d7 17 Nf3 Bb4
18 Re3 Rfd8 19 h4 Nge7

Kasparov's next move was considered a reflection of his respect for the computer's tactical abilities. In the July, 1996 issue of the *ICCA Journal*, Berliner looked at this position in some depth, concluding that 20 B×h7+ K×h7 21 Ng5+ wins more dramatically than the slower, but surer, line played by Kasparov. After 21 Ng5+, Black's 21 . . . Kg6 is met with 22 Qg4 f5 23 h5+ Kf6 24 Qh4. White then chases Black's bishop away from the a5-e1 diagonal and then increases pressure on e6 with Rae1 leading to a win: 24 . . . Re8 25 a3 Ba5 26 b4 Bc7 27 Rce1 Ng8 28 N×e6+ Kf7 29 Qg5 R×e6 30 R×e6 Q×e6 31 R×e6 K×e6 32 c×d5+ K×d5 33 Q×f5+! According to Berliner, Black's 21 . . . Kg8 is refuted with 22 Qh5 Nf5 23 c×d5 where White is now threatening to play d×e6 on the next move leaving Black's king in deep trouble. For example, 23 . . . N×e3 24 d×e6 f×e6 25 f×e3, threatening Rf1 and Qh7+ which is a bit too much for Black.

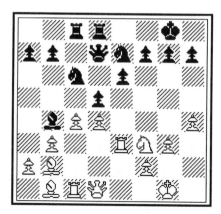

Figure 9.22. Position after 19 . . . Nge7.

20 . . . a3

Hsu fed the wrong information into the computer here, causing a crash and a loss of several minutes. Kasparov, in a good position and feeling confident, appeared relaxed, unlike his demeanor in previous games. He barely reacted to this final mistake by Hsu.

20 . . . Ba5 21 b4 Bc7

Kasparov had DEEP BLUE in a very cramped position and was slowly controlling more and more space.

22 c5 Rde8 23 Qd3 g6 24 Re2 Nf5 25 Bc3 h5 26 b5 Nce7 27 Bd2 Kg7 28 a4 Ra8 29 a5 a6
30 b6 Bb8 31 Bc2 Nc6 32 Ba4 Re7 33 Bc3 Ne5 34 d×e5 Q×a4 35 Nd4 N×d4 36 Q×d4 Qd7

Black was hopelessly tied up.

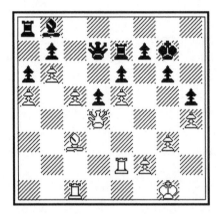

Figure 9.23. Position after 36 . . . Qd7.

37 Bd2 Re8 38 Bg5 Rc8 39 Bf6+ Kh7 40 c6 b×c6 41 Qc5 Kh6 42 Rb2 Qb7
43 Rb4 Black resigns.

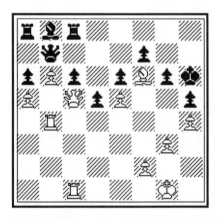

Figure 9.24. Position after 43 Rb4, Black resigns.

Black has little choice but to play 43 . . . Kh7 and then faces 44 Qe7 Q×e7
45 B×e7. If 45 . . . B×e5 or 45 . . . Re8, then White continues with 46 b7.
Seirawan suggested Kasparov could force victory with a king-side attack:
43 . . . Kh7 44 Kg2 Kh6 45 f3 Kh7 46 g4 h×g4 47 R×g4 threatening to
push the h-pawn.

Kasparov was swarmed by the press as soon as he stood up from the table. A press conference followed with about one hundred representatives of the media in attendance. Kasparov was very happy about the results and congratulated the Deep Blue team for its outstanding performance. Following the press conference he went into the commentary room, where he was greeted with loud applause and a standing ovation. He had indeed survived the tentacles of the Deep Blue monster.

At the ACM awards dinner later that evening, the ACM presented Kasparov with a check for $400,000. On behalf of the Deep Blue team, Tan accepted a check for $100,000, which would go to cover the high costs of developing new supercomputers at IBM, supercomputers that may be programmed to play chess or solve other related problems. Kasparov was obviously in top spirits and made an impromptu thank-you speech that delighted the five hundred ACM members.

Garry Kasparov and Yasser Seirawan on stage and in good spirits
following the final game of the ACM Chess Challenge.

The following day, Kasparov and entourage went by limousine to Ken Thompson's home for the remainder of the weekend. Kasparov was last reported to be relaxing and watching gory science fiction movies on Thompson's large TV.

The DEEP BLUE team was also delighted with the results. DEEP BLUE put on a terrific performance. It won the first game, lost the second with a bit of an alibi—part of its opening book was not connected to the rest of the system correctly and so, at minimum, cost the program valuable time calculating moves that might better have been selected from book—and drew the third and fourth games. Any doubt that Kasparov was coasting in the match was dispelled in the fourth game when he found himself short on time and in a position that he could best draw. In the fifth game, the DEEP BLUE team might have accepted Kasparov's draw offer. They would then have played the final game with the match tied at 2.5–2.5 apiece, a real dramatic climax. Thus, while the score was 4-2 for Kasparov, the match was very close. Hsu, Campbell, Hoane, Brody, Benjamin, and Tan returned to IBM the following Monday as heroes.

References

The match was covered extensively in many newspapers across the United States. *USA Today* (James Kim), the *New York Times* (Bruce Weber), and the *Philadelphia Inquirer* (Bill Macklin) reported daily on the activities.

J. W. H. M. Uiterwijk, "The Kasparov-DEEP BLUE Match," *ICCA Journal* 19, no. 1 (March 1996): 38–41.

Y. Seirawan, "The Kasparov-DEEP BLUE games," *ICCA Journal* 19, no. 1 (March 1996): 41–57.

H. J. Berliner, "Why did Kasparov blink?" *ICCA Journal* 19, no. 2 (June 1996): 99–100.

M. Antonoff, "Curtains for Kasparov?" *Popular Science* (March 1996): 41–46.

For those with access to the Internet, the results of the match can be found at http://www.chess.ibm.park.org.

10 The Future

It is most natural that man finds a way for his newest, greatest tool, the computer, to compete, and the game of chess is the ideal medium for the competition. Chess may serve the computer industry as auto racing has the auto industry. Many advances in the auto world were first tried on racing models and then after refinement incorporated into commercial vehicles. This may be the pattern in the computer field, too, where techniques used by computers to play chess are on the cutting edge of developments in complex problem-solving. Of course, there are many ways in which computers can compete. We have seen robot mice working their ways through mazes, computers competing with one another as artists and musicians and even as poets. There have been programming contests involving hundreds of participants. But at least for the near future, chess is likely to remain the primary battlefield and testing ground for computers.

The lessons of computer chess are relevant to a large class of important problems in computer science, problems that depend on search such as automated reasoning, molecular synthesis, scheduling problems, and even in the design of computers themselves. In automated reasoning—as was touched on in Chapter 4 when discussing automated theorem proving—a computer is given a set of statements about some problem and asked to draw some conclusion. The computer might be given information, for example, about the objects in a room and asked whether a robot can navigate from one side to the other. In chess, the computer searches for the optimal move; for the robot, the computer also searches for the optimal move, though it is a very difficult type of move. In molecular synthesis, one wants

to design a molecule with a particular property, and the computer must explore millions of possible configurations of atoms searching for just the right combination. Scheduling problems occur everywhere, from the airline industry trying to optimize flight times to universities trying to minimize final examination conflicts. In computer design, there are VLSI layout problems and logic circuit minimization problems for both combinational and sequential circuits. Search is a fundamental tool for solving such complex problems, and those interested in solving them have much to learn from the creators of chess-playing systems.

We are at a point in the history of computer chess where the abilities of the top players and the strongest computers are comparable. For the first quarter-century of progress in computer chess, computers were clearly inferior. For the last five years, they have been battling on a relatively even footing with the top players, and the two combatants will probably remain fairly equal for the next several years. But the day is not too far off when the best players will no longer be serious competition. Computers will simply consider too many possibilities and set up positions that are too complex for mere mortals to cope with.

Will the top players improve to meet the challenge? They certainly will improve some. Track and field records have continually improved because of better training techniques and because of human breeding; the same is happening in the world of chess. Children now have chess programs available that play at the master level. They serve as outstanding sparring partners and teachers. In the past, it was a rare occasion for a beginner to have an opportunity to compete with a master, but now anyone can do so. Further, just as athletes seem to breed athletes, chess players tend to breed chess players. However, when compared to the rapid improvement by computers, man's progress will be slow and modest. There are limitations on the information processing capabilities of the human mind that cannot change overnight.

Will Kasparov learn to defeat future programs as he seems to have done with DEEP BLUE? To some degree, and in the short term, this will happen. The style of computers is currently too rigorous and gives itself away after a number of games. Nevertheless, there seems to be a limit on how much such learning can yield. Currently, players with rating less than 2400 have little chance against DEEP BLUE no matter how many games they play. For Kasparov to have no chance, DEEP BLUE has a long way to go, but the day keeps getting nearer.

The Future

Perhaps eventually the game will become programming chess. There have been somewhere around one hundred thousand chess programs written since Shannon first described how to do it. Many were class projects at universities that went no further. A thousand or so have developed to the point where they have competed in tournaments around the world. Robert Hyatt's new program, CRAFTY, is available over the Internet (hyatt@cis.uab.edu), and he has provided forty thousand copies of the source code to interested individuals. The source code to GNUCHESS is also available, but it is not of the same quality. More programming effort has been invested in computer chess than in controlling the rocket ships that have gone into space. Anyone who has developed a game-playing program understands its addictive pull. Just ask Berliner or Donskoy or Thompson or Slate or Marsland. It's almost like giving birth to a child, where the creation exhibits a style of play that is a reflection of its creators. You always feel you can improve the program with a bit of work, and the work is never finished.

How will programs improve? Certainly scoring functions will slowly improve with chess knowledge cleverly encoded in special-purpose circuity, as has been done by Berliner's HITECH. Large opening books will be used, some generated by special programs developed for this purpose. Endgame databases will continue to grow, and eventually all six- and seven-piece endgames will be solved. A hundred years from now, all eight-piece endgames may be solved as well. Techniques for parallel search will improve, and the number of processors available for carrying out parallel search will grow from the current number of several hundred to millions and more. Just as we now have computers with megabytes of memory, in one hundred years we will have megaprocessor computers with each processor more powerful than current PCs and no larger than a pinhead.

Computers will soon defeat the best humans at chess, but some argue that the Japanese game of go will yield much more slowly. Go, it is argued, will not succumb to the techniques used for chess. Currently, the best go programs are far from competing with the top humans, but the effort invested by go programmers has been far less than that invested by chess programmers. It is reasonable to assume that strong go programs will be developed in the coming years and that they will be more similar to than different from chess programs. Parallel search techniques and large hash tables will be more effective in go programs than in chess programs. Move generation is also simpler, but developing good scoring functions is currently the bottleneck to major progress.

For the short term, Kasparov remains the challenge. A rematch with DEEP BLUE some time in the next year seems possible, and the odds are excellent that the computer will put on an even stronger performance than it did this year. If DEEP BLUE happens to win, Kasparov is entitled to a rematch. If it loses, it will try again and again and again!

Appendix A

History of Major Computer Chess Championships

WORLD CHAMPIONSHIPS

Year	City	Winner	Runner-Up
1974	Stockholm	KAISSA; Donskoy, Arlazarov, ICL 4/70	CHESS 4.0; Slate, Atkin, CDC 6600
1977	Toronto	CHESS 4.6; Slate, Atkin, CDC Cyber 176	DUCHESS; Truscott, Wright, Jensen, IBM 370/165
1980	Linz	BELLE; Thompson, Condon, PDP 11/23 with chess circuitry	CHAOS; Alexander, Swartz, Berman, O'Keefe, Amdahl 470
1983	New York	CRAY BLITZ; Hyatt, Gower, Nelson, Cray XMP/48	BEBE; Scherzer, Chess engine
1986	Cologne	CRAY BLITZ; Hyatt, Gower, Nelson, Cray XMP/48	HITECH; Berliner, et al., SUN workstation with chess circuitry
1989	Edmonton	DEEP THOUGHT; Hsu, Anantharaman, Browne, Campbell, Jansen, Nowatzyk, SUN with VLSI chess hardware	BEBE; Scherzer, Scherzer, Chess Engine
1992	Madrid	CHESS MACHINE/SCHRÖDER; Schröder, ARM2	ZUGZWANG; Feldmann, Mysliwietz, Parsytec T-800
1995	Hong Kong	FRITZ 3; Morsch, de Gorter, Feist, 90Mhz Pentium PC	STAR SOCRATES; Dailey, Joerg, Kuszmaul, Leiserson, Blumofe, Frigo, Kaufman, Randall, Riesen, Zhou, 1824-node Intel Paragon

ACM INTERNATIONAL COMPUTER CHESS CHAMPIONSHIPS

This championship was initially called the ACM United States Computer Chess Championship. It was renamed the ACM North American Computer Chess Championship in 1975, and renamed again the ACM International Computer Chess Championship in 1991. In 1983, the ACM hosted the fourth World Computer Chess Championship instead of its usual event. In 1992, the event was not held. In 1995, the ACM partially sponsored the world championship in Hong Kong.

Year	City	Winner	Runner-Up
1970	New York	CHESS 3.0; Slate, Atkin, Gorlen, CDC 6400	DALY CHESS PROGRAM; Daly, King, Varian 620/i
1971	Chicago	CHESS 3.5; Slate, Atkin, Gorlen, CDC 6400	TECH; Gillogly, PDP 10
1972	Boston	CHESS 3.6; Slate, Atkin, Gorlen, CDC 6400	OSTRICH; Arnold, Newborn, DG Supernova
1973	Atlanta	CHESS 4.0; Slate, Atkin, Gorlen, CDC 6400	TECH II; Baisley, PDP 10
1974	San Diego	RIBBIT; Hansen, Crook, Parry, H'well 6050	CHESS 4.0; Slate, Atkin, CDC 6400
1975	Minneapolis	CHESS 4.4; Slate, Atkin, CDC Cyber 175	TREEFROG; Hansen, Calnek, Crook, Honeywell 6080
1976	Houston	CHESS 4.5; Slate, Atkin, CDC Cyber 176	CHAOS; Swartz, Berman, Alexander, Ruben, Toikka, Winograd, Amdahl 470
1977	Seattle	CHESS 4.6; Slate, Atkin, CDC Cyber 176	DUCHESS; Truscott, Wright, Jensen, IBM 370/168
1978	Washington	BELLE; Thompson, Condon, PDP 11/70 w/ chess hardware	CHESS 4.7; Slate, Atkin, CDC Cyber 176
1979	Detroit	CHESS 4.9; Slate, Atkin, CDC Cyber 176	BELLE; Thompson, Condon, PDP 11/70 with chess hardware
1980	Nashville	BELLE; Thompson, Condon, PDP 11/70 w/ chess hardware	CHAOS; Alexander, O'Keefe, Swartz, Berman, Amdahl 470
1981	Los Angeles	BELLE; Thompson, Condon, PDP 11/23 w/ chess hardware	NUCHESS; Blanchard, Slate, CDC Cyber 176
1982	Dallas	BELLE; Thompson, Condon, PDP 11/23 w/ chess hardware	CRAY BLITZ; Hyatt, Gower, Nelson, Cray 1

1983		Not held as the ACM NACCC that year but as the fourth world championship. See World Championships.	
1984	San Francisco	CRAY BLITZ; Hyatt, Gower, Nelson, Cray XMP/4	BEBE; Scherzer, Chess Engine, and CHESS CHALLENGER; Spracklen, Spracklen, Fidelity machine
1985	Denver	HITECH; Ebeling, Berliner, Goetsch, Paley, Campbell, Slomer, SUN w/ chess hardware	BEBE; Scherzer, Chess engine
1986	Dallas	BELLE; Thompson, Condon, 11/23 w/ chess hardware	LACHEX; Wendroff, Cray XMP
1987	Dallas	CHIPTEST-M; Anantharaman, Hsu, Campbell, SUN 3 with VLSI chess hardware	CRAY BLITZ; Hyatt, Nelson, Gower, Cray XMP/48
1988	Orlando	DEEP THOUGHT 0.02; Hsu, Anatharaman, Browne, Campbell, Nowatzyk, SUN 3 w/ VLSI chess hardware	CHESS CHALLENGER; Spracklen, Spracklen, Nelson, Fidelity machine with Motorola 68030 microprocessor
1989	Reno	HITECH*; Ebeling, Berliner, Goetsch, Paley, Campbell, Slomer, SUN w/ chess hardware	DEEP THOUGHT*; Hsu, Anantharaman, Browne, Campbell, Nowatzyk, 3 SUN 4s w/ VLSI chess hardware
1990	New York	DEEP THOUGHT/88; Hsu, Anantharaman, Jansen, Campbell, Nowatzyk, SUN 4 w/two VLSI chess circuits	MEPHISTO; Lang, 68030 microprocessor MEPHISTO machine
1991	Albuquerque	DEEP THOUGHT II; Hsu, Campbell, RS/6000 550 + 24 chess processors	MCHESS; Hirsch, IBM PC Clone/486.
1993	Indianapolis	SOCRATES II; Dailey, Kaufman, IBM PC	CRAY BLITZ; Hyatt, Gower, Nelson, Cray XMP/48
1994	Cape May	DEEP THOUGHT II; Hsu, Campbell, Hoane, RS/6000 580 + 12 chess processors	ZARKOV; Stanback, HP735

---

*Denotes first-place tie.

Appendix B

Rules Governing the ACM Chess Challenge

When the contracts for the match were signed in May 1995 in Hong Kong by the parties involved, the rules governing the match were set. A slight condensation of the rules is presented here and this is followed by an explanation of some of them.

1 The ICCA

The Match is being held under the auspices of ICCA.

2 Number of Games and Schedule of Play

2.1 The Match consists of six games, all of which will be played. A win scores 1 point, a draw scores 0.5 points and a loss scores 0 points. The player who accumulates the most points at the end of the Match shall be declared the winner. The Match will be declared drawn if both players score three points.

2.2 All games will commence at 3:00 p.m., local Philadelphia time.

2.3 Game 1 will be played on February 10th, 1996, Game 2 will be played on February 11th, 1996, Game 3 will be played on February 13th,

1996, Game 4 will be played on February 14th, 1996, Game 5 will be played on February 16th, 1996, Game 6 will be played on February 17th, 1996.

2.4 Neither player can ask for a postponement of any game. If one player does not play any of the above games, then that player forfeits that game.

3 Rate of Play and the Chess Clock

3.1 The rate of play shall be 40 moves/player in the first two hours of that player's time, then 20 moves/player in the next one hour of that player's time, then all the remaining moves in an additional 30 minutes per player. Time not consumed during one period is carried forward to the next.

3.2 Kasparov has the right of choice of the chess clock to be used during the Match, but in the event of there being a faulty clock and if a replacement of the same type of clock is unavailable, then ICCA has the right to substitute a chess clock of a different type.

4 Award Ceremony and Prizes

The prize fund will be US $500,000 which will be split 80% to the winner and 20% to the loser. If the score of the Match is 3-3, the prize money will be shared equally between Kasparov and DEEP BLUE.

5 Logistics and Rules of Play

5.1 DEEP BLUE shall be operated by an operator provided for this purpose by IBM.

5.2 When he chooses, the operator shall sit at the chess table facing Kasparov. Although the operator is free to leave the table or move about in a non-distracting manner when it is DEEP BLUE's turn to move, when it is Kasparov's turn to move, the operator, if he chooses to sit at the chess table, may not leave the table or move in a distracting manner until it becomes DEEP BLUE's turn to move.

5.3 Provided that it is not Kasparov's turn to move, the operator may be replaced at any time or times during the game at DEEP BLUE's sole discretion.

5.4 In the event of a technical fault or problem relating in any way to Deep Blue the operator may, provided that it is not Kasparov's turn to move, communicate with any person he chooses in such a manner as to avoid any distraction which may reasonably be regarded as disturbing to Kasparov.

5.5 When it is the program's turn to move, Deep Blue's chess clock must remain running at all times even though there may be a technical fault (excluding power failure, discussed below) which prevents Deep Blue's move from being made in the normal way.

5.6 When Kasparov has made his move, the operator may communicate this move to Deep Blue via equipment provided for this purpose, such equipment to operate in a manner which can not reasonably be regarded as disturbing to Kasparov.

5.7 When Deep Blue has made its move and communicated its move to the operator, the operator shall make Deep Blue's move on the chess board and then press Deep Blue's side of the chess clock.

5.8 If the operator makes a mistake either in communicating Kasparov's move to Deep Blue or in making Deep Blue's move on the chess board, when this mistake is discovered the position immediately before the mistake is set up on the chess board and the players' clock times are adjusted. If it is possible for the arbiter to determine the times that should be showing on the players' clocks then he shall adjust the clocks accordingly, but if this is not possible then each player shall be allotted a time proportional to that indicated by his clock when the error was discovered such that the proportion is the same as the ratio of the number of moves made by that player up to the time the error was made divided by the number of moves made by that player up to the time the error was discovered.

5.9 Kasparov and the operator shall both keep a written record of the moves of the game at least up to move 60, after which it is optional for each of them to do as he wishes. Deep Blue's operator will provide the arbiter a computer printout of the game within one hour of the completion of each game.

5.10 When Deep Blue is on the move, the operator may tell Deep Blue the time remaining on either or both sides of the chess clock provided that the computer initiates the request for such information.

5.11 If, during play, DEEP BLUE is unable to perform in the expected manner, for example being unable to accept a legal move, then the operator may set up in the computer the current board position and status along with the clock times of both players and any other information required by the program, but all such work is permitted only while it is not Kasparov's turn to move.

5.12 At any time during play IBM may replace any or all of the computer hardware and/or software being used to play the games provided that any such work carried out in the playing hall is carried out only when it is not Kasparov's turn to move.

5.13 The operator may offer a draw, accept a draw or resign on behalf of DEEP BLUE. This may be done with or without consulting DEEP BLUE.

5.14 During the opening ceremony, Kasparov will draw lots to determine his color in the first game of the match and thereafter the colors will alternate.

5.15 In all matters concerning the laws of chess and their interpretation, including those matters referred to in points **5.0 to 5.14** inclusive, the decision of the arbiter shall be final.

6 The Arbiter

The arbiter is Mike Valvo. If he is unwell or unable to officiate for any reason then the ICCA may at its sole discretion appoint a replacement arbiter but shall, if practical, consult with the players or their representatives over the choice of replacement arbiter.

7 The Official Rules

The rules presented here are a condensation of the official rules in the contract drawn between Kasparov and IBM and only are meant to be a guide for the audience.

* * * * * *

It was fitting that the match be played under the auspices of the ICCA, given the ICCA's role and stature in the world of computer chess. In addition, the ICCA played an important role in bringing the two parties into agreement on the contracts related to the match.

A match of six-games duration was agreed upon early in the negotiations. The 3:00 p.m. starting times were requested by Kasparov as it best fits his biological clock. Taking a day off after the second and fourth games was agreed upon by both sides with each having different intentions for the use of this time. The DEEP BLUE team would use it to modify their book and correct any bugs found during previous games. Kasparov would use it to study previously played games looking for ways to take advantage of DEEP BLUE's inflexible style of play. It turned out that the fourth game was the most strenuous for Kasparov, and a day off following that game was at least partially used to recover. Rule 2.4 was suggested by Kasparov and agreed upon by the DEEP BLUE team to keep matters simple. The rate of play, in particular, limiting a game to seven hours in duration, was established to avoid adjudications.

The prize fund was set at $500,000 at the beginning of the negotiations but the split was a subject of some discussion. While a 5/8–3/8 split is the tradition in match play, there was no need to follow tradition here. Offering 80% to the winner was an extra incentive proposed by the organizers to Kasparov and to which the DEEP BLUE team agreed; Kasparov was confident that that would be his share of the $500,000.

The logistics and rules of play were based on those used in previous games between man and machine. Rule 5.8 is the messiest and was a factor several times during the match when the DEEP BLUE team made errors entering moves and interpreting the computer's replies. Rule 5.9 was established at the organizers' request. DEEP BLUE automatically recorded the moves of the game relieving Kasparov of any obligation on his part to do so after move 60 when he might find himself in time trouble. Rule 5.13 turned out to be the most contentious in retrospect, and should be expanded for future man-machine events. The operator should probably not be involved in responding to the draw request made by the human. The program should be modified to respond with a "yes" or "no" to any such request. As it was, requests for a draw by Kasparov and accepted by the DEEP BLUE operator ended games three and four, while Kasparov's request in game 5 was turned down by the DEEP BLUE operator even though the computer thought it was marginally behind.

Appendix C

Deep Blue Diary

This appendix chronicles the travels of DEEP BLUE from its first tournament in 1986, when it was called CHIPTEST to its latest six-game match with Garry Kasparov. Twenty-eight events are listed, beginning with its first performance in the seventeenth ACM North American Computer Chess Championship through the 1996 ACM Chess Challenge. Games presented in Chapters 8 and 9 are marked with a (G) following the result.

Dates: November 2–5, 1986
Location: Dallas, Texas
Event: 17th ACM NACCC
Time Control: 40/2, 20/1 thereafter
Results: 2.5/5
Performance Rating: 1761

White	Black	Result
BEBE	CHIPTEST	Lost
CHIPTEST	OSTRICH	Lost (G)
CHIPTEST	REX	Won
MERLIN	CHIPTEST	Won
CHIPTEST	RECOM	Draw

Reference

D. Kopec and M. Newborn, "BELLE and MEPHISTO DALLAS Capture Computer Chess Titles at FJCC," *Communications of the ACM* 30 (July 1987): 640–44.

Dates: October 25–27, 1987
Location: Dallas, Texas
Event: 18th ACM NACCC
Time Control: 40/2, 20/1 thereafter
Results: 4/4 (Winner of event)
Performance Rating: 2574

White	Black	Result
CHIPTEST-M	CYRUS	Won
LACHEX	CHIPTEST-M	Won
CRAY BLITZ	CHIPTEST-M	Won (G)
CHIPTEST-M	SUN PHOENIX	Won

Reference

M. Newborn and D. Kopec, "Results of ACM's Eighteenth Computer Chess Championship," *Communications of the ACM* 31 (August 1988): 992–95.

Dates: May 28–30, 1988
Location: Carnegie Mellon University
Event: 1988 Fredkin Masters Open
Time Control: 40/2, 20/1 thereafter
Performance Ratings: DEEP THOUGHT 0.01: 2571; CHIPTEST-M: 2506

Both CHIPTEST-M and DEEP THOUGHT 0.01 participated. Alexander Ivanov won the event, DEEP THOUGHT 0.01 finished tied for second through fourth, and CHIPTEST-M finished tied for fifth through eighth.

White	Black	Result
Bruce Leverett	CHIPTEST-M	Won
CHIPTEST-M	Kimball Nedved	Draw
Ronald Burnett	CHIPTEST-M	Won
Mark Eidemiller	CHIPTEST-M	Draw
CHIPTEST-M	Vivek Rao	Won
CHIPTEST-M	Klaus Pohl	Lost
DEEP THOUGHT 0.01	Ross Sprague	Won
Tom Martinak	DEEP THOUGHT 0.01	Draw
Kimball Nedved	DEEP THOUGHT 0.01	Won
DEEP THOUGHT 0.01	Roumel Reyes	Won
Alexander Ivanov	DEEP THOUGHT 0.01	Lost (G)
DEEP THOUGHT 0.01	Vivek Rao	Won (G)

Reference

M. Campbell, F.-h. Hsu and G. Goetsch, "Report on the 1988 Fredkin Masters Open," *ICCA Journal* 11, nos. 2/3 (June/September 1988): 105–10.

Dates: August 7–19, 1988
Location: Boston
Event: U. S. Open
Time Control: 40/2, 20/1 thereafter
Results: DEEP THOUGHT 0.01 was plagued by bugs,
but nevertheless defeated international master Igor Ivanov in round 9.

Reference

D. Maddox, "Flowers refuse to burn . . . Gurevich sizzles in Boston," *Chess Life,* (December 1988): 26–30.

Dates: November 13–15, 1988
Location: Orlando, Florida
Event: 19th ACM NACCC
Time Control: 40/2, 20/1 thereafter
Results: 3.5/4 (Winner of event)

White	Black	Result
DEEP THOUGHT 0.02	CHESS CHALLENGER	Draw
SUN PHOENIX	DEEP THOUGHT 0.02	Won
DEEP THOUGHT 0.02	HITECH	Won (G)
MEPHISTO	DEEP THOUGHT 0.02	Won

References

M. Newborn and D. Kopec, "Results of the 19th ACM North American Computer Chess Championship," *Communications of the ACM* 32 (October 1989): 1225–30.

D. Kopec and M. Valvo, "Report on the ACM 19th North American Computer-Chess Championship," *ICCA Journal* 11, no. 3 (December 1988): 181–86.

R. Keene, "MEPHISTO vs. DEEP THOUGHT analyzed," *ICCA Journal* 11, no. 4 (December 1988): 189–91.

E. Gufeld, "DEEP THOUGHT vs. HITECH analyzed," *ICCA Journal* 11, no. 4 (December 1988): 193–95.

Dates: November 13–15, 1988
Location: Long Beach, California
Event: Software Toolworks Chess Championship
Time Control: 40/2, 20/1 thereafter
Results: 6.5/8 (Tied for first place
with international grandmaster Tony Miles)
Performance Rating: 2745

White	Black	Result
Alexandre LeSiege	DEEP THOUGHT 0.02	Won
DEEP THOUGHT 0.02	David Glicksman	Won
Bent Larsen	DEEP THOUGHT 0.02	Won (G)
DEEP THOUGHT 0.02	Walter Browne	Lost (G)
Vince McCambridge	DEEP THOUGHT 0.02	Draw
DEEP THOUGHT 0.02	Rob Salgado	Won
DEEP THOUGHT 0.02	Alex Fishbein	Won
Jeremy Silman	DEEP THOUGHT 0.02	Won

References

J. Hanken, "Deep Thought has Miles to go before it sleeps," *Chess Life* (March 1989): 22–28.

F.-h. Hsu, "The Software Toolworks Open Championship," *ICCA Journal* 11, no. 3 (December 1988): 199–200.

D. Levy, "Computer Beats Grandmaster," *ICCA Journal* 11, no. 3 (December 1988): 168–170.

Dates: November 1988–March 1989
Location: On the Net at rec.games.chess
Event: Match with international master Mike Valvo
Time Control: One move every three days
Results: Valvo 2, DEEP THOUGHT 0.02 0

White	Black	Result
Mike Valvo	DEEP THOUGHT 0.02	Lost (G)
DEEP THOUGHT	Mike Valvo	Lost (G)

Reference

M. Valvo, "The Valvo-DEEP THOUGHT UNIX Mail Match," *ICCA Journal* 12, no. 3 (September 1989): 183–90.

Appendix C

Date: April 9, 1989
Location: Hilversum, the Netherlands
Event: The Netherlands versus the Computer World
Time Control: 60/1, then 60/1, then adjudication
Results: 0–1

CHIPTEST-M lost on Board 1 to international grandmaster John van der Wiel.

Reference

D. Levy, "The Netherlands versus the computer world," *ICCA Journal* 12, no. 2 (June 1989): 111–12.

Dates: May 28–31, 1989
Location: Edmonton, Alberta, Canada
Event: The Sixth World Computer Chess Championship
Time Control: 40/2, 20/1 thereafter
Results: 5/5 (won world championship)

White	Black	Result
MOBY	DEEP THOUGHT	Won
DEEP THOUGHT 0.02	REBEL	Won
CHESS CHALLENGER	DEEP THOUGHT	Won
DEEP THOUGHT 0.02	CRAY BLITZ	Won
HITECH	DEEP THOUGHT	Won (G)

References

G. E. Courtois, Jr., "The 6th World Computer-Chess Championship," *ICCA Journal* 12, no. 2 (June 1989): 84–99.

R. Keene, "Deep Thoughts from Edmonton," *ICCA Journal* 12, no. 2 (June 1989): 108–110.

Date: May 31, 1989
Location: Edmonton, Alberta, Canada
Event: Exhibition match with international grandmaster Kevin Spraggett
Time Control: 1st Game: All/30 minutes; 2nd Game: All/10 minutes
Results: Spraggett 1.5, DEEP THOUGHT .5

White	Black	Result
DEEP THOUGHT	Kevin Spraggett	Draw (G)
Kevin Spraggett	DEEP THOUGHT	Lost (G)

Reference

The editors, "DEEP THOUGHT vs. Spraggett exhibition games," *ICCA Journal* 12, no. 2 (June 1989): 99.

Dates: August 23 and September 2, 1989
Location: Carnegie Mellon University
Event: Exhibition match with international grandmaster Robert Byrne
Time Control: 40/2, then all/30 minutes
Results: DEEP THOUGHT 1, Byrne 1

White	Black	Result
DEEP THOUGHT	Robert Byrne IGM	Won (G)
Robert Byrne IGM	DEEP THOUGHT	Lost (G)

Reference

R. Byrne, *New York Times*, September 26, 1989.

The DT team, "DEEP THOUGHT versus Byrne," *ICCA Journal* 12, no. 3 (September 1989): 191.

Date: October 23, 1989
Location: New York Academy of Art, New York City
Event: Exhibition match with world champion Garry Kasparov
Time Control: All/90 minutes
Results: Kasparov 2, DEEP THOUGHT 0

White	Black	Result
DEEP THOUGHT	Garry Kasparov	Lost (G)
Garry Kasparov	DEEP THOUGHT	Lost (G)

References

The editors, "Champ meets champ," *ICCA Journal* 11, no. 4 (December 1989): 230.

R. Byrne, *New York Times*, September 26, 1989.

Date: October 29, 1989
Location: Harvard University
Event: The first Harvard Cup
Time Control: All/30 minutes
Results: DEEP THOUGHT 1/4, CHIPTEST-M 0/4

White	Black	Result
Boris Gulko	DEEP THOUGHT	Lost
DEEP THOUGHT	Maxim Dlugy	Won (G)

Colors are not available for the third and fourth round games. DEEP THOUGHT lost to Lev Alburt and Michael Rohde. CHIPTEST-M lost to Gulko, Dlugy, Alburt and Rohde.

Reference

C. Chabris, "The Harvard Cup Man-Versus-Machine Chess Challenge," *ICCA Journal* 16, no. 1 (March 1993): 57–61.

Dates: November 11–14, 1989
Location: Reno, Nevada
Event: 20th ACM NACCC
Time Control: 40/2, 20/1 thereafter
Results: 4/5 (Tie for first place with HITECH)
Performance Rating: 2508

White	Black	Result
SUN PHOENIX	DEEP THOUGHT	Won (G)
DEEP THOUGHT	BP	Won
HITECH	DEEP THOUGHT	Won
DEEP THOUGHT	REBEL 89	Won
MEPHISTO	DEEP THOUGHT	Loss (G)

References

M. Newborn and D. Kopec, "The 20th Annual ACM North American Computer Chess Championship," *Communications of the ACM* 33 (July 1990): 94–103.

D. Levy, "The ACM 20th North American Computer-Chess Championship," *ICCA Journal* 11, no. 4 (December 1989): 238–243.

L. Evans, "The key game," *ICCA Journal* 11, no. 4 (December 1989): 244–45.

B. Mittman, "Deep preparations," *ICCA Journal* 12, no. 4 (December 1989): 246–47.

Dates: December, 1989
Location: London
Event: Exhibition match with international master David Levy
Time Control: 40/2, 20/1 thereafter
Results: DEEP THOUGHT 4, Levy 0

White	Black	Result
DEEP THOUGHT	David Levy	Won (G)
David Levy	DEEP THOUGHT	Won (G)
DEEP THOUGHT	David Levy	Won (G)
David Levy	DEEP THOUGHT	Won (G)

Reference

D. Levy, "The end of an era," *ICCA Journal* 13, no. 1 (March 1990): 34–36.

Date: February 2, 1990
Location: Harvard University, Boston, Massachusetts
Event: Exhibition match with international grandmaster and former
world champion Anatoly Karpov
Time Control: All/1
Results: Karpov 1, DEEP THOUGHT 0

White	Black	Result
Anatoly Karpov	DEEP THOUGHT	Lost (G)

Reference

M. Valvo, "Moral victory: Karpov versus DEEP THOUGHT at Harvard," *ICCA Journal* 12, no. 1 (March 1990): 37–40.

F.-h. Hsu, T. Anantharaman, M. Campbell, and A. Nowatzyk, "A Grandmaster chess machine," *Scientific American* 263, no. 4 (October 1990): 44–50.

Appendix C

Dates: February, 1990
Location: Germany
Event: Exhibition match with international grandmaster Helmut Pfleger
Time Control: 40/2, 20/1 thereafter
Results: DEEP THOUGHT 1—Pfleger 1

White	Black	Result
Helmut Pfleger	DEEP THOUGHT	Draw (G)
DEEP THOUGHT	Helmut Pfleger	Draw

Reference

F. Friedel, "Pfleger versus DEEP THOUGHT," *ICCA Journal* 13, no. 1 (March 1990): 40.

Dates: November 11–14, 1990
Location: New York
Event: 21st ACM NACCC
Time Control: All/2
Results: 4–5 (Tied for first place with MEPHISTO)
Performance Rating: 2586

White	Black	Result
DEEP THOUGHT/88	BEBE	Won
BELLE	DEEP THOUGHT/88	Won
DEEP THOUGHT/88	MEPHISTO	Won
HITECH	DEEP THOUGHT/88	Lost (G)
DEEP THOUGHT/88	ZARKOV	Won

References

M. Newborn and D. Kopec, "The 21st ACM North American Computer Chess Championship," *Communications of the ACM* 34, no. 11 (November 1991): 85–92.

R. Levinson, "The ACM 21st North American Computer-Chess Championship," *ICCA Journal* 12, no. 4 (December 1990): 208–14.

Dates: May, 1991
Location: Hanover, Germany
Event: Hanover grandmaster event
Time Control: 40/2, 20/1 thereafter
Results: 2.5/7

White	Black	Result
Hans Ulrich Grunberg	DEEP THOUGHT II	Won
DEEP THOUGHT II	Klaus Bischoff	Draw
Eric Lobron	DEEP THOUGHT II	Lost
DEEP THOUGHT II	Uwe Bonsch	Won (G)
Wolfgang Unzicker	DEEP THOUGHT II	Lost
DEEP THOUGHT II	Matthias Wahls	Lost
Raj Tischbierek	DEEP THOUGHT II	Lost

Reference

F. Friedel, "Not the mother of all machines," *ICCA Journal* 14, no. 2 (June 1991): 101–107.

Date: August 28, 1991
Location: Sydney, Australia
Event: IJCAI exhibition match
with international master Darryl Johansen
Time Control: All/1
Results: DEEP THOUGHT II 1, Darryl Johansen 1

White	Black	Result
DEEP THOUGHT II	Darryl Johansen	Won (G)
Darryl Johansen	DEEP THOUGHT II	Lost (G)

References

R. Levinson, "Man and machine, theory and practice square off in Sydney," *ICCA Journal* 14, no. 3 (September 1991): 150–52.

ICCA editorial board, "Johansen vs. DEEP THOUGHT II: A correction," *ICCA Journal* 14, no. 4 (December 1991): 233.

Dates: November 17–20, 1991
Location: Albuquerque, New Mexico
Event: 22nd ACM ICCC
Time Control: 40/2, 20/1 thereafter
Results: 5/5 (Winner of event)

White	Black	Result
DEEP THOUGHT II	ZARKOV	Won
MCHESS	DEEP THOUGHT II	Won
DEEP THOUGHT II	HITECH	Won (G)
CRAY BLITZ	DEEP THOUGHT II	Won
DEEP THOUGHT II	CHESS MACHINE/SCHRÖDER	Won

Reference

D. Kopec, M. Newborn, and M. Valvo, "The 22nd ACM International Computer Chess Championship," *Communications of the ACM 35*, no. 11 (November 1992): 100–110.

D. Beal, "Report on the 22nd ACM International Computer Chess Championship," *ICCA Journal 14*, no. 4 (December 1991): 214–222.

Dates: February 24–28, 1993
Location: Copenhagen, Denmark
Event: There were two matches
(1) Four-Game match between NORDIC DEEP BLUE and international grandmaster Bent Larsen
(2) Four-Game match between NORDIC DEEP BLUE and Danish National Team
Time Control: Some games were played 40/2, 20/1, then sudden death in 1. Others were played 40/2, All/1 or 40/2, 20/1, All/30.
Results: (1) Larson 2.5, NORDIC DEEP BLUE 1.5
(2) NORDIC DEEP BLUE 2.5, Danish National Team 1.5
NOTE: A total of seven games were played in the two matches; Larsen's fourth game counted in both matches.

White	Black	Result
Bent Larsen	NORDIC DEEP BLUE	Lost (G)
NORDIC DEEP BLUE	Bent Larsen	Draw
Bent Larsen	NORDIC DEEP BLUE	Draw
NORDIC DEEP BLUE	Bent Larsen	Draw (G)
Henrik Danielsen, IM	NORDIC DEEP BLUE	Won
NORDIC DEEP BLUE	Carsten Hoi, IM	Draw
Lars Bo Hansen, GM	NORDIC DEEP BLUE	Draw

Reference

F.-h. Hsu, "IBM DEEP BLUE in Copenhagen," *ICCA Journal* 16, no. 1 (March 1993): 53–56.

Date: April 20, 1993
Location: New York University, New York
Event: The DEEP BLUE Challenge
Time Control: 40/2, 20/1 thereafter
Results: DEEP BLUE PROTOTYPE 1—Rohde 0

White	Black	Result
DEEP BLUE PROTOTYPE	Michael Rohde	Won (G)

Reference

M. Ginsburg, "The DEEP BLUE Challenge," *ICCA Journal* 16, no. 2 (June 1993): 111–13.

Date: August 20, 1993
Location: IBM T. J. Watson Research Center,
Yorktown Heights, New York
Event: Exhibition match
with international grandmaster Judit Polgar
Time Control: All/30 minutes
Results: DEEP BLUE PROTOTYPE 1.5—Polgar .5

White	Black	Result
DEEP BLUE PROTOTYPE	Judit Polgar	Won (G)
Judit Polgar	DEEP BLUE PROTOTYPE	Draw (G)

Reference

F.-h. Hsu, "DEEP THOUGHT vs. Judit Polgar," *ICCA Journal* 15, no. 3 (September 1993): 150–51.

Appendix C

Dates: June 25–27, 1994
Location: Cape May, New Jersey
Event: 24th ACM ICCC
Time Control: 40/2, 20/1 thereafter
Results: 4–5 (First place)

White	Black	Result
DEEP BLUE PROTOTYPE	ZARKOV	Won
MCHESS	DEEP BLUE PROTOTYPE	Lost (on Forfeit)
DEEP BLUE PROTOTYPE	WCHESS	Won
STAR SOCRATES	DEEP BLUE PROTOTYPE	Won (G)
DEEP BLUE PROTOTYPE	MCHESS	Won

Reference

M. Newborn, "The 24th ACM International Computer-Chess Championship," *ICCA Journal* 17, no. 3 (September 1994): 159–64.

Dates: May 25–30, 1995
Location: The Chinese University of Hong Kong, Hong Kong
Event: The 8th World Computer Chess Championship
Time Control: 40/2, 40/1 thereafter
Results: 3.5/5, Tied for third in field of 24

White	Black	Result
DEEP BLUE PROTOTYPE	STAR SOCRATES	Won
HITECH	DEEP BLUE PROTOTYPE	Won (G)
DEEP BLUE PROTOTYPE	CHEIRON	Won
WCHESS	DEEP BLUE PROTOTYPE	Draw (G)
DEEP BLUE PROTOTYPE	FRITZ 3	Lost (G)

Reference

H. K. Tsang and D. Beal, "The 8th World Computer-Chess Championship," *ICCA Journal* 18, no. 2 (June 1995): 93–111.

Dates: July, 1995
Location: Barcelona, Spain
Event: Exhibition match with international grandmaster Miguel Illescas
Time Control: 40/2, Fischer clock
Results: Illescas 1.5, DEEP BLUE PROTOTYPE 0.5

White	Black	Result
DEEP BLUE PROTOTYPE	Miguel Illescas	Draw (G)
Miguel Illescas	DEEP BLUE PROTOTYPE	Lost* (G)
*on time		

Reference

http://www.chess.ibm.park.org

Dates: February 10–17, 1996
Location: Pennsylvania Convention Center, Philadelphia
Event: ACM Chess Challenge
Time Control: 40/2, 40/1, then all/30 minutes
Results: Kasparov 4, DEEP BLUE 2

White	Black	Result
DEEP BLUE	Garry Kasparov	Won (G)
Garry Kasparov	DEEP BLUE	Lost (G)
DEEP BLUE	Garry Kasparov	Draw (G)
Garry Kasparov	DEEP BLUE	Draw (G)
DEEP BLUE	Garry Kasparov	Lost (G)
Garry Kasparov	DEEP BLUE	Lost (G)

References

J. W. H. M. Uiterwijk, "The Kasparov—DEEP BLUE Match," *ICCA Journal* 19, no. 1 (March 1996): 38–41.

Y. Seirawan, "The Kasparov—DEEP BLUE games," *ICCA Journal* 19, no. 1 (March 1996): 41–57.

H. J. Berliner, "Why did Kasparov blink?" *ICCA Journal* 19, no. 2 (June 1996): 99–100.

M. Antonoff, "Curtains for Kasparov?" *Popular Science* (March 1996): 41–46.

For those with access to the Internet, the results of the match can be found at http://www.chess.ibm.park.org.

Appendix D

Diary of Kasparov versus Computers

Garry Kasparov's path has crossed with computers a number of times. In Appendix C, two events with DEEP BLUE are chronicled. This appendix chronicles six others.

Date: 1985
Location: Hamburg
Event: Simultaneous exhibition against 32 computers
Results: Kasparov 32, Computers 0

Reference

The editors, "Chess Grandmasters versus Chess Computers," *ICCA Journal* 8, no. 1 (March 1986): 51–53.

Date: October 28, 1989
Location: Harvard University
Event: Harvard Chess Festival, a simultaneous exhibition
Results: Kasparov blanked eight opponents, seven humans,
and SARGON IV.

References

C. Chabris, "The Harvard Cup Man-Versus-Machine Chess Challenge," *ICCA Journal* 16, no. 1 (March 1993): 57–61.

Dates: May 1994
Location: Munich
Event: Intel World Chess Express Challenge
Time Control: All/5 minutes for FRITZ *3; All/6 minutes for Kasparov*
Results: Kasparov and FRITZ *3 tied for 1st in 12-round event,*
Kasparov won playoff.

Dates: August 31, 1994
Location: London
Event: Intel Speed Chess Grand Prix
Time Control: All in 30 minutes
Results: PENTIUM CHESS GENIUS *1, Kasparov 0*
Kasparov took on PENTIUM CHESS GENIUS,
running on a 100Mhz Pentium PC.

White	Black	Result
Garry Kasparov	PENTIUM CHESS GENIUS	Lost

References

F. Friedel, "Pentium Genius Beats Kasparov," *ICCA Journal* 17, no. 3 (September 1994): 153–58.

Dates: May 1995
Location: Cologne
Event: Intel World Chess WDR
Time Control: All in 30 minutes
Results: 1.5–0.5
Kasparov took on PENTIUM CHESS GENIUS,
running on a 100Mhz Pentium PC.

White	Black	Result
Garry Kasparov	PENTIUM CHESS GENIUS	Won
PENTIUM CHESS GENIUS	Garry Kasparov	Draw

Reference

O. Weiner, "A vengeful return," *ICCA Journal* 18, no. 2 (June 1995): 125–26.

Appendix D

Date: December 14, 1995
Location: London
Event: Intel-sponsored match with FRITZ 4
Time Control: All in 30 minutes
Results: Kasparov 1.5, FRITZ 4 0.5

White	Black	Result
FRITZ 4	Kasparov	Won
Kasparov	FRITZ 4	Draw

Reference

F. Friedel, private correspondence, March 1996.

Appendix E

Algebraic Chess Notation

The games in this book are described using algebraic chess notation. This notation is described in this appendix. To begin, the eight rows, eight columns, and sixty-four squares of the chessboard are assigned names as shown in Figure E.1. The pieces in the game of chess are the king, queen, rook, bishop, knight, and pawn. The moves and the notation to describe each of the eight types of moves follows.

(1) Transfer from one square to another by a nonpawn.

The moving piece is named, followed by the destination square. If two pieces can move to the same square, the original column of the moving piece is given before the destination square. If that leaves the move ambiguous, the row is given instead.*

(2) Transfer from one square to another by a pawn.

The new square of the advancing pawn describes the move.

(3) Capture by a non-pawn.

The moving piece is named, followed by an ×, followed by the destination square. If two pieces can move to the same square, the original

---

*If there are three knights or three queens of the same color on the board, a move could still be am-
biguous requiring both row and column to be given; that did not occur in the games in this book.

Rows

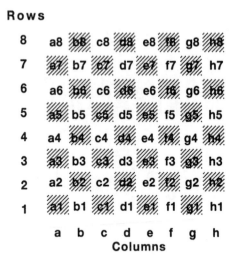

Figure E.1. Naming of the squares of the chessboard.

column of the moving piece is given before the destination square. If that leaves the move ambiguous, the row is given instead.

(4) Capture by a pawn.

The original column of the capturing pawn is given, followed by an "×," followed by the destination square. This format is also adequate for *en passant* captures.

Figure E.2. An unusual position.

(5) Castling move.

Kingside: O-O; Queenside: O-O-O.

(6) Promotions.

The name of the new piece, a Q, R, B or N, is added at the end of the move.

(7) Checking moves.

A "+" is appended to the end of the move description.

(8) Mating moves.

A "#" is appended to the end of the description.

Consider the position shown in Figure E.2. Assume that Black last advanced its pawn from h7 to h5, or in ou. notation played h5. Then White's possible moves are Kb8, b8Q, b8R, b8B, b8N, b×c8Q#, b×c8R#, b×c8B, b×c8N, Rd×e6+, Rd7, Rd8#, Re×e6+, d×e6, Bd8, Be7, Bg7, B×h8, f×e6, g7, g×h6.

Index

Index

Index

Index